The Journey Within

Extraordinary Conversations with Uncommon People

by

Kim Hughes

Interior font: Garamond

Cover design by Samantha Weiskopff

Cover photography by Kim Hughes

ISBN 9780986334306

First Edition

Lexingford Series in Spirituality, Meditation, and Peace Studies

Library of Congress Control Number 2014959587

L

Lexingford Publishing

New York

www.lexingfordpublishing.yolasite.com

THE JOURNEY WITHIN

Preface

In this book, you will hear from 16 practitioners of meditation as they reflect upon their meditation practice, the changes that have taken place, and their "journeys within." Three to four people are interviewed for each of the sections of the book: Getting Started, Lifestyle Changes, Master and the Spiritual World, Living in the Heart, and Hope for the Future.

The spiritual master referred to in this book, affectionately known as Chariji, gave his permission for me to start this book in December of 2012. This series of interviews and discussions about heart-based meditation and spirituality allowed the opportunity to interview nearly 30 practitioners of the Sahaj Marg (Natural Path) meditation practice. The first to be interviewed was the meditation trainer in Macau (S.A.R. China), where I live and work. Two interviews were done over the next few months by Skype. The great majority, however, were done face-to-face at the headquarters for the Shri Ram Chandra Mission (SRCM) on the ashram grounds in Manapakkam, Chennai, India in July of 2013. The interviews began in February of 2013, with the final one conducted in February of 2014. Interviews were typically about one hour. All were recorded, transcribed, and checked for accuracy.

Informants were from a variety of continents and cultures. They were mixed in age, gender and occupation. They also varied widely in their experience with meditation. Some mentioned grandparents who meditated, while others were only a few months into the practice.

Please note that all those interviewed follow the Sahaj Marg method of meditation, although some have tried other techniques. It is thought this is the most efficient and most natural method considering today's hectic and stressful lifestyle – and the writer is a follower of this method and thus had access to people using this practice. However, it should be clear that those interviewed do not promote only Sahaj Marg but rather any serious attempt to go inward in a search for the purpose of life and to connect with the heart in our search for the Divine.

In the chapters which follow, you will hear answers to a number of questions a newcomer would have about meditation and spiritual practice. Very basic principles such as when and how to meditate are covered as well as esoteric concepts such as the difference between religion and spirituality. In these extraordinary conversations, you will hear the interviewees' hopes and dreams for a brighter future for humankind, one based on tolerance and love. Besides giving you a similar hope for the future, the main purpose of this book is to encourage you to think about how to lead a life oriented toward growing inward. Rather than focusing so much attention on those things with which we are bombarded each day -- acquisitions, self-indulgences, all aspects of materialism – we can seek to find inner pathways through tuning in to our hearts. This book should help you to begin the process of learning how to go, grow, and continue journeys within.

Meet Kim Hughes

Dr. Kim, as she is known by her students, has been a language educator and teacher trainer for over 30 years, living and working over half her life overseas. She and her family lived one year in Hong Kong, four years in Malaysia (where her second son was born), one year in Indonesia while on a Fulbright Senior Fellowship, and now over 12 years in Macau. She has also lived and worked for shorter periods as a consultant in Austria and Japan. Kim was a tenured professor at Southern Illinois University in Carbondale for a decade in the 1990's and is currently employed at the University of Macau, S.A.R. China. She has Master's degrees in Secondary Education and in Applied Linguistics/Teaching English as a Second or Foreign Language and holds a Ph.D. in Language Education. She is a frequent presenter at international conferences, most recently invited to give plenary speeches for international teacher education conferences in Malaysia (2013) and in South Korea (2014).

Although she has conducted and published academic research, this is Kim's first step into publishing for the general public. She started this project as someone new to meditation who wanted to learn more and to share what she had learned. Stress release, peace of mind, and lower blood pressure are but a few of the benefits she has noted personally. She was curious to learn if others had similar experiences. Seemingly, although a meditation "practice," this approach was becoming for her a "lifestyle," which was unexpected.

At that time, there was very little information available for people before actually starting the practice. She thought that the insights shared here (and in the second book of the series) would help both newcomers and those more experienced.

In her leisure time, Kim enjoys spending quiet time with her husband of over 30 years and their two sons, both in their mid-20's. She enjoys travel, cooking, reading and learning languages. Increasingly, more and more of her personal time is oriented toward meditation on the heart.

THE JOURNEY WITHIN

THE JOURNEY WITHIN

Acknowledgments

Our Master and my Tender, Chariji. His Master, Babuji Maharaj.

All the brothers and sisters who were willing to be interviewed for this book.

Meditation Brothers and Sisters

Michelle-Elaine Sidwell and Claire Gormley, without whose enthusiasm, connections and support this book never would have happened.

Hari Venkatesan, Judith Polston, Martin Worthy and Alice Tesler for their advice and expertise.

Brother Kamlesh Patel and Sister Elizabeth Denley, for your help and attention to detail.

Family and Relatives

Betts Hughes (mother) and Tom (husband), with special thanks to their editing pencils.

Devin and Renata, Kelsey and Joana (sons and their special ladies), much love and happy reading. Ana Claudia and Abbi, as well.

Kaye (sister) and Bruce and Craig (brothers) and their families.

Terry and Greg, Jim (in-laws) and our wonderful nieces and nephews (special thanks to Heather, Dan and Michael).

Marion Hughes (father), Tony and Pat Wilhelm, Joey Wilhelm, Peggy Quirk, Mary Wilhelm, and Sean Beall, watching over us from the Brighter World.

THE JOURNEY WITHIN

Colleagues

Department of English and English Language Centre, University of Macau and the Department of English and Center for English as a Second Language, Southern Illinois University at Carbondale for the lessons learned and for your support of my career and this project. Special thanks to dear Ming Cheang and wonderful Teresa Lacuna.

Paul Angelis, Jodi Crandall, Jun Liu, Harry Gradman, James Mahan, Marlin Howard, Susan Greer, Dr. Haz and Anabel Newman for mentoring and support.

Joseph Sommerville and Marie Mater, Terry and Ellie Cohen, Vicki and Tang, Rando and Mike, Faridah Pawan, Manuela and Tony Sotero, Kelly and Kris Walsh, the Frenches, the Bobays, the Bodnars, Robbey Byers, Chris Backs and Eric, Alan and Cathy, Gloria Ulloa, April Bonar, Georgia Creedon, Stephanie Lam, Gala and Konstantin, Glenn Timmermans, Nina and Gary, Lua Wilson and Bill Guthrie for being true-blue, forever friends.

Art Bell and Dayle Smith, for believing in this project.

The production staff of Lexingford Publishing, for a job well done!

Dedication

Dedicated to all those beginning to question the purpose of life and those turning toward spirituality as the driving force of human life. To the living Master of Sahaj Marg and all the Masters who have gone before to pave our pathway in pursuit of mergence with the Divine. May we all evolve.

THE JOURNEY WITHIN

Table of Contents

Introduction

Another incredibly busy day at the ashram in Manapakkam, Chennai, India. As one sister put it, "Considering we sit around meditating all day, this sure is exhausting." I smile to myself as I crawl out of bed and make it to my meditation chair, foot rug and pillows already in place for maximum support. My back aches from a bent posture and I wonder if I can find someone to give me a much-needed massage. I am such a softie – and it is amazing how hard a tile floor can be after an hour with motionless feet. I feel happy I am able to talk myself into getting up before dawn, considering dawn comes at 4:30 a.m. these days. I try to get a precious hour of morning meditation at home before the sun rises, then walk the short distance to the ashram and mission headquarters in plenty of time for 6:30 group meditation, called satsangh. An hour now will put me in just the right state to "absorb" and be in tune with the group session in the huge meditation hall.

A little over an hour later, refreshed and peaceful, I emerge onto busy morning streets. Large busses and trucks joust with bicycles and multitudinous motorcycles and rickshaws. Horns are blaring continuously. Motorcycles enter my roadside pathway dangerously, weaving side to side. Cows and their calves loiter at garbage piles, generally making a mess while foraging for food. I try to not get too close to any hind hooves as I hurry as best I can to the ashram main gate, show my membership badge, and enter a peaceful world of bird calls and gardens as I head toward the meditation hall. Smiling to the volunteers, I relinquish my mobile phone, making sure it is set to silent, and again offer my pass for attendance purposes before entering the hall. Finding a quiet seat in the shade, I settle happily to meditate another hour with the whole group.

An hour later, we surface. Some stay on to enjoy their meditative state while others, me included, head to the nearby ashram café. There, morning conversation mixes with chai masala (hot spiced Indian tea). Some watch the children play cricket and soccer as they wait for their school bus to depart. Oftentimes, I wash dishes for an hour while waiting for the next meditation to begin at 9 a.m. After the 9 a.m. meditation, we are free until evening meditation, which usually begins at 5 p.m. Usually those hours are spent in quiet study, in 1:1 sittings, in volunteer work, or taking care of practical concerns such as banking or shopping. After 5 p.m. group meditation, we again gather at the café or wait for the dinner bell to announce dinner for ashram guests. The adventurous among us might go into the city for dinner, but most prefer to linger on the ashram grounds, hoping for a glimpse of the spiritual master, Chariji, or to even be allowed to sit with him in his garden. By 9 p.m., most of us abhyasis [ah-by-ah-sees] have retired to do evening cleaning and the evening prayer before tumbling into bed. This is our normal routine, one I have enjoyed the previous 3 times I have visited the ashram on meditation retreat. This time, however, I am here on a working holiday, so every minute seems full.

Armed with voice recorder, phone recorder as backup and interview questions, I interview 3-4 people each day, ending with nearly thirty interviews of one hour each. Organized into two books, these collections of interviews with people practicing Sahaj Marg (The Natural Way) meditation will, I hope, help to answer some of the questions a person might have if just starting to be interested in spirituality. A transcription was prepared after each interview, with some rewriting done to omit superfluous language, to connect topics, and to make the writing more reader-friendly. In the case of non-native speakers of English, some words and phrases from the interviews were changed in order to be true to intended speaker meaning and to provide a more standard form of English, suitable for publication. In regard to transcription conventions, brackets [ ] indicate additions by the author. Several terms are used throughout these chapters, including *abhyasi* (a meditation practitioner, or follower) and *sadhana* (the practices involved in this system of meditation). A glossary follows of the special terms used.

Thank you for reading this book and please share it with others. It is particularly appropriate for those wondering about and starting to be interested in pursuing meditation and spirituality. Enjoy, discover, evolve. Blessings upon your journeys!

THE JOURNEY WITHIN

Glossary of Terms

If not sourced, definitions are taken from:
https://www.sahajmarg.org/abhyasi

abhyasi (abhyaasi) - Aspirant; one who practices yoga in order to achieve union with God

ashram or **ashrama** - "Ashram" comes from the Sanskrit "Shreyas" which applies, in the spiritual sense, to the growth of benefits which are connected to the higher level. An ashram is also a kind of refuge, a place of retreat from today's life. Ashrams in Sahaj Marg are dedicated to meditation only, all other activities are normally not allowed in the Ashram. An Ashram is usually charged by the Master, who creates a special atmosphere of spirituality conducive to meditation.

bhandara – a spiritual gathering or celebration (usually for a celebration such as the birth or death anniversary of one of the masters; typically 2-3 days under open tents)

chakras -- In Hindu metaphysical tradition and other belief systems *chakras* are points in the human body, i.e. major plexuses of arteries, veins and nerves, that are centers of life force (prana), or vital energy. Please refer to: http://en.wikipedia.org/wiki/Chakra

guru - Master who transmits light, knowledge; a spiritual teacher.

Jainism /ˈdʒeɪnɪz(ə)m/, traditionally known as Jaina dharma, is an Indian religion that prescribes a path of non-violence towards all living beings and emphasizes spiritual independence and equality between all forms of life. Practitioners believe that non-violence and self-control are the means by which they can obtain liberation. Retrieved 5 December 2013 from http://en.wikipedia.org/wiki/Jainism

karma - The Pali term Karma literally means action or doing. Any kind of intentional action whether mental, verbal, or physical, is regarded as Karma. It covers all that is included in the phrase "thought, word and deed." Generally speaking, all good and bad action constitutes Karma. http://www.buddhanet.net/e-learning/karma.htm#1

pranahuti - Process of yogic transmission; derived from *prana* meaning life and *ahuti* meaning offering. Offering of the life force by the Guru into the disciple's heart.

preceptor or **prefect**: An abhyasi chosen, prepared, and permitted by the Master to impart spiritual training through the utilization of pranahuti or yogic transmission.

sadhana – the practice, in all its components

Sahaj Marg - Literally: natural path, simple path. A simple practice of meditation on the heart derived from the ancient Indian system of raja yoga. "The true aim of this highly effective training in spirituality is to take the seeker to the highest goal of human existence – God realization or Self realization." See https://www.sahajmarg.org/sm/what-is-spirituality

samskaras - Impressions; grossness.

satsangh (satsang) - Spiritual assembly; being with reality.

sitting - A session of meditation, usually lasting from 30 minutes to an hour, in which the Master or a preceptor/prefect/prefector meditates with a group or an individual for the purpose of cleaning and transmission.

Part I: **Getting Started**

In this section of the book, Getting Started, we focus on some of the practical methods involved in the practice, as well as the need to focus on the heart. This is a rather big issue for many people, to get "out of the head," building the ability to quieten or ignore the brain so that the divine "spark" in our hearts can be fanned into a living flame. This involves behavioral conditioning, which is why it is recommended to be consistent in the meditation practice, for example meditating at about the same time each morning and evening, sitting in the same place, and under the same conditions.

Our first interviewee, Michel, is an uncommon man, I'm sure you will agree. Involved for nearly 40 years in infrastructure development for some of the poorest countries around the world, he has been in meditation practice less than a year. He brings to us the insights of a newcomer along with the experience of a globetrotter and "high roller," as one friend called him. His story is intriguing, not only because of his life story but also how he came to Sahaj Marg, in particular.

We next meet Bani, a housewife, mother, and meditation trainer, who explains in detail the meditation practice itself and how all the components go together to foster constant remembrance of the love we all carry in our hearts. She explains the purpose of the three introductory sittings, morning meditation, and evening cleaning. She also discusses the goals of our time on this Earth as we try to cleanse ourselves, to subsume the ego, and to grow in our capacities for kindness, tolerance and love. As a prefect (meditation trainer) for Sahaj Marg meditation practice, Bani travels often to Central and South America.

Our final interviewee in this section, Mathew is a university student from China's mainland. Age eighteen, he has only been meditating for two months. He touchingly talks about loneliness and how the meditation practice has made him appreciate this wider group of "brothers and sisters" who truly care for and try to help each other. All three discuss their perceptions of the practice and how it feels to

THE JOURNEY WITHIN

get started. I leave you, dear reader, to their explanations and sound advice.

THE JOURNEY WITHIN

Chapter 1   **It's Worth It**

Michel

International citizen, French nationality, early 60's, infrastructure development consultant

Preface: Michel admits that he probably "should have been an international banker" but instead decided to contribute to making the world a better place. For 40 years, he has worked with infrastructure development in some of the world's poorest counties and under the most difficult conditions. He tells a very interesting story of being introduced to this form of meditation less than a year ago.

We meet in the living room of my friend's apartment a few days after our return from the bhandara celebration in Tiruppur in July. We are still vibrating from the energy generated in this huge gathering of over 20,000 people. Michel arrives a little late, having slept poorly and nursing a cold. Dressed in blue jeans, hip, energetic, and forever young, Michel wouldn't let a small thing like a cold keep him down, however. As I bring him a cup of tea, he is ready to be interviewed and eager to share his thoughts. I trust you will enjoy Michel's interview and admire his sense of altruism. He seeks to balance practical support efforts for the poorest and neediest of human beings with his personal goals to grow in tolerance, love and spirituality.

Kim: Could you tell us a little about yourself and how you became involved with spirituality?

I grew up in Latin America and West Africa, and then went back to Europe to study. I finished my studies in the U.S.A., England and Spain. I'm from a very strict Catholic background and did military service in the French Navy. I was on an aircraft carrier and decided in Djibouti that life would be different for me [so] I dropped the family ring in the middle of the Indian Ocean so as to say, 'That's where it's going to start." With a background like that, I should have been an international banker but I decided to give a year of my life to try to understand what is going on in the world.

I was sent to Lebanon on the U.N. team that was supposed to work on the reconstruction of Lebanon. Two weeks after we arrived, war started again and, because of my background as a Navy officer in charge of commanders and stuff like that, the UN asked me if I would be interested (instead of flying back to New York like everyone else) in staying to help in relief operations. I was 24 or 25, a bachelor, and decided to stay. I got involved in a children's program that the UN was financing at the time, rebuilt villages in south Lebanon, took care of refugees and went through a year of incredible experiences which changed my life. That was nearly forty years ago and I'm still in this line of business.

For years, I worked in consulting and management for countries and organizations. In 2009, I decided to open my own company, mostly putting development programs together (investment and infrastructure). We work mostly now for the poorest countries in the world such as Haiti, Madagascar, Senegal - these types of countries. What I am trying to do is still make money because I still have some duties towards my family, so I am trying to make money in infrastructure and at the same time help put together social programs in some of these countries.

At the same time, outside the job we do, we are trying to do things which can be useful to the less favored people. This work is being done with colleagues from those countries. We are trying to contribute to the operation of a few schools for the poor, taking care of orphans.

THE JOURNEY WITHIN

The plan is to put together a full-scale orphanage somewhere in the world... probably one of the poorest countries in the world. It's a magnificent location and the kids are quite amazing.

Normally I should be getting to the time when retirement should be the gift of life, but I'm not planning to retire. For years, I've had the feeling that I'm not really working. I'm having a life which is very different. When you do this kind of work it's kind of a commitment where it's not really serving humanity, but it's trying to be useful and not useless. Let's put it that way. Sometimes you sense that you are maybe not that useful and maybe sometimes that you're counterproductive when you don't approach the problem the right way. You can't be successful all the time. Let's say that if you have a 50, 60, 70 percent success rate, that's already an amazing success. That's why I say that it's more a life than a job.

Kim: So what about spirituality? You were raised Roman Catholic, is that right?

A very Catholic family. From the beginning, I was involved with the Church. Twice in my life, I wondered if I shouldn't become a priest. The last time was when I was 23 or 24. What I had seen in life earlier on, especially in Lebanon, where the Christians were fighting with the Muslims at the time I was there, made me lose faith, I believe. But the education I received probably made me decide that, as a decent human being, you have a duty towards others. It's close to what the Catholic Church called charity, but to be honest, I don't think we should call it charity. It's a duty. You cannot be happy when you know that the majority of people around the world are suffering.

Even if my life was not dedicated to any faith over the last thirty-something years I still try to stay a decent human being, understanding that we have a duty towards others.

THE JOURNEY WITHIN

Kim: Is this your first experience with meditation and what led you to be here?

I studied meditation very early in my life. I think the first time was probably 30 years ago. I was on an Indonesian mission and met a few wise old men who introduced me to Buddhism. I was (in and out) involved with meditation for years. I used [it] a lot in my job because it helped me to look at suffering a different way. Suffering is a part of life and it can bring growth -- but compared to what I am discovering now, which is really spirituality, it was very different.

Over the last five years I could feel the limits of what I was practicing because it is very difficult when you are dealing with the very worst post-conflict countries (like Afghanistan, Angola or the DRC: Democratic Republic of Congo) and situations. So over the past five years, if I couldn't find something to bring me to a higher level, I would have had to stop working and retire like everybody else -- go and play golf -- but that was not me.

I was very lucky that 40 years ago I had an incredible relationship with a lady who joined me at one stage in Lebanon at the beginning of my professional life. She had a different approach to life. She said, if you want to change the world, you need to take care of the soul of the people. [But] I was into action. So we separated and I went for 35 years of action and she moved into spirituality.

The way I found her again after 40 years is quite interesting. One day when I was in the middle of the Ivory Coast, I had a dream. I woke up, knew she was in my dream, and had to talk to her. I was trying to find somebody after 35 years when I'd been all over the world (I wasn't living in France any more and was based in the United States). I went through the internet, put her name in and, nothing. Then I went through the images and finally, after a few days, I found somebody who could be her. She looked exactly the same, just 35 years older. I found an email address, sent her an email and said that if (a specific

THE JOURNEY WITHIN

name) "clicks" in your head, please send me an email at that address. The next day I had an email with a phone number. We talked and I learned she was very involved in spirituality and that's how I discovered Sahaj Marg.

Kim: So you followed your dream; the dream said that she had the answer for you, right?

Kind of. I was in a situation where I knew I needed to find something. One night she came in a dream and when I woke up, I knew that I had to talk to her. A few weeks after I talked to her, I was in France. She was giving a seminar somewhere in the south of France, so I took a motorcycle and joined her. She initiated me and did four sittings (I guess I had a lot of heavy stuff that she needed to clean). When she saw me again she even said, "It's not going to be three, it's going to be four."

Kim: She said that even before the first session?

Yes. At the fourth one, I had this incredible experience. Afterward, I drove the motorcycle for something like 750 kilometers. It was raining... and I felt I was plugged into this most amazing energy all the way back, nearly 24 hours.

Kim: Twenty-four hours on a motorcycle in the rain and you didn't care!

I didn't care. I was plugged into this energy that she made me discover. It's a beautiful story. That was in June and this is February, so seven months [ago].

THE JOURNEY WITHIN

Kim: So here you are in India.

I started practicing while traveling all over the world. It is quite difficult, so I decided the best way would be for me to find a way to come [here]. I came to Manapakkam just after Christmas for two weeks, went to the ashram every day and tried to understand better. I started really meditating. Then I left for a mission and found again that it was difficult to practice when you're traveling all the time and so on. So I am back again for the second time. I found that there could be a way for me to go on with my job, at least for the next year. Instead of flying back to the States or flying back to France, I could fly back to India for 10 to 15 days per month, ideally, and get more involved in ashram life, meditation and all that.

Kim: It's been six or seven months. Do you feel there has been a change?

I think it's too early, but I experienced a few things recently. I was in a country in West Africa helping the government put together a drainage program in the poorest areas of the capital city. They had a lot of floods with people dying every rainy season. Strangely, after I had been initiated into Sahaj Marg, I looked at the problem differently. I couldn't satisfy myself by just trying to find a certain amount of money for the development phase. For some reason, there was something in myself which was pushing me to put the real issue on the table. That's what I did instead of doing the normal approach. It gave me a new approach in dealing with the problems in poor countries. Is it spirituality or is it that I'm ready for that stage? I don't know. I felt that spirituality was quite a trigger for that, but it's too early after seven months.

Kim: I know you are very new, but sometimes people who are very new are the best to give advice. It doesn't have to be Sahaj Marg in particular, but imagine a young person today questioning materiality, starting to say, "Is this all there is? What's going on? Is this what we are put on Earth to do?" What kind of advice would

THE JOURNEY WITHIN

you give somebody who is just starting to look around at his or her life and say, "Isn't there more?"

In my case, I was quite lucky to have an incident which changed my life. I was supposed to be an international banker which is exactly what you are describing - money, house, regular family, vacation, retirement, golf. I meet a lot of young people who come to me now because they probably feel that I am quite happy in the life I have, in the professional life I have. If I can give advice, I'd say, "It's worth giving." If they can give a year or a few months, that's what real life is about.

In the Western world, we don't really deal with real life most of the time, even if we could discover it there. I've given this advice to a few people and, yes, if they can spend a few months somewhere in the world or somewhere outside where they grew up to try and discover how difficult life can be for a lot of our fellow brother and sister human beings, this would certainly help them a lot. One way or the other it ends up as something that is very close to spirituality.

Kim: I'm going to ask you this because you have experience with the Catholic religion and spirituality, including Buddhism. Is Sahaj Marg more effective or more important than religion?

The Master wrote a book on that which is on religion and spirituality (I'm supposed to read it!).

Kim: Where religion leaves off, spirituality begins?

Maybe. Spirituality comes at a much higher level than religion; trying to find a union with God in yourself, which is not always the case in

THE JOURNEY WITHIN

religion. This brings you to understand that God, the Divine, is within you. If you work on that, discover it, then your life has a totally different sense.

Religion is not about that. Religion is about that there is God and there is the human race. Between the two, there are all kinds of rules and ways of getting in touch and getting involved. It's not a global approach to your contact with the Divine. Spirituality brings you to that level. At the beginning, it's a day-to-day feeling through regular contact. My understanding is [that] practicing more, this feeling gets more into you and becomes a 24-hour experience.

If you take the best monastic human beings, they have been very close to that, but in religion, it's reserved for those people. What you understand here is that it could be for everybody. It's just a question of deciding to move ahead and to do it, to practice and then to experience it.

Kim: Have you had to give up anything? Is there anything that's really challenging for you with the practice?

For me what is challenging (I am sure I will find a solution) is traveling the world for my job and making sure I can have a decent way of practicing enough so I can move forward. That's why the experience of regularly being back next to the ashram, where there is no other option than to be who you are, is probably going to help me recover after a few days of non-practice outside.

Kim: Like trying to meditate in a jeep in the desert?

THE JOURNEY WITHIN

I had that kind of experience in the north of Chad. When you work, it's a tough schedule and your mind and your brain are really dedicated to what you are supposed to do. I met an amazing man a few hours ago. He joined in 1978 and, for whatever reason, he came and sat next to me. He wanted to explain to me what the practice was, and how I was supposed to focus to discover my soul. I believe this man was sent to me by the Master. In the two hours we spent together, he taught me so much; that the simplest as well as the more difficult is there…"Try to stay with the basics, the basics of who you are. Then you are going to progress." I think he's right. He gave me a few tips and, after listening to him, I can probably have a much better practice outside India even when I'm traveling for my job.

Kim: Do you think you have to be pure to be spiritual?

That's a very good question. When you begin, you feel that purity is not something coming very quickly…but if you experience feeling during meditation, you feel that the next step is to be sure you do something so that you become pure. You feel that purity is part of the element that is going to help you maybe go faster and go deeper into your soul. That's what I feel.

Kim: I know you haven't been in the practice very long, but do you have any special stories to tell? Any special experiences that would help people know what it feels like inside?

What I can tell you is that this is not the first time meditating, but the way I was meditating before never brought me this feeling of transmission. In my case, I was lucky enough to feel this transmission after the fourth cleaning that this preceptor friend of mine gave me. I felt I was plugged into this energy all the way back for hours and hours and hours! During the trip back, I had thoughts of forgiveness and deep human involvement on real essential things. If you're not too stupid, you feel that, with practice, you can have this. [Maybe] not be in this state of mind all the time, but re-discover it from time to time.

Now, after only six or seven months I have moments (not as deep as what happened to me the first time, but I have moments) where I feel my soul is bringing me harmony -- and purity -- to what I'm supposed to do in life. That's what this old man confirmed a few hours ago; that with simple practice, with a simple life, purity of feelings and thoughts, you can have that more and more often. If this is the case, it's really worth practicing.

My understanding is that the cleaning process is really crucial. Even after seven months, I can feel that, if I clean before a meditation, I can feel much more during the meditation. It seems to me that this is the essential part. This old man made a lot of sense. If you want this energy to come into you, you need to be sure it has space. So you need to clean whatever is there before this Divine energy can come in.

Kim: Maybe you've already answered this, but what's your ultimate goal?

It's a very basic goal. I'm not trying to find Nirvana. I've got this professional life, a life where I can eventually be useful to those who are less lucky than we are. Being human and certainly not one of the best, I've got limitations. This means that after 35, 40 years of this type of work you get frustrated, you get tired, sometimes you get impatient-- and I knew for the past five, seven years that I needed to find something that would help me get over that and go on. Let's hope that I have 10-15 years of intelligent life still in front of me. For humanity it's probably better that I go ahead with the experience that I have and be useful to those who are less lucky than we are, instead of paying a very expensive green fee to play golf or whatever. (laughs)

THE JOURNEY WITHIN

So my first goal was to find a new energy to go on another 10-15 years, if possible. What I'm discovering is what I wanted to find -- a new energy which would help me look at things differently. I could have looked at it 20 or 35 years ago while being young, enthusiastic and idealistic but I'm discovering that I might find something even deeper that will fill me for the rest of my life.

So overall, it looks like an immense gift. I could have fulfilled the goal that I had to overcome the limits that stopped me from taking a plane and going to live in difficult countries from time to time. But through doing that [work], I might get the super gift of having something that is fulfilling myself. That's great if it happens. I'll tell you in ten years, but for the moment, it's a bit too early.

Kim: One final question, unless you have something you would like to add. Some people see Sahaj Marg as kind of a social movement, as maybe hope for humanity for the future. What's your take on that? Do you see Sahaj Marg as a sort of hope for the future?

I'm still too young in the movement, on the path, to have an opinion on that. What I can feel is that this Divine energy circulating in Sahaj Marg is certainly the beginning of an answer for the future of the world. I'm not a specialist in spirituality so I cannot tell you that this is the only movement, but what I can feel is that it certainly has the basis for what you said. Like any organization of human beings, you've got good and bad aspects -- and Sahaj Marg is not an exception. But you can see that you've got a lot of very good souls along the path, probably more than anywhere else.

The approach that Sahaj Marg is offering is certainly the right thing for the future... The simplicity in what's been offered could make the difference because you don't need to be highly educated, you don't need to be speaking ten languages or be from a special social environment to feel what Sahaj Marg is offering. So, it could spread quickly. One of the dangers is that people [may] try to interpret the rules or push to try and segregate people. Again, I'm not a specialist and still quite new, but the fundamentals of what I feel could make a difference in the future. That's for sure, for me, and that's why I'm interested in being part of that.

Kim: I understand this is your first bhandara. What's a bhandara like?

It's a crushing experience. In our case, we had 25,000 people. When you've been around the world, 25,000 people in the same place without any incident is already a miracle. You have these moments of intense energy around you when all these people are meditating together. [It's] just fascinating. Comfort is the other side of the thing, but for what you get during the day, it really doesn't matter. It's just a smashing, enhancing, fabulous experience. If you do it early on your spiritual path, you can imagine what the future could be for you. It's amazing, honestly.

Kim: Do you have anything else to add?

I'm brand new to it, but I can feel things already. I think there is something that is a bit specific in Sahaj Marg. If you are lucky (and maybe I'm lucky), you can quickly feel the Divine energy in you and, once you have felt that, you are at the beginning of something that can only grow… The beauty of Sahaj Marg is that it is very simple. You don't have to do anything very special. You just have to follow the basic thing, which is to practice and clean so as to be able to meditate properly. As we heard in the bhandara, what is one hour a day? We lose at least one hour a day doing stupid stuff. I think it's worth it. Thank you.

THE JOURNEY WITHIN

Chapter 2 **A Beautiful Future for Humanity**

Bani

Indian living in the U.S.A., female, 50's, prefect for SRCM (U.S.A. and South America)

Preface: Bani and I meet on a hot afternoon in the education center of the ashram. Fans whirl overhead and construction workers haul supplies on the street outside. She is at the ashram for only a short time and is in high demand due to her responsibilities for the USA and South America. Nevertheless, she cheerfully meets with me, squeezing me in between two other appointments. She looks pretty and fresh despite the heat. I'm interested to learn she has daughters just a little older than my sons and is expecting her first grandchild. I hang on each word. This woman has presence.

In words both simple and penetrating, Bani discusses the fundamentals and components of meditation practice (according to Sahaj Marg), emphasizing that each component is of equal importance to this "beautiful practice" as a whole. With honesty and humor, she recalls early perceptions when visiting the ashram in India and meeting "Master," her guru and spiritual teacher. She touches upon the importance of both discipline and guidance. She emphasizes the goal of constant remembrance, the need to nurture the divine alive in our hearts, and the concept of cleansing ourselves of samskaras, or "impressions." Perhaps most importantly, she affirms her belief in "a beautiful future for humanity."

Kim: Could you begin by telling us a little about yourself and how you became interested in meditation?

I was born in India but, at six years old, I moved to Venezuela, South America, because my dad worked for the United Nations. I lived there for ten years then I moved to the U.S.A., where I studied, married, [and now live]. I was first introduced to Sahaj Marg [meditation practice] in Detroit, Michigan in 1987. I am a prefect for the SRCM U.S.A. mission and I do work in South America. I coordinate the activities for Mexico, Nicaragua, Panama, Venezuela, Colombia and Ecuador, traveling quite often to all these places. I have beautiful experiences whenever I go to participate in the seminars and training for the prefects in South America. Mostly [my role is] encouraging and helping to motivate them, but also to make sure they do the practice correctly, as it is prescribed. They get distracted, deviate, and want to incorporate other techniques, so we have to make sure and follow up and tell them that the techniques of the practice have to be preserved.

Kim: Can you explain in detail what one is expected to do in the meditation practice?

We have to make the thought that we have divine essence in our heart and maintain that thought for the duration of the meditation. If other thoughts come, we have to try to not focus on those. It's just like reading a book [when] you're totally involved in that book and the information it's giving you; you're not paying any attention to what's going on around you. The same with meditation: you're just paying attention to that divine presence that is in every one of us – in every living being – maintain[ing] that thought throughout the period of the meditation. It's like we are inviting that presence [to be with us] for that one hour.

When first joining Sahaj Marg, I used to be always wondering, "Is there really a God? Is there somebody looking after me? I feel so lonely. If

THE JOURNEY WITHIN

there is a God, why don't I feel him?" And I prayed so much to have some guidance as to how to find him. [However], it's not really finding him; he's there all the time (chuckles). It's just feeling, knowing, in your heart, really accepting that he is with us all the time. He's watching over us -- every thought that we have, every action that we do -- it's known by him. We go on in this world thinking that we are alone and [that] our thoughts are only ours and nobody knows. We go on in our lives that way; creating more samskaras, on and on. We don't realize that. Only when I came to Sahaj Marg did I feel that I was not lonely.

Kim: Can you briefly describe what the practice is? I know there are normally three introductory sittings with a prefect, then regular morning meditation and evening cleaning. Can you explain more?

Many ask why it is necessary to take the introductory sittings. It is to prepare us for the process, because we're not used to this meditation. It prepares us to receive the transmissions (the divine energy) from our Master. Once we are prepared, it's easier for us to meditate. So then, they tell us to sit and meditate for at least an hour with the thought that we have divine presence or divine light in our heart. If thoughts come, just brush them aside gently and go back to meditating. Meditating is simply thinking of one thought for a period of time. Most of us, we are not able to maintain that thought at the beginning, even for a few minutes, because we have not trained our minds; we have not disciplined our minds.

So, we have to start some place; just start, just sit. Even if we are able to meditate for [only] five or ten minutes, that's great progress. Then slowly, slowly as we meditate and we do the practice, we notice that we can be with the thought of the Divine presence in our hearts. We can meditate for one hour and we are surprised because the time concept changes. Sometimes we meditate for an hour and it seems as if it's only five minutes. Other times we meditate only for five minutes and it seems like it's one hour. So the time concept also changes when we start this practice. The more we meditate, the more we go deeper and the more we experience the divine presence. [When] we come to a state where we feel that perfect condition, where everything is balanced; that is when we achieve the perfect meditation.

Then there is the process of cleaning which is very different compared to meditation. It's an integral part of the practice because, without it, our meditations are not as effective. We need to empty out from our system all the impressions, anything unnecessary to achieving balance. Master says we have to empty the vessel to be able to fill it up. We do this cleaning for half an hour every day in the evening. It is suggested that we do this as soon as we finish our daily activities because every day we accumulate some impressions. We should not distinguish between whether it is a good impression or a bad impression; we are not able to evaluate what is good and bad. You just have to have the idea that all impressions are going out of our system and, in its place, we are filling up with divine energy, with divine essence. This process we do for half an hour every evening. That is very important because, when we don't do the cleaning, we can see the effect the next day when our meditation somehow is not as effective. So it's very important to do this cleaning. We know this ourselves because, if we do it properly, after the cleaning, we feel some lightness; we feel some calmness and peace -- and then we can have our dinner with a calm and balanced condition and be able to absorb what we eat.

At night, we have a nighttime prayer. This is a beautiful prayer because, in the traditional sense, prayer is always begging of our God, something or the other -- but this prayer is unique because we're not asking for anything or begging for anything. We're just stating the situation that we are in right now and we definitely need the help of God himself, and of our guru, to be able to overcome our situation right now. We're just stating a fact; and we're reminding ourselves every night why it is that we are doing this practice, because we tend to forget. We create also a condition so that, during our sleep even, we are in touch with divinity -- until the next day in the morning again when we start with our meditation.

THE JOURNEY WITHIN

So it's a beautiful practice that is a whole that has its components -- and each component is as important as the other. We have to do all of it; each complements the other. You will see that, if you do each part of it with discipline, in no time at all, you will see an equilibrium in yourself. You'll see a balanced state in yourself; you can observe it yourself. Nobody has to tell you about it because this is an experiment by yourself, on yourself, for yourself.

Kim: Isn't it difficult to sit still for an hour?

The tendency of the human mind is to figure out the easiest way to get out of things (laughter) and, if we don't do it for an hour, from the beginning -- if we try to do it for five minutes or 10 minutes -- then it's not effective. It takes time at the beginning, and we need to discipline ourselves and use will power to sit for that one hour. Even our Brother Kamlesh gave a speech which was printed in the quarterly magazine Constant Remembrance. He saw that he was in a rush to get to work and did not do his meditation in the morning effectively. However, once he made up his mind that, "Yes, I'm going to get up earlier and take that one hour to do the meditation," the rest of the day goes so smoothly. We need to create that condition during the meditation so that we can keep that peaceful condition throughout the day. If we don't start out the day properly, our day will not continue properly. It's not that we won't face the difficulties that we have to face in the destiny of our lives, but we are given the tools to deal with those problems in a much better way when we do the practice as prescribed.

When we have constant remembrance [constantly in a balanced state, remembering the divine], we are able to make the right decision when we are faced with a situation with so many choices... Only when we are connected to the divine does the thought come to us and we make the right choice. Then we do not have to face the consequences that

THE JOURNEY WITHIN

might create more samskaras for us. The whole purpose is not to create more samskaras. We want to be able to deal with the load of samskaras we have and not create any more. This is the way we become liberated. We exhaust all of our samskaras. That's what Master does; he cleans us of our samskaras every time he gives us a sitting. When we go to a prefect for an individual sitting, they do the deeper cleaning so that most of our samskaras are cleaned out and only a small reserve is there that we have to go through. Master has sometimes given an example that, if we're in an accident, instead of suffering great pain or even losing our life, we may just break our hand or a leg. We have to go through that suffering, but it would have been worse if we hadn't cleaned out the samskaras. We may even have to go through another life again. So the whole purpose is to not have to have another life, to be able to exhaust all our samskaras in this life itself, and to reach that point of liberation.

Kim: Can you explain what a samskara is?

Samskaras are impressions. They may be good or bad. If you have done good deeds, the consequences could be that you reap those benefits. If you've done something bad, you'll reap the consequences of those bad actions too and you have to undergo it. What stops the creation of these consequences is to not do any more actions -- but how you don't do any more of those actions is to be always in the remembrance of God. [Without this practice] in each one of our lives, we accumulate these samskaras and the load gets heavier and heavier. Let's say you don't believe that there are several lives that we go through, reincarnation -- even just this life, let's say you have to appear for an exam and you do not study. What is the consequence? You will not pass and you'll have to suffer the consequence. If you study, you will pass and you'll reap the benefits. Everything that we do in this life creates a consequence -- action and cause and reaction.

Then we have something we do that's not for ourselves. It's a nine o'clock universal prayer, when we pray for all of our brothers and sisters, that they will also grow in the faith and love in their hearts for the divine. So for 10 to 15 minutes every day we do this prayer so that others may also benefit. That is the individual practice. Every two weeks (at least once in a month), they do need to go and have an individual sitting with a prefect. This is very important wherever there is a prefect; it's important to go and have the individual sittings because they do the deeper cleaning. When we do the cleaning every day it's the daily cleaning, the events that happened that day -- but what about the events that happened a long time back that have been hardened? Those are more difficult to clean, so the prefect has been prepared by Master to clear those samskaras. That [1:1 sittings] has to be done every two weeks or every so often, at least once a month. [Finally], we have the group meditations every Wednesday evening and every Sunday morning. We get together in a group and meditate together -- because the multiple, the collective group (the whole is bigger than the parts) -- and also because we are in the presence of Master. Master can see us and he can work upon us, too. It's a beautiful system that can be tested and we can see how effective it is.

I have seen throughout the years how my character has changed and I have seen progress in this spiritual practice. I have changed in the sense that I used to have a lot of anger -- very impatient, very insecure. I used to feel very shy; I couldn't even say two sentences together. [Now] here I am going to countries, talking to groups of people about the mission and about the Master. Whenever I do it, it's not me who is talking; I feel it is some divine energy that is flowing. The words come from me and I don't know where they come from. It's amazing all the information that is given to the group. A lot of patience has developed in me. It's taught me so many things.

Kim: Do you think it's essential to meet Master, in person?

Yes. At least once in your lifetime. I wanted to see, at least for my own conviction, "Who is this person? Who is this person who is going to guide me? I need to know. I need to see him." I was very lucky

THE JOURNEY WITHIN

that, after two weeks of joining the mission, I was able to meet Master. He was traveling and he was in Montréal and I could go and meet him. The moment I saw him, there was a conviction in my heart: "Yes, this is the path I want to follow. This is the master for me." Before that I had met many gurus.

Kim: Could you talk about that a little? How did you get involved in spirituality?

I started out with the Catholic church in Venezuela, going to Catholic schools but with so many questions that were never answered for me. My mother was a very religious Hindu idol worshiper. I remember when I was a child and asking my mother, "Why are you praying to those idols? What's there? They are just dolls. How can God be in those dolls?" She used to get so upset at me, partly because she didn't know how to answer. Later on, she became a devotee of Sai Baba (see references). We did go and visit Sai Baba. He used to do a lot of miracles, [also helping through] hospitals, social work, things like that -- but that did not satisfy me. I used to ask, "Okay you do miracles, you do all this, but what do I gain out of it?" Where is God? What do I experience out of all of this? It doesn't benefit me in any way." So I was not that attracted to that system. After I got married (it was an arranged marriage, from my region in India), my husband was an idol worshiper and he was very much into it. He was also crying and wanting to see God. We used to have different gods' pictures all over the house and we had a closet that was set up like a temple for us -- but that did not satisfy me. And then, at one point, I took all the idols and everything and I threw them in the trash -- I literally threw it all out -- and I told my husband and I prayed to God, "This is not it. Show me. Show me your presence. I'm not satisfied with this. " A few days later, my friends came and they talked to me about Sahaj Marg.

That evening when they came, it was such a wonderful time. I used to go to a lot of parties, social events; every weekend full of events. I used to fill my life with things, people and activities, because I was so empty inside. But that day when they came and they talked about Sahaj

THE JOURNEY WITHIN

Marg was the first day that I felt so happy. I was filled with such happiness that I didn't know what this was. I was intrigued to find out -- what is this? I was especially interested in the idea of cleaning. The prefect kept saying cleaning, cleaning -- that was the one topic I was so intrigued about. I wanted to know, "What is cleaning?" Because I'd never heard of it -- meditation, yes, it's a common thing -- but cleaning? It's so new.

So after a few days I called the prefect, started the practice, and in the first sitting itself I knew, "This is it. This is what I was searching for." The experience was incredible, almost like a bolt of lightning going through my body. It was incredible; I never experienced this in my life. I took the three sittings and in two weeks my prefect called me (they're a little shy to talk about the Masters in the beginning because they don't know what you may think, especially in the United States where it's not such an accepted thing), so very shyly she says, "You know, the Master who's giving this practice is traveling to Montréal." I said, "Oh really?" and she said "Yes. I'm going. I have a ticket on this flight and I'm going these days." I said, "Okay fine" and I hung up and then I thought, "I need to see who this guy is." I called the airline, I booked the ticket and I called the prefect and said, "I'm going with you on the same flight." I took my daughter, who was four years old, and we flew to Montréal. My husband later on decided that he would come so he drove up to Montréal from Detroit with the prefect's husband; both of them came.

The event was scheduled in a university campus. Master and his wife were sitting alone in the meditation hall; nobody was there at all yet, a very special opportunity. My prefect introduced me and Master gave me a chocolate, [putting it] in my hand and, when he gave me the chocolate, it was like a confirmation: "Yes, finally you have come to the path that you had to be in, and welcome." I just felt as if I had come into a family that I knew about! I was so comfortable. The prefect was making sure that I was not alone, that I was taken care of – but I felt so comfortable; nobody had to do anything. It was like my brothers and sisters, I felt like I knew them before for some reason. It was a beautiful experience -- the sittings with Master -- I had no idea

THE JOURNEY WITHIN

what I was getting into. I was just happy. I knew, "This is my Master. He is mine." And that was it. My husband came and he also joined when he came. His story is a different one.

So, yes, I do think it's important to meet Master – and that's why he travels so much -- to meet with the people. Once he was in Europe and he made a trip across the border from France to Switzerland. He was in some cafeteria in a small town and a lady came to serve them and somehow that lady knew about Sahaj Marg, and she talked to Master. The whole trip was just to meet her. She didn't know about Master and he didn't know about her – and he didn't know why he was going there -- but it was to meet that one lady. He traveled all around the world.

Kim: He's being directed?

I think, he's being <u>attracted</u> by people, by the call of their hearts.

Kim: Do you think there is a group in the brighter world that is working to guide our living Master and to help us?

Yes, sure. See, the soul does not die.

Kim: Do you think Jesus Christ is there with the group?

Yes, all the great teachers -- Grand Buddha, Krishna -- they're all working for the upliftment of human kind. And they send, from time to time, Masters to teach us and to uplift us -- and those souls that are ready to help. But we have to <u>ask</u> for that help, we have to be ready

THE JOURNEY WITHIN

for that) -- because we have the free will, the will power. So unless we allow them, [unless] we permit them to help us, they won't be able to. And this meditation, this practice, is a preparation, a willingness to say, "Yes, we are preparing ourselves. Please help us." Then they come and they do help us.

Kim: Is it hard work?

No, because it all has to come from the heart. It's not so much what we do or what we think. If we do sincerely feel it in our heart (that is most important); we have to connect with our heart. It's no use just saying with our mind, "Yes, I want a Master and I want his help here, and I want to do this practice." Even the practice cannot be done that way. It has to be done with sincerity, humility, and a <u>real craving</u> that comes from our heart. Only that [craving] is what the Masters respond to – and it's not an intellectual process, it's not an intellectual exercise at all.

Kim: What advice would you have for someone who's new to the concept of spirituality?

To sincerely ask with their heart (it doesn't have to be in a temple or church or anywhere); if you long for it, long for the answer, it comes, it will come. It's like a mother, you know? When a child cries in a group of children, how does the mother know it is her child that is crying? It's that connection, it's that love -- and when we cry sincerely from our heart: "Oh God I want to be with you," he shows us the way. There are no two ways about it. He responds immediately.

Kim: Talking about being a mother, about raising children in the U.S.A... Do you think in some ways people from a more conservative culture have an advantage

THE JOURNEY WITHIN

over people from a more free culture? How important is it to have a pure lifestyle?
Do people from a pure background have an advantage when coming to Sahaj Marg?

Not necessarily so. Anybody can join Sahaj Marg, no matter what background.

In the upbringing of children (it doesn't matter what society it is), they do need discipline, they do need guidance; that's what the parents are there for. I remember my oldest daughter (I used to be quite a disciplinarian with my children); after she grew up, she told me, "I'm so glad you were so strict with me because if you had not been I would have been lost. I wouldn't know what choices to make. Even though I hated you for it at the time, later on, I really appreciated it and thank you for guiding me." So this idea that they have in the (mostly the Occidental societies), that children have to experiment on their own, they have to make their own choices, it's a little bit sad because you don't have to learn everything on your own. You should have some learning, some experiences of others who have already gone through that path, and build upon that.

There is confusion about liberty and freedom and living your life and making your choices in these countries, because you can have liberty and free choice also when you have discipline or a disciplined way of life. It's not constricted; it's not a type of imprisonment. It's actually a type of a protection that's being given to you -- when you're given guidance, when you're given certain rules of a way of life -- and this most religions try to give, even Christianity. Jesus tries to teach to love your neighbor as your own; don't covet other people's things. These are basic principles that have somehow been distorted by societal thinking, "We are free. We should be able to enjoy everything, be able to experience everything, even sexual activities. But it's gone to an extreme. Certain rules have been given to society to be protected and we are distorting that. We are distorting those ideas, and that is what most of the masters, the gurus, are sad about, you know?

THE JOURNEY WITHIN

Take a simple thing like a traffic light. What are they there for? You can say, "Oh, it's constricting my freedom to drive as I would like." It's there to protect us so that we don't get into an accident. Simple! The same way, children have to be given guidelines, some direction. Most children, when they come home there are no parents to give them any guidance. The parents, when they come, are too tired; they don't spend any time with their children. They [children] are left on their own to grow. It's too much pressure for a child to be on its own. They need guidance -- and unfortunately, parents think that it is the school that has to do it, and it's not. It's not the school's responsibility to do that. It's the parents' responsibility to take care of that child, guide them to make the right choices within their own free will -- and they will make those choices -- but they need some guidance to get there.

Kim: Do you have any special memories about Master or anything else that you'd like to share?

I'll give you an experience [from] 1992 when I came to India. It was the first time I was coming to India to meet Master [P. Rajagopalachari] and I came with my two daughters. My youngest was a one-year-old and the oldest was seven years old. I was staying with my husband's family and I called Master and I asked him what is his schedule, that I'd like to come and visit him -- and he says, "Don't ask me those kind of questions, I don't know what I'm doing the next minute. But you can come to Hyderabad for the Silver Jubilee [celebration, gathering] and from there you can come with me to Manapakkam ashram." And I said, "Oh, but Master, it's so hot!" (I was so naïve in those days.) And he said, "Where are you right now? Is it any different? You'd better come to Hyderabad." "OK, Master." So I made arrangements and I stayed in a minister's house because this minister is a relative of my husband's family – beautiful, air-conditioned house; chauffeur-driven car dropped me off at the ashram and picked me up. [It was] so comfortable at the house and I could leave my children and go for satsanghs [group meditations]. I didn't tell anyone where I was staying

THE JOURNEY WITHIN

or anything but, I kept going for the satsanghs [2-3 per day] and coming back.

I was supposed to go from Hyderabad to Manapakkam that night and was in the minister's house packing when I received a call that afternoon. Somebody called from the ashram, saying, "You have to change your ticket. Master's not going tonight; he's going tomorrow morning." I thought, "What? How did they find out I am here? Nobody knows this phone number, nothing. Is this some crank call or something?" So I called the ashram to make sure: "I want to talk to Master." I could hear Master in the background talking to abhyasis and the person on the phone refused: "No, Master is busy." "But I need to talk to him and find out if he is going tonight or tomorrow morning." "He's going tomorrow morning, sister." And I hear Master asking who is calling and says I have to change my ticket. So I go off that afternoon to change my ticket for the next day morning flight – and I'm 35th on the waiting list. "Oh, my gosh. I won't be able to go with Master." "No, you have to come back tomorrow morning to the airport, you are 35; there are no seats now."

So I have to pack up everything and, in the morning I go to the airport, and am still number 35 on the list. Nothing had changed. So I'm wondering, "Is there another flight? How am I going to go?" -- And I am so confused because I'd never traveled in India; I'd never been in India before. It was very confusing for me, the whole situation.

Then Master comes and he passes by and says, "Bani, did you change your ticket?" And I said, "No, I don't have a ticket, Master. I'm on the waiting list." "Oh." and he smiled and went off. Then, after a few minutes, somebody comes with three tickets for us. "Here, here, here. You can go." "But what happened? I was 35 on the waiting list. All 35 got tickets?" Somebody came and told me, "Master wanted you on the flight so they asked other abhayasis to stay back but put her on the flight." When I heard that, I thought, "Oh, Master is taking care of

THE JOURNEY WITHIN

me!" (You know how the ego works? You feel elated, special, and it's nothing.)

So we land in Chennai airport and Master, of course, with his entourage goes off in his car and I'm left alone with these two kids. I don't even have the address of the ashram, I don't know where to go, and everybody's almost gone. Then I see one lady that I know is an abhyasi so I run to her, "Are you going to the ashram?" "Yes." "Can I come with you? I don't know where it is." " Yes, yes, yes." She finds an auto-rickshaw; the three of us with all our luggage. Can you imagine? From the minister's house with a chauffeured car, here I am in an auto-rickshaw with this lady arguing with the auto-rickshaw guy that she'll pay only this and not that and he says, "No, you have to pay this." Finally, we reach the ashram, the driver is so mad at this lady, and I was so afraid that he would even do something to us; I was trying to calm her down and say we'll pay whatever he wants, but she said it was the principle of the thing and she didn't want to pay any more. So when she gave him the money and we got down (thank God we were out of the rickshaw before she gave the money) -- he was so mad he threw the money at her. He didn't take any of the money and he went off. I was like, "Oh, my goodness. What is this?"

It is so hot -- and then I turn around and I see only vacant land with one coconut tree somewhere in the distance and another coconut tree with a palm tree growing out of the middle, and a shed-like thing and a hut-like thing made out of palm leaves -- and I thought, "Oh my God. Where am I? What is this?" They tell me, "OK. That is the meditation hall." It's an open-air with an asbestos roof and I think, "How could I stay under an asbestos roof; it's cancer-producing, don't they know? Why are they doing this? How dare they put me here?" And it's so hot and there is no fan and it's open air and there are no trees. This was in 1992 and it was nothing like it is now. [Just] vacant, bare land. It was a hole, a hole in the ground. Master's quarters were on one side of the meditation hall and we slept in the meditation hall. My youngest daughter inevitably, every night, she would cry. She was the crying baby.

THE JOURNEY WITHIN

So the first day at the ashram when I saw Master in the evening he was having a great day -- and I was so miserable, ready to take the next plane out of here. With two kids, how am I going to stay here? I was just beside myself. He didn't even look at me because he knew I was so mad. We were all sitting there with the Master and I was like, "I can't wait to get out of here. I don't want to be here." My oldest daughter goes to him and he says, "So how do you like this place?" "Not much." "Don't worry; you will like it better later." It was almost like telling me through my daughter that I would be fine. That was the first day.

I stayed one month. I didn't want to leave this place. It was just so wonderful to be here, even with all the discomforts, all the mosquitoes, my daughter crying at night, not much to eat, didn't feel like eating with all the spices. Just being here was such a training for me. Master [was] training me during that time to be in tune with whatever is available, just get adjusted. My daughters also loved it. Our trips were to Master's house and back. That was it. Otherwise, we'd be at the ashram.

One time we went to Master's house and there was this prefect who said, "Oh I'm staying in a hotel and my wife and I are going shopping. I'll take you there. You can rest there and then go back to the ashram." So he took us to this AC room and we slept for four hours straight (laughter). It was such a luxury. But then, as soon as we got up, (ah!) we missed the ashram and had to go back. We rushed back to the ashram. It was so lovely to be in that barren, infested mosquito park -- unbearable place – most uncomfortable place ever. Even to take a shower was such a big deal for me because, there are no showers -- you have to use a bucket in a small cubicle. Everything is wet; don't know where to hang the clothes, everything is dirty or looks dirty. It was such an experience. One month of bliss in that condition -- and Master's presence is felt throughout.

THE JOURNEY WITHIN

Kim: What are the short-term goals of the mission – or are there short-term goals?

The purpose of the mission is to serve humanity. Those souls that are seeking will surely find this place. We don't advertise, we don't promote; it's all word-of-mouth. Those who are seeking, those who are really truly seeking, they come and they find this mission. [There are] stories of abhyasis from far away -- they've told me the stories of how they find Sahaj Marg; each one of them have incredible stories. It's so funny because, when we asked people to write the history of how the practice started, people in one of the countries in South America wrote, "Master came to Chile through the heart of this abhyasi from Colombia who visited us. So Master comes to all these places. It's amazing how, throughout the world, people are finding the practice. It's because they're seeking it, and Master has not been to those countries at all.

Kim: Do you have any concerns that he is getting older and will pass on?

Well that is life -- but he has lived it to the fullest. If you watch him, you will see that, every minute, he is utilizing it to the utmost. It's as if, in one minute, there is infinity -- and how much he does in that one minute, it's incredible. We have no clue, because constantly he is working. Every moment he is working. Even in his sleep he is working. So he has done so much work; one day he has to get some rest and his successor will have to take over and we, as his disciples, as his abhyasis, we need to take up the work and continue. It's such noble work that he's doing, so full of love. I have never experienced this type of love anywhere -- not even from my parents.

Kim: What do you see as the role of Sahaj Marg for the future?

THE JOURNEY WITHIN

It is a social movement in a way, a silent movement. Each one of us, we are changing, and that is going to change society and I hope it is for the better. I don't see why it should be a Doomsday if we are all working for it. I think it will be a beautiful future for humanity.

Chapter 3 **Meditate Together**

Matthew

Chinese (People's Republic of China), 18 years old, male, studying Political Science & Law in Beijing

Preface: In this chapter, we hear from a young man from China who is new to meditation, having started only two months previously. He talks about his generation in the PRC and his feelings of loneliness. He also shares experiences of learning to meditate, encouraging others to give themselves time to adapt to the practice. Finally, he discusses his feelings of fellowship as he enjoys the warmth and kindness extended by meditation brothers and sisters.

Matthew and I met through his sister, who came up and introduced herself after meditation one morning. With our China connection and with her upcoming move to New York City to study for a Master's degree, we have much to discuss. I ask to interview both her and her brother. Matthew and I meet at the canteen and enjoy a simple lunch of rice and lentil gravy before settling near the children's merry-go-round to talk. We enjoy the children's laughter while proceeding with the interview. Apologetic about his sometimes halting English, Matthew impresses with his sensitivity and insights about society as well as his perspectives about starting meditation.

Kim: So could you just tell a little bit about yourself?

My father is a government officer and my mother used to be a nurse but now she works for an electronics company. I'm here in India for the first time with my older sister. I am a new abhayasi.

Kim: Isn't it a little unusual that there are two children in your family?

Yes, especially in mainland China. I was born in 1994 and, especially in 1994, the one-child policy was very strict -- so I experienced many things other children didn't experience. If I was found by a government officer, my mother and my father would lose their jobs and have to pay a lot of money. So they hid me. Sometimes I would spend one month in the countryside or maybe I would go live with my aunt and uncle, so they shifted me around so nobody found out.

Kim: But now no problem?

Maybe, maybe not. Because now, not everybody knows I am my father's son. Some of his colleagues don't know. But I think it's okay; not a serious problem now.

Kim: That's an interesting story. Brave parents, right?

Yes. And one lucky thing is my sister, younger sister --maybe you would say my cousin -- she is the daughter of my aunt. She was born just ten days after me. So they told everybody we are twins.

Kim: So you spent more time with your aunt and not as much time with your parents?

THE JOURNEY WITHIN

Actually, with my grandparents; together with my cousin, we lived with them.

Kim: And that's very common in China, right, that the grandparents help to raise the children?

Yes, always.

Kim: Well, very interesting background. We are lucky you are here. We are lucky you were born.

Yes. I think I really experience many things, but some things I don't want to experience.

Kim: Some difficulties?

Yes, because the feeling that you can't go with your mother, go with your father on the street. If you go, there comes their colleague and my parents will tell me, "Go away to the other side of the street." I think it's not a good feeling.

Kim: You feel like you don't belong. Wow, what a shame. Especially since boys are so -- everybody is so happy to have a boy.

THE JOURNEY WITHIN

Yes, especially in China. I asked my grandparents, my mother and father -- especially my grandparents – why did they even have me? They said the reason is they wanted a boy.

Kim: So could you tell the story of getting involved with spirituality and meditation?

Yes. You know, I don't know why I am very nervous – I find it easy to get stressed out, you know, and I always pay much attention to the outside and not to my heart. I always focus on what somebody else will do to me. So I talked to my sister, and my sister told me she does meditation and it takes her to a peaceful situation -- so she introduced it to me. I'm still new. I've only been doing it about one or two months.

Kim: So why did you decide to come here, to India? Most people wait maybe one year and then they come. Did you feel the need to come and see master or...?

Maybe because my sister decided to come and it was a good chance for me. And I wanted to see India. I know things here are just like at the source. Everything starts from here and [goes out] to the world. So I wanted to get to the source to see. Today I saw the master and did meditation with him. It's really good. I am a lucky boy. And somebody introduced us to master and he shook hands with us. It gave me a big surprise. And in meditation with Master real near, I think maybe you are so close to the source, so it is very unique and strong.

Kim: How do you feel when you meditate? Can you feel anything inside?

As you know, I'm new. So sometimes, because you are new, when you do meditation, you always have some thoughts enter your mind. You

THE JOURNEY WITHIN

will think about what happened in the past or you will think about the future, or you will think what happened between you and your friends and so on. So a lot of things just flood to my mind. So my prefect told me, "You should keep your mind focused on the heart." So I try my best to do it, but maybe because I am new, I still have lot of things on my mind. And it is hard to sit still. Sometimes there is back or neck pain and I want just to move all the time. I remember the first time I had a sitting with the prefect, because the room was really hot and there were flies distracting me, and I had never [before] sat or rested in one position for one hour. That was new for me. So it was challenging. But now it's easier than before.

Kim: Have you changed since you started meditating?

I think I have a better spirit. Before I did meditation, I was always stressed out, nervous, and not confident about myself. So after doing meditation, maybe I think I am more at peace -- and I don't feel desire to get many things...

Young people are changing in China. In my generation -- maybe it's related to the one-child policy. Every family can only have one child. So in my generation, parents will give them what they want and a lot of love. They don't need to share with their brother or sisters -- all is just for one person. So maybe it's different from the last generations, our parents or grandparents. But the good thing is, you know, China has changed a lot so we can see more things, get more things, maybe be more talented than before. Maybe in our past generations, our parents just can't know -- knowledge was limited in their world. For instance, very few of them had the chance to take lessons, like how to play the violin. But now, it seems everybody can paint well, play the violin well, and they get good knowledge. They can go to university, they can get further education and they can go to foreign countries to learn more. In my generation, the boys and girls are more talented and open-minded. And their ideas are more open. In past generations, my parents and their colleagues don't know how to speak English. They

THE JOURNEY WITHIN

can't communicate with foreigners like we can. But now it's common that everybody speaks English. Some may learn when they are older; some may be skillful while others just can make basic conversation. But that's OK. It means they can communicate with the outside, not only within their country.

Kim: Do you think people in China are also becoming more open to the idea of spirituality?

Meditation. Yes, yes. Our parents, they don't know about meditation, "What is it?" And they never know why I should do meditation and they don't know it is good -- but in this generation, they know, and they can understand it. Maybe because they know there is yoga in India and many people do meditation, and it is important to people's life so they will be more open to it.

Kim: Do you have any advice -- let's say a friend of yours is just maybe starting to think about meditating. Would you have any advice for them?

I think the first time, the second time, third time, somebody who tries meditation will find it easy to drop it. They should hold onto it ... insist on it.

Kim: Don't quit.

Yes, keep [doing] it. After six or seven times, they will be fine.

Kim: Do you think Sahaj Marg can change the world?

THE JOURNEY WITHIN

Change the world? I think it could because -- you know, everybody here, even though strangers, they will say "sister or brothers." Maybe in the city, you face a stranger, you will think, "Will he be dangerous for me, will he cheat me?" It's not a good phenomenon for human beings. I think human beings should just be like when at home; you should love each other in a unit together. Maybe if Sahaj Marg is all over the world, whomever you see, [you'll think], "She is my sister, he is my brother. I shouldn't cheat him. I shouldn't fight with him. I shouldn't start a war to invade his land." Right?

Kim: Right. Will you try to persuade your friends to try?

Persuade. Maybe I will present it to my roommate because, in the university, he is the person who trusts me most. Before I come to India, my friends told me, "Please tell us what happens in India" and they want me to teach them meditation.

Kim: Do you have anything else you want to tell me, anything you want to share?

I want to say… I think in our generation, maybe it's a lonely generation. Even though I have a sister -- and that is better than other children -- but when I was a teenager, my sister went to Shanghai and I then went to school in Beijing. When I came home, my sister was still in Shanghai. Our parents always have work, you know. So always, I stayed alone at home. I feel lonely. And I think competition in the younger generation is more serious than in the last, older generation. So we always feel stressed out. When I was young, our parents told us, "You should study hard, you should make your personality more strong and you should study and learn more skills." So we feel very stressed out. We have a lot of stress, just like a mountain on our back.

THE JOURNEY WITHIN

Kim: Crushing you, yes. So this is a way to not feel so lonely? Sahaj Marg, does it help you not feel so lonely?

Yes, because we do meditation in groups. And if you see others, they will call you brother or sister. They are very kind if you are in trouble. Yes. If you are in the city and you have trouble, maybe only somebody warm-hearted will help you. But many people, they will imagine how they can get more money, get a higher position or how to get more power. Maybe your trouble is just not important to others. But, you know, everybody has troubles. So we should meditate together.

Kim: Yes, one big family on earth.

Yes, yes, yes.

Part II: **Lifestyle Changes**

A number of lifestyle changes have taken place since I started meditation. Establishing a new routine was a first, practical change. Depending on my work schedule, I try to sit for meditation for an hour at sunrise and sit for evening cleaning for at least half an hour at sunset. This has meant getting up earlier in the morning to have quiet time before the family rises. Evening cleaning normally involves "hiding" in my bedroom to better concentrate while others are arriving home after work or socializing before dinner. I have also found it important to give time for an evening prayer before reclining to sleep. This settles my mind, opens my heart to the divine source, and puts me in a "zone" conducive to sound sleep. These changes in schedule have affected family life very little but have had a great deal of impact on my personal life. I sleep better, I am calmer and somehow "removed" from emotional involvement, and I feel more inner peace and happiness. I feel I am simply able to cope more positively with life.

The most important change for me personally has been a more balanced and unemotional reaction to problems and stress. Have "feelings, not emotions," I was advised. To emote is to spew out our feelings, thus creating impressions on ourselves and on others; this is to be avoided. An important part of learning to meditate is to be able to "go to zero," or to become centered with the brain turned off (or humming along silently, passively). Inner focus and sensitivity should become increasingly centered on the heart, with random thoughts dismissed like unwanted visitors. The meditation trainer in Macau, Hari, explains that we want to be like a pendulum hanging straight down because, if we feel extreme joy (a high emotional swing to one side), then the pendulum will certainly swing back to the other side and we will likewise feel extreme pain. The goal is to be in balance so that we don't create impressions. He explains this and other important concepts in the Living in the Heart section of this book.

THE JOURNEY WITHIN

With an improved ability to "go to zero," I can respond more neutrally to stimuli. I am better able to simply "not engage" when addressed with hostility or anger, even when someone is pushing all the right "buttons" to bring me to anger. Increasingly, I am able to observe the situation from a removed position, to analyze more clearly what is happening and what the issues are, and to react in a non-combative, more loving and peace-making manner. This has obviously created an improved home life and has transformed my interactions with my husband. We are able to treat each other with mutual respect and kindness. We both have improved our abilities to handle strife with equanimity, maturity and a dose of humor. Many of the interviewees in this book discuss this aspect of a lifestyle change. In the interviews which immediately follow, you will find that Jyoti, a mother and wife, describes similar changes in family relationships and lifestyle. Her words will strike a chord with all the busy wives and mothers out there.

A very difficult concept for me has been the need to subsume the ego. I was just entering college at the height of the second wave of the feminist movement in the U.S.A.. I have worked most of my career in male-dominated contexts. As a woman and, usually, as a foreigner, it has been important to build a strong ego and sense of self-confidence. However, in the meditation practice, our goal is to merge with the divine energy, thus diminishing our individualism. Some describe a process similar to osmosis as we "blend" with the divine energy found in each of our hearts. This has been a big hurdle for me as much of my adult life has been spent building the ego. Coming from academia, I think it also difficult to be humble, having been given, especially in Asia, high status and respect due to my position as a university professor. So now I am in the process of breaking down any feelings of superiority, learning how to be more humble, and simply learning how to be quiet. I have found that being silent definitely helps in my progress as I work on various aspects of character development.

Other lifestyle changes have been to lead a "cleaner, purer" lifestyle by avoiding smoking, drinking, foul language, and negative influences such as books or movies that disturb a serene condition. I used to be a voracious reader and, having lived often in countries where books in

English are not readily available, didn't mind reading almost anything I could get my hands on, including murder or adventure stories with graphic descriptions of some of humankind's baser emotions. Now I find I simply cannot tolerate or "waste time" on such stories; neither can I afford to have them influence my peace of mind.

It is recommended that we not eat meat and, while I was not a huge meat-eater before, I live with three active men from the Midwest who are not yet ready to go totally vegetarian. Meat is actually a pretty big part of our cultural upbringing, as evidenced by turkey dinner for holidays, barbeque parties, and meals centered around meat as the main dish. My father, a farmer, raised a herd of beef cattle, in fact. When I first started meditation, I tried to be strict with myself about vegetarianism, feeling very guilty if I did try some fish or meat occasionally. I had identical feelings and issues with drinking alcohol. Macau was a Portuguese colony for 99 years, so wine is a big part of the social culture here. Many business lunches, for example, feature a bottle of wine with the meal and port with dessert.

So, when interviewing others, I wanted to find out what lifestyle changes had occurred for them and what processes were involved. I wanted to know for personal reasons, for myself and for my family. I hope to attract my sons to start meditation and have concerns about the lifestyles of young people in their early 20's. Is it necessary to have a pure lifestyle in order to grow in spirituality? This seems to me an important question for those considering or new to the practice.

This section features John, a French Canadian who describes fairly heavy involvement with a recreational drug before he started meditation. John is someone young people can relate to, especially young males. He gives good advice regarding lifestyle changes and talks contentedly about his involvement in the practice and his relationship with a spiritual master. John's chapter is followed by a conversation with Gilles (pronounced the same as "Jill"), who discusses a total change in career and lifestyle through immersion in the practice. Gilles switched from a lucrative career "selling fear," as he puts it (security systems) to becoming a psychotherapist engaged in lifestyle coaching and group therapy.

I hope you will enjoy these three stories as you ponder lifestyle changes you have been wanting to make in your own life. I have found that many changes happen naturally. In this book, you will hear others similarly talk about bad habits "falling away" as they proceed in the practice. A change in one aspect of your life may lead to automatic change in another. For example, more time in meditation means you need to stretch and be active in maintaining a good posture; otherwise, you are likely to have spinal or neck stress. So meditation can lead to involvement in yoga or physical activity to strengthen those muscles. Reducing meat intake can lead to improved physical health. Replacing wine with healthy fruit or vegetable beverages is helping me to reduce alcohol consumption. Will power is part of the mix, of course. Gilles also mentions the need for self-forgiveness and a recognition that all of life's experiences help us to learn and evolve. I leave you to our interviewees, John, Gilles and Jyoti.

Chapter 4   **The Wild Child**

John

French Canadian, male, late 30's, banking executive

Preface: In this deeply personal and frank chapter, John shares his background as a "wild child" with no limits, one who liked to "push the envelope," consistently breaking adult rules relating to sexuality, drugs, and life success. He talks freely about early experiences with marijuana use and the changes brought when he started meditation practice. He encourages us to "just start" a meditation practice and see what it will do in our lives. He also expresses deep feelings for his personal Master and teacher, Chariji.

We make ourselves comfortable in the air-conditioned bedroom of a friend, hiding from the dust and heat that seem so oppressive. We're just hoping the electricity doesn't go out, as it seems to during "nap time" most afternoons. I'm impressed by John's easy friendliness, his ability to express deep, intimate feelings, and his willingness to share his "wild child" entry into meditation. Here is someone young people can relate to and older people appreciate. He has a zest for life that is impressive.

Kim: How did you become interested in spirituality?

I live in Montréal, the French part of Canada. Spirituality came to me at a very young age, bit by bit, basically through my mother, who was interested in spirituality. I remember having different books about

Indians, about supra-mental consciousness. When I was 14, I attended a conference about supra-mentalists. I was the only young guy there and was always questioning.

My background was two-sided. From my mother I got spirituality and from my father, concern with the material [world]. A lot of people don't understand how I could live with this duality because my internal and my external tendencies are sometimes much different. [For example], growing up, I had a very strong pull by and toward women and, like a lot of young boys, a love for acquisition and a love for doing business and making money. At the age of 12, I would say I had the maturity of a boy of 17 or 18. I was quite mature and different experiences came to me at a very young age. I had my first girlfriend and sexual experiences when very young.

Also, in my generation, marijuana was booming. I was not ever really into alcohol – probably because my father was an alcoholic – [but] I was very passionate about marijuana and started [it] very young. At the same time, however, I was doing a lot of sports. I was known at school as a person who had no limits in any area. I would come to school stoned yet always had a lot of respect from my teachers and got good grades. I coped well with it all, so I never had a problem – except that I did not like to go to school.

Kim: So you got okay grades even though you were stoned?

That's right.

Kim: Were you popular?

THE JOURNEY WITHIN

I wasn't that popular, but I was the kind of guy everyone respected. I was on "middle ground." I had no specific gang but I was [accepted] by all.

Kim: You were the sort of person we would say likes to "push the envelope"?

That's right. I had my own car at the age of 16 and even tried to drive at 14, which I wasn't supposed to do. I just wanted to do what I wanted to do. Sexuality and physicality were important – to impress women and for my own belief in myself. All this meant that, by the age of 17 or18, I was at the peak of loving marijuana and tripping. When I was stoned, I thought a lot about life -- life in general -- and love. I remember looking at the sky and having a very strong feeling that we are not alone in this universe. I got such a very strong feeling about this that tears came to my eyes; it was a very nice experience. Once when I was 14-years-old while lying in the grass one night, I felt that I was the whole world, the whole universe.

I was never really attracted to strong drugs. So I just took a little bit and understood that, if I passed the limit, there would be no way back, because I loved it too much. I put in some self-discipline that helped me in the future for the stability of my mind. [I tried to] not cross the line where permanent effects would harm me for the rest of my life.

My parents divorced when I was 12 and I think that was the point where I decided to be the guy who did whatever he wanted. I became a man very fast -- too fast, I guess.

Kim: Whom did you live with?

THE JOURNEY WITHIN

My mother. It's a strange thing with my father: I had a very strong love of him and I think he loved me but he found me uncontrollable. I was too strong for him in terms of character (that's what he always said, anyway). So he left me with my mother and she had what I call an "intelligent heart," meaning she taught me to use my intelligence to make good choices. She never constrained me. That's why I never put myself in bad situations from which I could not return; I never crossed the critical point. That was very important. When I look at young people today: you can do a lot of things but you have to know inside that you shouldn't go beyond a certain point. I saw the damage that the new chemical drugs can bring, changing dramatically the only life you possess. At the age of about 19, I loved marijuana like heroin. I was still functioning in society, but I knew I was using the minimum of my potential…

At the same time, something very important was happening in my life. I just talked about the supra-mentalist conference I went to at the age of 14 and 15. There was such an energy. I know now, after the experiences I have had over the past 30 years, that something was transmitted at that time and place, to the people there. It was only a long time afterwards that I realized it, but I think there was a [spiritual] pull. We know that the heart works on the mind and, through science, we have discovered that meditation does the same thing. I realized a long time afterwards that I had a craving for something – and that I was putting that into a craving for drugs.

During supper, my father would look at me worried because I was stoned 24 hours a day – but I would tell my family, "Accept me this way or not at all. That's it!" I was doing things my way. But there was a switch one day. He told me, "You know your auntie is starting to do meditation. Maybe you should try this. It has changed her life; it has changed her character." He said that to me quite innocently, like a child. So I said to myself, "Okay, why not? Let's try this." So he gave me the phone number of a preceptor, which at that time was a person in charge of introducing people to that [meditation] system.

THE JOURNEY WITHIN

I remember the first time I went for a sitting, meaning sitting with somebody and meditating together. I had spoken to him (the meditation tutor) over the phone and he explained the process to me very quickly. He said nothing about spirituality, nothing about anything, just to come to his house and have a talk. I remember at that time I was smoking a joint but I told my friend, "I have an appointment. I have to go." So I took my car and, when I entered the place, I was received by someone with a feeling that I didn't even get in my own family.

Kim: So you felt close to this person?

Very, very rapidly, and his way of receiving me with love -- I didn't know it was love -- I just felt, when I entered this atmosphere, comfortable and at home. We talked and he said, "Just sit." I didn't know what we were doing or what we were going to do; I was still affected by the vapors of smoking. So he said, "Just close your eyes and put your attention on the heart region. Just imagine divine light is in the heart." So I said, "Okay, I can try." All of a sudden I [felt a] merging in me, where I completely lost consciousness; I did not know where or what I was. I was completely lost when I heard him call time. I couldn't believe it was already finished (in fact half an hour was completed). I closed my eyes and felt completely relaxed, with an empty mind! When he tapped me on my knee and said, "That's all." I said, "What?" I could not come back. He tapped me a few times before I came back. I felt I was in a special place. Afterwards I said, "Oh my God! What is this?" So he invited me for supper, which does not always happen when you meet a preceptor for the first time -- but he did and for some reason it touched me; it touched my heart.

He asked me to come back three days in a row and I agreed. I went back to my old stuff but, for some reason, I didn't feel the need to smoke. I remember that night I was with my "drug friend." I didn't know if he felt something was wrong with me, but he said, "Something is different with you. What happened?" He wanted to go on a trip to

THE JOURNEY WITHIN

St. John Lake. Normally I would just say "yes" right away. He just got his paycheck and would have paid for everything. But when he said, "Let's go!" for some reason I said, "No, I have an appointment." I don't know where this will came from, but I decided to go to the second sitting. And I think that was the pivotal point of my life (I would only understand this a long time afterwards). This second sitting was so important that, if I hadn't gone to it, who knows what would have happened?

I went again and had the same experience. Boom! I was nowhere. I said, "There's something in this." Something external entered me and, on the inside, I became better and better. I had a feeling of lightness in my heart. So the final story is that I got to the third sitting and I fell in love with this energy thing.

Kim: Something wholesome?

Yeah, exactly. It helped me. This preceptor said he wanted to see me more often and was very nice. He had children and I get along well with children; so I had a chance to connect with something that helped me. There were no questions about whether I should stop using drugs or anything. I never was a big meat-eater and so never had the craving for it. When he told me in this system it is good to be vegetarian, somehow I found myself becoming vegetarian almost instantly. I stopped eating red meat almost right away; something from inside was preventing me. I ate chicken for a further two years and [then] the taste for chicken just disappeared on its own.

With this system, I didn't feel confined or restricted. There was a freedom that any change that happens comes from inside, not from the outside -- so it worked well with my perception of the world and what I was doing with my life. So I continued with this system we call Sahaj Marg.

THE JOURNEY WITHIN

The world was changed… Up until then I never had any idea of what spirituality was or why I would seek out spirituality. I had no specific thing [goal] in mind, but for some reason I had the feeling that if I woke up every morning and tried [to meditate, tried] something small, it gave me something. Some people need time to get to the one hour [of morning meditation]. I remember it took me eight months to get to one hour. For a long time I got stuck at 45 minutes. It was okay and no-one told me, "This is bad." I loved it.

After six months, I felt no need to smoke again. It took six months, a long time. I was doing sittings, meditation and practicing but not always at 100%. I loved it so I did it. Things started to change. I started at university and got really high grades and, all of a sudden, I was always at the top of the class. I was just falling in love with what it had brought me. Looking at my background, I still had friends, many kinds of friends. But one-by-one, they all kind of disappeared for some reason or another. That would have been the one thing that prevented me from continuing; I could have been afraid of not wanting to lose my friends, but they just disappeared without any discussion, or fight or anything. It was just that life was changing. I made new friends, a different life, different vibration, different level and something just became. Whoosh!

When I was in the fourth or fifth year of a French course in high school, one of my teachers said, "You know what, John? You like to do as you please too much. So why don't you just go and work in McDonalds, because that's the only place you are ever going to work in your life." I remember this so clearly. It really struck my heart and I told myself, "No way! That's not going to happen. Believe me!" By doing this practice, life has brought me to where I could go back to that teacher to say, "You see? My life turned out well!" So I continued this practice from the age of 19 to now. I'm shortly turning 40.

THE JOURNEY WITHIN

But I would say the greatest experience didn't start there. The greatest experience started the first time I met the Master, Chariji. I remember I went to see him in Germany two years after I started; it was the first time I traveled. I went with my preceptor in 1994 and I remember it like it was yesterday. I remember going on the train to the place and when we entered there was a camp, with tents and canopies, [and I felt] some great lightness emanating from that place. I was very sensitive and I was fortunate to feel that. I thought, "Oh my God! What's going on here?" My meeting with him was a very simple one. I waited for him, someone introduced me and we shook hands in a businesslike way. He said, "Welcome" but that word "welcome "in his voice had so much depth; it was very special. At that time, Chariji could travel a lot. I am so grateful today for having the opportunity to travel with him and to be with somebody like that; it has such a deep meaning. There's a special feeling you have with such a teacher. It's the same feeling that I used to express to my girlfriend, "Just being with you is enough." It's also the same feeling that a mother has with her child.

People were telling me it would change my life but I didn't really understand and it wasn't that important. It didn't happen immediately. I guess I had a big load to clean up… believe me, I had a large emotional load to work on at a very deep level. One of the more difficult things is when you look at people who have done this work for 10 to 15 years. Sometimes you feel a bit depressed when you look at the huge amount of work in front of you. The craving of being there already makes you suffer! Then, at the end of it, you kind of see the "applause" and you're there.

So things continued on what I now call this spiritual path. I finished school, finished university, finished all of that, found a good job, and now am raising a family. There are times when things are tough and I feel pulled in many different directions: by money in one direction, society in another, my girlfriend, and by what we call the Mission, where the practice takes place. I am now living with someone who is not involved with the practice; although she's not really interested in spirituality, she has a lot of sensitivity and is in touch with feelings…

THE JOURNEY WITHIN

Kim: So she's not meditating?

Not meditating and not interested. She's a very dynamic person who feels that when we meditate we do nothing. She is the kind of person who cannot feel she is doing nothing. She has two nice kids who I have the privilege of helping her raise at the moment. No one knows what the future will bring, but there is nothing to stop someone from following his own path.

I look at youth today and cannot tell you how much I would like to transmit and support them with my experience. I will never really know what this Master did for my life and I will never really capture the entire picture. Sometimes my mother tells me, "Why don't you just leave this and try something else?" There's nothing to try if you have found your own way, when you have found a person that has helped you in every single part of your life. There's nothing more to say. I am just grateful to Chariji, my Master. Today I can call him this because I feel that he is the person in charge of my life. Twenty years ago, I couldn't think like this. It's just a matter of experience and [I know] he has transformed me over the years. When I look at it, I came from a Christian background with a belief about the Christ miracle. For me, the real miracle was when a system, a Master, imprints your life by just being with you.

I see rich, intelligent, beautiful people and their lives -- but I wouldn't swap [that] for any of my past with my Master. I just yearn to see him again and again and feel very grateful that I can. With his age now, it is becoming more and more difficult to see him and that gives sorrow.

Kim: My next and final question, unless you have something to add, is how important is it to be physically with Master? You talked about traveling with him and seeing him. I'm a new abhyasi and it's becoming increasingly difficult; I don't

THE JOURNEY WITHIN

have a personal relationship with him and see him from a distance although, in my heart, I feel I have a relationship. But, in terms of the conventional idea of a personal relationship, could you comment on that? I think it's increasingly difficult to have access to this person.

That's an interesting question and you may or may not like the answer. One of the things about this practice was [a feeling of suffering by] not being able to see him more than I was doing, such suffering for so many years. Believe me… today I know I was blessed. If I compare myself to new abhyasis in the system, I was blessed like no other; there's no amount of money, nothing that would come close to that.

Kim: To be with him 24 hours a day.

Today I can say that. Twenty years back, it was not the same. At times I was angry with him; [I also] wanted to guard this very personal relationship and would really love him to be my father, the one that I never had. I had a mother but my father was absent. A lot of people have different experiences with the Master, depending on what they have to learn.

I suffered by not being able to see him. It was like being a barking dog at his door. I thought that he was not listening, but he always gave me a small gift when I was least expecting it, a little sign, just amazing. I wouldn't have got that smile, that love even from my own mother. It could be a five-second thing that just blows you out in your heart for weeks and weeks, so just imagine the strength and energy that you receive! So yes, I could have got more and from the bottom of my soul, I would have loved to have had more, but that's how it was for me.

THE JOURNEY WITHIN

At the same time, there are new people arriving who are fortunate in having many opportunities to see him. Others have little opportunity to see much of him and do you know what? For some, it's not that important, because for them the internal connection is very strong. The system of Sahaj Marg is evolving. Just as the universe has expanded, so too has Sahaj Marg; evolution is also [involved]. What we transmit and what the Master transmits to abhyasis has a certain evolutionary quality and refinement. For me, this evolutionary quality is becoming more and more subtle; so less contact is sometimes necessary to do the same work.

Let me tell you something interesting. Sometimes I see abhyasis who have been in the Mission for two or three years. They have such a light. You may yourself even sometimes see it in the mirror. That means He can give everything from a distance at any moment. So I think what is important is to see him for the first time. That first contact with him is very, very important. It must be done. After that, it unfolds according to each personality, in each person's life, and things come as they come.

I do remember one thing Master told me, (and I don't remember everything he told me because you're in a kind of state where you don't remember everything afterwards) when I was in a north Indian city. My heart was pounding and I said, "Master, I have a question to ask you. How can I become like you?" He said very simply, "Accept things as they are." This seems very simple; it's linked with not only Sahaj Marg but with all spiritual teachers. Everyone talks about this but it took me years and years to understand this. Accept things as they are.

Today if I see him once or five times, I'm happy; happiness is there all the time. In one sitting, he will give you what another will receive in ten. So numbers are no longer important, but being in his presence when you can is a very important thing because it gives certain things you may not be able to receive at a distance. So even now, in 2013, I

THE JOURNEY WITHIN

think it is still important to spend time with him. Maybe Sahaj Marg will evolve, as a society things will change, and you won't be able to be close to him. Maybe in 20 or 30 years from now, things will be done directly at a distance. Who knows?

Kim: Let's talk more about the human role in evolution. Looking at the Earth today and everything going on, there seems to be a lot of cataclysmic change coming our way. Do you see Sahaj Marg as a social movement, as a way of life for the future that can take us in a new direction as a species?

Yeah. I love your question. I have to be frank. Because I was linked to the extra-terrestrial movement with my mother when I was young, [those ideas were] not new for me. I knew that inside me: it's not that I "see" people but I always knew that there were other forms of life elsewhere. I always knew. People can say, "You don't have proof." They can say that science says this and that, but if you look at the size of the universe, it would be a sign of low intelligence to think that we are alone. I don't want to make a judgment about this but I would even go as far to say that this belief [that we are alone in the universe] is Americanized (since I consider myself an American, I include myself). So we think we own the world. We think we rule the world and allow ourselves to do as we please with the world, but in a way, we are so very small.

So coming back to what's going to happen. Everyone knows they have a sixth sense and people have a profound feeling that things are happening now. There is a lot of change. How will it occur? Will it be a disaster? Will it be nuclear? There are definitely things that are happening, big changes in the way life is lived. Civilizations have gone through it [before]; it's just change. We're not better, we're not worse; we are what we are.

Sahaj Marg came into the picture. I don't think of myself as part of a great movement -- not at all, because to think that would be self-

THE JOURNEY WITHIN

centered. I really think, when I see the way it works in this system, that there's a pull that everything originates from that helps us act when we're linked to that pull. When we are linked to that pull, we are part of a protective entity; we are linked to the center, linked to a puzzle that's completely done.

I know that this lightening, this subtle energy, which is being brought to us, is at another level of vibration and it helps a lot as we go through either small emotions or big things in life. It helps to minimize certain things. Along with that, it brings a real feeling of community and maybe love… One thing I know is that, when the time is right, we are going to be linked and I think we are definitely going to be able to help each other with this center that will connect us as one. In that sense we are going to be safer -- not because we are going to be protected and so on, no -- it's more like hearts linked together making things happen; you become a part of the whole process.

The way you live your life is the most important thing. If I can live my life, come to seminars, and see my Master, see my European friends, see my American friends and see my friends from all over the world -- this feeling of affection, of love and of connection is great. This is priceless and I would give away all my money for that. A lot of my old friends have never had this experience of consciousness and the experience of this transmission that he is giving us. Oh my God, such Grace!

Kim: Do you have anything else to add? Any advice, final stories?

This is not really advice as it just comes from my experiences. Whenever we feel pulled in some new direction, just take the first step because you just never know what that first step will bring you -- regardless of the kind of spiritual system [or] even for a job -- you never know where the first step will take you. Leave your fears aside

THE JOURNEY WITHIN

and take the first step and you will be amazed at what it will bring you. Thank you.

Chapter 5   Non-Separation

Gilles

French, male, 60's, psychotherapist

Preface: In this chapter, Gilles talks about changing his life completely as a consequence of learning about spirituality. He gave up a lucrative career selling security systems because he felt he was "selling fear." Now a psychotherapist, he draws upon the quantic field to help his clients see that we are all connected through the divine matrix. He discusses "stepping stones" to spirituality, the need to forgive oneself, the importance of "non-separation," and the role of a living Master.

Gilles and I meet mid-morning in a garden near the ashram which has a raised block patio. We share the comfortable sofa set with mosquitoes and cats while observing the inordinate number of snails that make the garden their home. Gilles is at the ashram with his wife, Pascale, and I had enjoyed their company socially before asking for an interview. I'm eager to learn more about Gille's career, as well as get his perspective on the lifestyle changes he himself has experienced since starting Sahaj Marg meditation. He has read and thought about my questions ahead of time and is ready to begin.

Kim: Can you tell us a little bit about yourself?

I'd like to begin at the beginning. I came to Sahaj Marg after meeting and getting to know Pascale (now my wife), who was healing me at the time. She was my doctor. At the time, I didn't really know what the

THE JOURNEY WITHIN

word "spirituality" meant. In French, "spiritual" means somebody with a lot of spirit, someone who is energetic.

I had a business and I worked in my own company for 15 years. I specialized in sales and was very good at selling, good at making money. In fact, this company still exists. It was bought by an international group and is now listed on the stock exchange.

Then I met the Master for the first time in France. He was supposed to come to Switzerland to do a seminar there but he cancelled, so I said, "I have 15 days' vacation. Let's go to India." I bought two tickets. This was in August of 1991.

Kim: Were you married then?

Boyfriend/girlfriend; we weren't married. We had just met in April and this was in August, so we had been together four months. I had my first sitting on the day of her birthday, the seventh of June.

Kim: So the question was, did you have your first sitting to please your girlfriend?

Not entirely. In fact, I would see her giving sittings because she's a preceptor and people would come to her house. One day I saw a lady who came out of the sitting with so much light in her eyes and a smile on her face. I jokingly asked my girlfriend, "What do you make them smoke?" She said, "We don't smoke. We meditate." So I said, "Okay then, I want to try (it)." So that's how I started. (laughs) I was 36 years old and I was still a child.

So (in India) we got a hotel near Master and spent 15 days there. I began to feel that I could no longer continue my work in the security company, which revolved around people's property and their personal security. My job was to sell fear in order to protect them. Inside myself, I felt I couldn't do that anymore. So before leaving, I went to speak to Master, asking, "Master, can I change jobs?" He said, "Yes, why not? On condition that you always make money because in Europe you need money."

Before getting on the airplane to go back to France, we had a sitting with the Master in a very small group. When we got on the airplane, for the first time ever, I was upgraded to first class. The hostess offered us some wine but Pascale advised, "I don't think you should drink. I don't think it's good for your condition." As a good Frenchman, I said, "A good glass of red wine can't hurt anyone." I drank my glass of wine and felt like a ton of bricks had fallen on my head. From then I understood that, even if the wine had a great taste, it wasn't good for my spiritual vibration so I eventually stopped drinking.

I understood that the first part of my life was imperfect, that I wasn't pure. I had a normal life as a human being and tried many things, but I knew it was a "school," or preparation. It was all these experiences that brought me to the Master and to God.

I did a lot of work on myself to accept the first part of my life as a stepping stone and to stop judging myself. This was the beginning of my personal development work which is still ongoing. It has been 22 years now. What I can say here is that, at the bottom of my heart, I feel good.

When I returned to France, I didn't know how to exit my company because my shares were worth a lot of money and my business partner didn't have the money to buy me out in cash. Even though it seemed

THE JOURNEY WITHIN

completely insane, I was convinced I could not continue and had no idea what I was going to do next. I also have a tendency to feel insecure in my character, so it was completely crazy to think of changing. Then a little miracle occurred. In a group meditation, the entire exit strategy of how to leave the company and how to present this to my partners came to me. I applied the strategy and two months later my business partner presented a proposal to buy me out. I lost a bit of money but I was happy and ready to leave the company. Within five years, I would have a salary and I would have some cash.

From there I started meeting different people and started a completely new professional life re-formed into helping human beings. I met doctors, professors and very quickly it started working very well for me. After I had earned my diplomas, I started teaching others in France, in Italy, and in Canada. I have become a professional coach, which is what I still do to this day.

Kim: I'd like to hear what you do in your own words.

My wife Pascale was working on autopsik, the re-education of the eyes, and I've been a psychotherapist for 20 years. A few years ago, we started working with groups and life coaching, specifically, and with family system constellations. We're now working on quantic constellations and quantic attitudes, [helping people] in France, all over Europe and in Canada. We hope to be at the service of the Grand Master.

We are working on consciousness, and our objective is to open the person to enlarge [their] consciousness of themselves and to gain a larger consciousness of life, of the Earth and of the Celestial. We are also working on non-separation, the idea that we are all linked. We are not separated, not from God and not from each other. For the people we work with, Pascale and I try to render unto them their responsibility and the power of creativity.

THE JOURNEY WITHIN

We use several practical tools to do this. For example, we ask that they purify their language. We use simple terms, abandoning psychiatric terms and mumbo-jumbo speech to work the way our ancestors used to work. In the Occident, we have been cut off from our capacity to heal ourselves and from the alchemistic capacity of transforming things. With inquisitiveness and having been initiated, we have the possibility of transforming ourselves, and therefore transforming Earth.

Kim: Do you work with individuals or groups?

Pascale works more with individuals and I work with groups. I worked with many individuals previously but now I work with groups.

Kim: Your training is in cognitive psychology? Did you have any formal training?

Yes, I did my psychotherapist training in psychoanalysis, systemic, PNL, hypnosis, study of dreams and many other kinds of training. I'm certified in America and hold French diplomas. I see myself as a coach because that is my job. I accompany people and guide them. I was officially a psychoanalyst for twenty years, but today I really have a different vocation. I would identify myself more closely as a coach.

Kim: And what do you do? So I come to you and I have a problem. In fact, the doctor I went to see said that I had some kind of trauma even in-utero and also during my life. What would you do?

There are three tools that I use. The first is the classic tool to understand the story of the person, but then we're still staying in the mind-intellectual analysis. We have more healing therapies and tools.

THE JOURNEY WITHIN

We know that all traumas come from childhood or from life in the uterus. Specifically, it manifests in the lymphatic system, the emotional mind and also the automatic/biological mind. The first traumatic imprints are created in childhood. We use a wonderful tool, which is also a quantic tool because it works on the morphic channels. It's called family systemic constellations. It's an acting out where people act out either their trauma or perhaps that of their family; your father, your husband, your children, your illness, your biological dysfunction. Whatever needs to be remedied can be discussed. Or your own family system -- you act it out like a play, you know?

It turns out that, when these people or systems in your life are represented/re-enacted, you then have access to the quantic or morphic field. In psychological terms, this would be termed the personal collective or family "subconscious." The people represented in your family are going to say things so that, without doubt, you know it's the truth, the reality. The dynamics then emerge, the nervousness, neuroses, anxieties or whatever needs to be healed. The wounds can be healed and there is the opportunity to change your beliefs and your vision of something. Healing is like a small "death." It's closure.

For example, it [this coaching] will permit acceptance of my parents, my dream of affection, my imperfections, their imperfections and [helps you] work to accept yourself and others. This is based on a biblical belief, a law, that you should not judge others. This law is very, very powerful because it is not to love your parents, but to honor them. This means, if you have been badly treated by your parents, you may not be able to love them, but you can achieve [a state of] not judging them. [Through] understanding the mechanics of why they treated you badly, you can come to understand and to honor them -- and honor our ancestors as you realize the constellation. This is the key to success in our life.

THE JOURNEY WITHIN

It's work and everybody comes to work for a specific objective. We can only help if the person has a specific objective. The therapist cannot decide; it's up to the person to wish help.

There's another tool that comes from America called the "Two Point Method." It was used by an American based on quantic laws and the work of physicians. Applications for daily use were created by working on the belief system, on your negative emotions, on your traumas, on your memories. [This work] enables transformation, alchemistic transformation.

The therapist is just a middle man providing love and information between the person that needs the consultation (the problem) and the quantic field, where everything and all solutions are possible. The only action of the therapist is to be in the heart and to serve the person for the betterment of all. We make a link, find the solution in the large store of the collective field, and bring it to the person.

It has been a real revelation to us, for Pascale and me, because we adapted this technique with the constellations and we now do quantic constellations. We created a method where we added various techniques in order to change people's inner beliefs, including the macular (eye movement) as well as the auditory, such as tapping. Neuroscience therapies have developed these and we have found they are very quick, efficient, and have profound effects. They work at a very deep level using different applications.

Kim: So is part of the idea that we take information through our senses, so therefore you're using those senses? The eye, taste, sound --?

No, no, no. Without making too many comparisons, it's exactly what our Master is doing in Sahaj Marg. He is the intermediary between the

Grand Master or the field of God and us. He cleanses us and
integrates new information within us at a higher level, but the principle
is quantic. Jesus Christ is a Grand Master and a great therapist who is
doing exactly the same thing. There are millions of healers in the world
who use this and don't even know that it is quantic. You don't need to
know it to have it work. Whether it be here in India or Native
Americans, or Indians in the north and the south, or the shamans or
the healers or the Christian mystics; all say the same thing, all function
in a very natural way using this physical reality of non-separation.

There is nothing that separates us and we just need to open our hearts.
You don't need diplomas because the quantic field is for everyone. It is
God and you don't need diplomas to access God. You just need to
open your heart and access this large field of love.

I can develop this as far as the brain is concerned. To be in the heart,
you have to be in the right side of the brain and not on the rational left
side, which is always in the future or in the past (always predicting the
future based on what it knows of the past). The left side of the brain is
concerned with the past and personal experiences. There are
techniques to calm the left side of the brain in order to allow more
space for the right side of the brain.

There is also meditation on the heart that permits a natural entry into
this space which is filled with peace and love. Everyone can experience
this.

*Kim: So what do you think of the role of the pineal gland in all this because they
say it's the only gland that does not go through the blood brain barrier, and it
connects the right and left hemisphere. They are starting to learn more and more
about this. I just wondered if you had heard much about it as it sounds quite
interesting to me.*

THE JOURNEY WITHIN

Yes, there are many interesting things about the brain and the pineal gland, which allows the link between both hemispheres. I am very interested in this. There's an American doctor who calls this the "D Point," like the "God-point." It is located in the temporal lobe. MRI scans have shown it to be active in certain people, particularly in people who have a spiritual path -- those that meditate, those who are mediums, clairvoyants and people who have had NDE's (Near Death Experiences). This Point is an opening into another space, like mediums have.

We don't really know very much about the brain -- just like we don't know very much about our consciousness -- and that's why we need a guide.

Kim: And how long have you been involved with Sahaj Marg?

Since 1991, twenty-two years. I have a Christian background and during childhood, I had several experiences with the Christ. I had difficulty integrating the concept of a Master because my Master was Christ and I always felt like I was betraying Christ -- until I came to India for the first time a year after starting. Then I had the wonderful opportunity of having an individual sitting with Pascale, just the two of us with the Master. I had the same experience as when I was a child, the same energy. The Christ and the Master are the same energy. One is alive and the other is dead. Who do I follow today? The one who is alive.

My heart told me it was true and definitely not a lie. There was no other proof needed.

THE JOURNEY WITHIN

I had other experiences with the Master in 1993. He gave me the Grace and allowed me to live unconditional love. That is an experience that still lives with me today.

Kim: I'm not sure I understand that part. He made you live by unconditional love?

He gave me the gift of the state of unconditional love. I was ten meters above earth, unafraid. [I was experiencing] only love. I understood that, when you remove the fear, you have access to love. So for the past twenty years I have been working on removing my fears with His help. It takes a lot of work (to work on your character) but it's a beautiful adventure. I can't imagine my life today without this adventure. It took me twenty years in Sahaj Marg to understand the luck of having a real, living Master. It really made me change my life when I realized what a gift it was.

Kim: And how have you changed?

"If you want to change something in your life, you have to change your life." It was an American who said that. So I changed things in my life. I changed habits, attitudes; I worked on my fears, my beliefs. It's not easy, but once you succeed, your life changes automatically. I can say there have been a lot of changes in my life since I met the Master, all changing quickly in a very positive direction.

Kim: So do you think you have to meet the Master and have a personal relationship with him?

I think that depends on each individual person. The wisdom says no, the Master is in our heart, but, on a human level, it is important to meet him and there are always times when something happens. I had

THE JOURNEY WITHIN

moments with the Master and other moments when he ignored me. The Master is a mirror, so he bothers your ego. It [your ego] has its own prerogatives and is attached to them. So yes, I feel you have to see the Master, even if it's difficult. When the heart is here and he's close, something happens.

I have been coming to India for twenty years, sometimes three to four times a year. Sometimes he comes to Europe. It's not always easy but it makes you grow. So for me it is the Master who makes the difference. That's what's important about Sahaj Marg compared to other systems; that there's a living Master who transmits this universal divine energy that transforms us. Therefore, meeting the Master when we can and if we need it, has been important for me.

Kim: You started with Babuji as living Master and now it is Chariji. What about when Master goes to the brighter world? Are they really the same entity? Is there a conflict in your heart?

I can only answer for myself. There's no conflict. I feel we know the future Master. I accepted him even before he becomes a Master. I know that the Master has chosen him and that he has been guided by all the preceding Masters, including Babuji and all the other Masters. It's the right person with the right skills and capacities to guide us.

Kim: And what do you see for the future of our "globe"?

Fantastic, if you have raised your consciousness and done what you have to do. Each of us has a job. Humanity has to find its inner harmony to integrate our lives on a practical basis. I feel that everything is moving. This apocalyptic time is offering us the opportunity to change; we all have to change. This world is not right

THE JOURNEY WITHIN

and we have a lot of attachments. The problem is always to change, but this time we won't have any other choice.

We are fortunate in having a Master who's giving us a direction to follow. It's the direction of love. Other Masters have given the same direction. For me, we have no other choice. Surrender to his will and try to live as close as possible to the principles he's given us. Stay linked to the soul that connects me to my Master. Have faith in his guidance and whatever happens.

I would recommend you see "The Divine Matrix" by Gregg Braden. He's an American.

There are a lot of books and there is a video on YouTube that you must see about the three experiments that "changed the world." If you go to my site (http://www.gilles-placet.com/ under "quantum attitude"), you will see this video of Gregg Braden www.greggbraden.com/videos. It's very simple. Eight minutes. You create your world. Master said that.

Chapter 6   Clouds Have Cleared

Jyoti

Indian, first generation USA American, female, early 30's, editor & writer

Preface: Jyoti's background is interesting in that she was raised by abhyasi parents and was, from an early age, involved in a meditation community in California. She joined Sahaj Marg in her early 20's, then dropped out and tried other methods. At the time of the interview, she had been living for eight months in India while her daughters attend the ashram-affiliated school. She is soon to return to the U.S.A., where her husband has remained. She shares the major changes Sahaj Marg has made in her life these last few months of regular practice.

Jyoti and I meet one morning while the children are in school. She is kind enough to invite me to her home and we share a cool drink and snacks while chatting. We had met about a week earlier over dinner with a large group of people. I enjoy children and ended up seated next to her younger daughter, coaxing her to eat her food and trying to help keep her entertained at, what for her, must have been a rather boring adult party. Jyoti and I focused our discussion on lifestyle changes, especially those having an impact on family life.

Kim: We were talking about Sahaj Marg and that you are a first generation Indian American (not native American). I think it's a pretty interesting story that you left the practice for eight years and then came back.

Right.

Kim: How do you think you've changed since practicing the method?

I guess you could say I had two lives with Sahaj Marg. Which one do we talk about?

Kim: Both.

Why don't we talk about the second life because that's more recent? I started practicing again not even a year ago, about nine months. It's been quite amazing the change that has happened in those nine months. The thing I see the most change with is in family life. I am less annoyed and yell at the kids less when they do something small which is just a kid-like thing. A lot of the time, we get irritated when we take care of them all day. Now I feel a lot more patient with them, which has been a progressive thing I've seen.

I've attended two major celebrations, Babuji's birthday in April and Charuji's birthday just last week. After both of them, I felt a big change in the way I relate to kids and my anger levels. I have more patience. I feel very, very happy about it. Who wouldn't, right?

I have been here in India for about eight months. I came here in July and started doing the practice in October. I returned to the U.S. for a short time in May and will return there soon to look for a job and so on.

THE JOURNEY WITHIN

I can see the difference in my relationship with my husband, also. For the first time he was saying that our marriage was not so bad (laughs). Somehow, I also felt the change in him too. I don't know if that was a reflection of me and/or I'm looking forward to more change.

I've only been practicing for nine months and I know I need to change more. I know that it's a reachable goal. I don't feel hopeless, like I did before. Even though he's not an abhyasi I still feel confident in my ability to change – and him changing through my reflection and, through him seeing the change in me, perhaps [he'll] become interested in the system as well. I do definitely see the way I talk to him [has changed]. I still do react sometimes -- but for the most part, I feel I'm able to step back a little bit. If you're not reacting, then the other person doesn't have anything to react to. That has created a lot more harmony and I see the kids are happier, too. It's not that everything has become harmonious in nine months, but there's a definite change and, as I say, I feel confident that there will be more change as long as I keep this practice up.

Kim: The hope is huge.

Yeah, it's huge. I'm really confident about it -- as long as I work on myself. This is what we are doing here; we are working on ourselves.

Kim: What's it like being an active full time mom with young children? How do you fit the practice in?

Sometimes it can be a challenge. I found that, when I was in the U.S., it was a little easier than in India because in India there are always so many things going on. It's about priorities and training kids. My kids are not so young. They are old enough to understand that this is my

THE JOURNEY WITHIN

time, and that they should respect that time and let Mommy meditate so that Mommy will be a better Mommy for you.

Sometimes it's easy to say "I can't" because I need to do this and that, but I find that, if we are a little disciplined and train them, then it not only benefits us, but them too. So it's just like taking that little bit of time out for yourself so you can be better with them later.

Kim: What are the repercussions?

It's like anything else. If you set yourself a goal of getting fit and you skip a week, there are repercussions and you get back on it. So it's like that. The practice is very flexible with mothers, too. You just do it for your benefit and you do what you can.

Kim: What would you suggest for someone who is maybe just considering a spiritual path, someone who is thinking, "Oh, gee I'm really not happy with the way my life is going"?

Try the method. I like this particular method. It's worked for me. I have looked into different methods and this one attracted me. I would say, try it for six months and see how you feel. There's no guilt or force involved; it's just there. You want to do it, it's there for you.

If you try it, try it properly. Try it with full willingness and put the time aside to do it. After six months, you want to evaluate it and you can only evaluate if you have done it. Try it sincerely and see if it's for you.

THE JOURNEY WITHIN

Kim: I've talked to several people whose real goal is not to be re-born, to finish earthly existence and hopefully never have to come back. Is that your goal?

That is the goal of Sahaj Marg and, I would say for me and other abhyasis is maybe there at the back of our minds, but it's not a predominant goal. I would say that my goal is, rather than be liberated at death, is to be liberated in this life. What that means is to be one with your inner self. What is the inner self? It is just the divine that is omnipresent; it exists everywhere. If you live like that, you can live a very harmonious life. At the time of death, you can continue that, so I don't think about the goal of getting liberated at death. I just want to be liberated here and now from all the daily troubles that we face, [those] which prevent us from enjoying a tranquil life.

Definitely, when you surrender, the divine takes over and kind of says that this person is leaving it all up to me. We have a lot of ego that prevents us from wanting to surrender. If you really think about it, none of us is really independent. We think we are, but we are actually very dependent. We're dependent on firstly, our parents when we grow up, [then] we're dependent on society, on government, on our families and our children. So we are not really as independent as we think we are.

When it comes to being dependent on a guru, it just sounds like too much for most of us. [So] it's not something that we have to force. We can take it slow. They use the word "subtle," subtle changes and suggestions. Even my preceptor won't make an instruction, he'll make a suggestion. When you think about it, suggestions usually work better than directives.

Kim: What do you think about Sahaj Marg as a social movement, as a kind of way to change the world?

THE JOURNEY WITHIN

I think that everybody and anybody knows the world needs to change. Just pick up the newspaper and, whether it's parents or government, everybody knows it. I think we have tried so many ways -- with political systems, wars, education -- and nothing has seemed to work. I do believe this -- because Sahaj Marg is about yourself and, when individuals change, families can change, communities can change and then societies can change.

Kim: Do you feel that you have had to give anything up?

No. I feel that because the things we "give" up we don't actually give up. They fall off and we become less interested in them. For example, I used to drink alcohol but now I am not interested in drinking alcohol. I don't feel like I have lost it. I don't feel like I want it. It's good to not want it because it's not really good for us. Growing up in the West, our thinking process can become very convoluted. We're not able to think clearly and make decisions well. When we make decisions, there are all these other things that come into the picture. We can't make a very good and direct decision. I think a lot of mind clearing has gone on with the meditation, which has to do with the unnecessary baggage that we carry. I used to feel like I couldn't reach myself. I know I'm in there somewhere but for all the clouds that are around me. People can probably relate to that, so I feel that all these clouds have been cleared and now I can reach myself better. Thank you.

Part III: Master and the Spiritual World

When I last visited India, over four months ago for the New Year, my husband came with me. This was a huge act of love on his part and a welcome expression of his support for my spiritual journey. His birthday is December 31, so he was missing both his birthday and welcoming in the New Year with our sons so as to join me. He had taken the three introductory sittings upon my urging, partly out of curiosity, partly out of respect and true interest, and partly out of his love for me. He was allowed to attend meditation at the ashram (mission headquarters for SRCM in Manapakkam, Chennai) and, for two weeks, really made an effort to be part of the experience there. He had several individual sittings with senior preceptors and began to attend the group meditations more regularly as time went on. Five months later, he occasionally attends Sunday morning satsangh and occasionally takes a sitting, but does not otherwise practice regularly.

I think that he may have first decided to accompany me to India because of worry that I was getting entangled with a "cult." (Jules, whom you will meet in the next section entitled Living in the Heart, shares similar reactions when he first was introduced to Sahaj Marg.) The danger of a cult was one concern, along with the idea of a "Master" representing God. My husband was raised Roman Catholic, including being an altar boy and having enjoyed a healthy dose of parochial schooling. So one early question was how God and Jesus Christ fit into all this. I think, regardless of cultural or religious background (Christian, Hindu, Muslim, Buddhist, etc.) this was an issue of concern for many of the people interviewed for this book. How does spirituality fit with religion? One early quote I heard by Ram Chandra, affectionately known as Babuji, helped and reassured me considerably: "The end of religion is the beginning of spirituality. The end of spirituality is the beginning of reality, and the end of reality is real Bliss. When that too is gone, we have reached the destination."

THE JOURNEY WITHIN

Faith and love are part of God's gift to humanity, directly given and accessible within our hearts and souls. It makes sense that religion is not required in order to connect with the Divine. In the first chapter of this section, Michelle goes into this topic in more detail, saying that, "Religion is speaking to God (prayer) and meditation is learning to listen to Him."

One interesting concept is that God has no mind, so therefore cannot "think" or respond to us. Instead God sends or radiates love, permeating the universes, as a sun would send warmth and light. God is always there, the divine essence which has always been in our hearts, part of our creation. It is up to us to tap into that divine source that is always available. Thus the help given through the practice to train us to locate and plunge into that divine source and to further be "divinized" through transmissions of the divine energy from the guru (Master, teacher, spiritual guide). In the final section of the book, Kali shares this quote by Rajagopalachari (2013, p. 24):

"So you see, that is the ultimate obedience – that I listen to my Self within me. And I can do this only when I have stopped listening to everything else. I shall find Him only when I have stopped looking for everything else, whether it be health, wealth, happiness, beauty, what have you. So it all comes down to this process of involution: going inwards, looking within, establishing contact…"

My whole family's reaction to me using the word "Master" was negative and I know myself, when first hearing practitioners going on about their Master, I had a visceral reaction against that term. This was, in fact, one of the questions I put to many of the interviewees and several comment and give helpful explanations. In an upcoming chapter, for example, Joseph explains that we don't find it unusual or uncomfortable to talk about a master carpenter or a master mechanic. Thomas, in the last section of the book, says it is useful to think about master and apprentice rather than "massah" and slave. If you need help with a medical problem, you try to go to the professional with the most knowledge and experience to help you with your problem. That

THE JOURNEY WITHIN

is the role of the spiritual master, to offer advanced, more evolved knowledge and experience, lovingly helping us along our paths to spiritual evolution.

Master (Chariji) himself asks that we perhaps substitute the term "Mother," as that is more of the nature of the relationship: nurturer and guide giving selfless love, suggestions, perhaps a little discipline at times, and so on. I actually prefer the term "Tender" and I like the fact that this is an ambiguous word in English, meaning "tender" as in "shepherd, caretaker" and "tender" as in "caring, loving." To me, to think of the living Master as my "Tender" fits most comfortably.

Another comfort has been to think of all the "greats" as Masters. Those who have moved beyond this world, I believe, are part of the divine unity that is trying to help us (Earthlings) evolve. They are watching over us from a brighter world and I truly do believe they respond to heartfelt love and unselfish prayers. The idea that our loved ones and the "Greats" are watching over us and able to help when asked just makes sense to me; it also explains some of the Near-Death Experiences (NDEs) and other rather fantastic stories in this book.

You will hear two such experiences from Michelle in the upcoming chapter. I was mesmerized by her stories of two NDEs, one as a child and one much more recently. She is adamant and persuasive in her encouragement to "plunge" into spirituality. Her story, that of a third-generation follower of Sahaj Marg, is truly remarkable. Michelle is followed by Jean Baptiste who, while the son of abhyasi parents, only recently took his three introductory sittings at age 20. He expresses concern that other young people today begin to look toward the spiritual world rather than the material world as a means to contribute to society and thereby gain contentment and happiness. He also discusses his personal relationship with his Master, saying how much confidence and encouragement he felt when Master learned of his plans to leave India so as to study permaculture in Australia.

THE JOURNEY WITHIN

In the final chapter for this section, an interview with Joseph, we again hear of the importance of a personal relationship with a guru, or Master. Raised in the Sahaj Marg network out of Europe, Joseph has been around Master (Chariji) most of his life, even thinking of him as a grandfather when a young child. He talks about the importance of the ashram as a means to show children how the world can be. I give you a little preview in this quote from his interview:

"… children coming to the ashram and experiencing that atmosphere (and young people also), they can see how the world can be, how the atmosphere can be, how you can create a society. [They can see] how love and non-judgmental nature and how empathy and all these kinds of things that we speak about very often but do not really practice - we can experience that when we go to the ashram. We can bring that into society and see how it's actually possible."

As you read these and other chapters, I hope they help to clarify any issues or concerns you may have as to the use of the term "Master" as well as some of the differences between religion and spirituality. I hope you seriously consider your life now and your sense of personal fulfillment while beginning to imagine a life oriented toward the spiritual world.

Chapter 7   Take the Plunge

Michelle

French-American living in India, female, 30's, real-estate agent

Preface: Working from the basic interview questions, which are included below, Michelle writes her own story, one of early and continued connectedness with the Divine and, in the case of two potentially crippling accidents, divine intervention as part of a near-death experience (NDE). A third-generation practitioner of Sahaj Marg, Michelle started out as a high-flying global executive searching for peace of mind in today's frenetic business world. Her personal experiences with trauma brought her to the realization that what is most important in life is the opportunity to be alive so that the soul can evolve. Michelle offers words of encouragement and advice to those who are searching for something more than material success in their lives.

Kim: Can you tell us a little about yourself and how you became interested in spirituality?

I was baptized Church of England, and since birth, my best friend has been God. I graduated magna cum laude from George Washington University in Washington, D.C. with a B.A. in International Affairs and Diplomacy and a minor in International Economics. I obtained my graduate degree from Harvard in International Business and Management.

I was very fortunate to be born into a spiritual family. Both my mother and grandmother follow the Sahaj Marg 'natural path.' In fact, my grandmother's last words to me were, "Do whatever you wish, my dear, yet please, I ask you, take Sahaj Marg seriously."

I met God for the first time truly when I fell from a roof, twelve meters, from the fourth floor of my neighbor's house. I landed on cement with my head in geraniums. I woke up for twenty seconds after my fall, just long enough to say my name and my address. After that, I left my body. Before I knew it, I was happy to be back in the brighter world and the souls there were very happy to see me too. I was as light as a feather and yet as fast as the speed of light. I felt like a transparent bubble filled with total joy.

The next thing I knew, I could see myself from above and surrounded by twelve doctors reviewing my case. I was 12 years old and had these wonderful red Adidas soccer shorts - I won all my soccer games in them. I had heard that "ADIDAS" stood for "All Day I Dream About Sex" - and every time I repeated this, everybody laughed. I had no idea what sex was or what this meant, but I enjoyed the fact that everybody chuckled, so I would often repeat this news. Anyway, from above, I saw the doctors start to cut my favorite shorts [to better see my injuries]. I screamed to my mother who was sitting by my hospital bed side, "Maman, please don't let them cut my shorts" and, all of a sudden, I heard my mum tell the doctors, "Please don't cut her shorts!" I was so happy she could hear me; I knew I had picked the right mother (grin). She was connected.

This is when the doctors told my mum that I would perhaps not come back and that, if I did, I would either be a vegetable or be paralyzed. I was a bit shocked and this is when I asked God (I saw no face, only felt A Higher Force) to please let me come back. I asked if I could please come back, with permission to please be able to ski all day and dance all night. I felt life was an exchange of give and take and so I added, "I promise to take care of Your People."

THE JOURNEY WITHIN

The next thing I knew, I woke up in my body. I still had divine consciousness, which means that I had access to total information about Every Thing and Every One. I knew the hospital had financial problems, that some of the doctors were cheating on their wives and that the wheel chair they wanted to sell my parents cost 47,896 francs. I told my Mum, "Please don't buy it. I don't need it. I made a deal with God. Besides, imagine all the shoes we can buy with this money, maman." (laughs) I asked her to please trust me. My mum looked at me in awe and then told the doctors, "Well, perhaps my daughter will be paralyzed but she is clearly not a vegetable."

Medically, I had fractured my first two vertebrates (sacrum and coccyx) and I broke my little left toe. After a few months of crutches, God was kind with me and I fully recovered. Never to be the same, I knew now that: i) life was a precious gift, and ii) I had made a vow to help humanity.

Kim: So from a young age you have been involved in spirituality and you had role models in your mother and grandmother.

Four years later I met the physical Master, Parthasarathi Rajagopalachari, affectionately called Chariji. I was 16 years old. My mother introduced my brother and me by saying, "Master, these are Your children." Master kindly gave me a white plane that could fix everything (the nose was glue, the back was a pair of scissors, the right wing was a ruler, the left an eraser, with paper clips and a stapler underneath). My brother Bruce, age 10, was given a Rubik's cube.

Later, after seven years of University, when I was managing seven call center companies in seven different European countries, I realized the impact of this gift. Master had given me the ability to fly to these companies; I naturally met with the employees but felt their problems and had the capability to fix the issues at hand -- and quickly move on. Regarding my brother, Master was also right; my brother definitely has a strategic business mind.

Our Mother would take my Grandmother, brother and I to Augerans (a large meditation center in France) as often as she could. It took me a long time to fully grasp the great fortune I had been given, to be a part of this growing spiritual family. At first I really saw mediation as an adult thing to do. I would always attend the European seminars and, of course, it is always a tremendous pleasure for me to meet our Great Master whenever He would come to Europe. I was not very regular with my practice, however -- sometimes, even not at all.

Later during my corporate career, I began living the problems of my company. We took the company public, and the more I worked, the less I slept and this vicious circle increased as time went on. I would explain this to my Mum, and she would always reply saying the same thing, "You need to see Master." Really, I felt my mother had no clue what stress I was undergoing. And her answer to Everything was always, 'MASTER, MASTER, MASTER."

Finally, Christmas came along and she bought plane tickets for all of us (my brother, his girlfriend, my mum and I) to go to India. After arriving at the ashram in Manapakkam, my true inner change began. She organized for me to have a meditation sitting with a senior preceptor. The humble brother coughed during most of the sitting. I was rather embarrassed. After this experience, my brother Bruce came by and asked me if I wanted to smoke a cigarette with him. I realized that I had not smoked in more than six hours. We went outside, I lit my cigarette, and as my lungs inhaled the smoke, I coughed, choked, and told my brother, "This is totally disgusting. I will never ever smoke again." In reality, I was allergic to smoke, but living in Paris, everybody smoked because smoking was in fashion at the time. I realized somehow that my smoke disturbed me less than the smoke of others -- and this is how an occasional habit becomes a constant one. I

THE JOURNEY WITHIN

had tried hypnosis to quit before but nothing was more efficient than that sitting -- every cell in my body screamed 'never again.'

After this I went to see my mum and I told her what I never told anyone before – that I had constant voices in my head, constant pressure pushing me to do things and to never forget other things. After the sitting, all that noise in my head magically disappeared. "What do I need to do to keep this peace in my mind?" I asked her. "You have to do your spiritual practice." I said, "That's all?" I mean, one and a half hours of mediation for twenty-four hours of peace and quiet! Wow! What a worthy and amazing way to spend my precious time. I immediately felt that the entire world needed to find out about this. She smiled and said, "This will be your job in the future."

A few years later, I began investing my energy for the Sahaj Marg Mission. I had sold my corporate shares and finally had more time to spare for my inner Self. I started by selling books on Sunday morning. One day, I was sitting in my apartment in Paris and I said in my heart, "God, Master, I promised You to Help Mankind. I always do everything I can to help everyone around me but, if I can do more, I am ready."

Quite incredibly, a few days later, in the Swiss ashram, one of the sisters told me that Master had sent a message and that He wanted me to become a prefect (a meditation teacher). I was stunned by how quickly He had replied to my heart-filled request. For two years, He placed me on the Committee of the Paris Meditation Center in order to facilitate the organization of the ashram. It is an honor and a true privilege for me to work for Him.

Kim: Do you have any special stories or memories to share with us?

THE JOURNEY WITHIN

In 2009, I had a very serious car accident. I was driving back from a center where I had given 27 sittings and completed nine introductions [introductory sittings required for newcomers]. I was tired and, what with the rain mixed with snow and ice, my fast convertible car went out of control on the highway. As I crashed into the wall, I was sure this was the end of my life. I let go of the steering wall and closed my eyes and began to thank My Master, to thank God for the lovely parents, family, friends, for all the wonderful sisters and brothers I have met around the world, people whom I loved and cared for so much. I thanked Him for my chance to Live -- and for allowing me to go now, when I had no children and no husband to harm.

Next thing I knew, the sequence of time changed. One second lasted a very long time; my hand movement looked fragmented. I felt as if I was placed in a little cocoon filled with Light. I really felt like my Master was with me. In fact, I said to Him in my heart, "You never cease to amaze me with your magical powers." After three or four flips and turns of my car, I asked Master, "Please, can we stop this accident now?" Immediately, the car stopped rolling and crashed into the side of a wall. "Wow. Thank you, Master." I looked in the mirror and saw my teeth and nose were intact. Thus, come what may, I felt this was only a small bump on the road. Turns out, it was a big bump. My rib cage was fractured, my solar plexus was cracked, my shoulder and finger were broken - and my lip was ripped -- nevertheless, I smiled and thanked God that I was still alive. A meditation brother kindly helped me leave the hospital.

It took eight months before I could fly again. My recovery has been spent in Chennai, India (at the headquarters of our spiritual mission). Since, I have made a conscious decision to prioritize the purification of my soul and focus on my inner growth. In my opinion, Sahaj Marg is the simplest and most efficient system to spiritual progress. My experience has proven it to me. Now, my heartfelt desire is to spread this well-kept secret of Sahaj Marg among as many heart-sensitive humans as possible.

THE JOURNEY WITHIN

Kim: Do you have any advice for someone who is new to spirituality?

Just as it is difficult to explain the taste of chocolate, it is nearly impossible to explain the effects of transmission, which truly transforms us from within. Sahaj Marg allows us to connect to our soul. This is the purpose of our existence and the reason for our being. I urge everyone to take the 'natural path.' Please plunge.

It's free. We function on donations.

All that is needed is discipline, to be 18 or over, and to have the will to truly succeed in your life. As your inner transformation takes place, your outer views will alter. Slowly but surely, your outlook on life is bound to change and so will everything else. Listening to the inner voice in the heart takes perseverance. Our mind is disturbed, filled with thoughts - yes, no, maybe so… As Mathieu Ricard says (the personal secretary for the Dalai Lama), "The mind is like a crazy monkey, which we need to learn to control." Once the mind is quiet, the Heart can lead our path. This is what Sahaj Marg teaches us. Yes, it takes time, it takes patience. It takes Love. It takes discipline, obedience, courage. It takes strength and it takes wisdom. It takes our time and yet, every second involved gives us so much more in return. Only the soul is of eternal value. Everything else we have, we will leave behind: our beautiful muscles, our cars, our toys, even our loved ones.

Earth is an educational playground - our time is better spent on raising our universal consciousness, cleaning our vibration and loving others. We have all wasted time -- and yet it is never too late to start now. Money comes and goes, but the light that grows in our heart remains forever.

THE JOURNEY WITHIN

I highly recommend you try Sahaj Marg seriously for six months at least - as it takes time to learn to swim, it takes time to quieten the mind. Once you learn to observe yourself through your daily journal after your morning meditation, you will realize so much about your character. Learn about your true self, who you are and how you react to outside events.

Everything and everyone is just a mirror for us to learn from -- or not -- the freedom to choose is always there. Originally, I wanted to be a psychiatrist for children. In psychology, we dissect human issues; in spirituality, we transcend them.

I heard somewhere, "At the time of your death, you will realize how important your soul is. " Don't be afraid of the inevitable, don't be afraid to die. Your soul will carry on. Only your body will cease to exist. Learn to love your inner self, please find the TIME and the patience to Love Yourself enough, to connect to your soul within. Sahaj Marg will help you find Your Inner Home. As we advance spiritually, many of our illusions disappear as a clearer understanding of what is truly important arises.

Kim: Do you have anything else to share?

After my near death experience (NDE), I can honestly say-- Life is a True Gift from God, a Lucky chance given to us for our soul to Evolve. We need to purify our thoughts, let go of our prejudices and release our judgments. We need to be freed from our past, from our belief system, and as Eckhart Tolle (2004) says, only "live the now."

We co-create our life with our thoughts and this is why thoughts need to be purified (cleaned).

THE JOURNEY WITHIN

I highly recommend a book I just read called <u>Laws of the Spirit World</u> (Khorshed, 2009) written with a medium by two young Indian men who died. The book consists of messages sent by them from "heaven" to their mother, for the most part. I agree with what is relayed: we picked our mother, our story.

The greatest gift that can be given to every human being is this chance to grow spiritually - especially with a high caliber master. We progress much faster than ever possible alone. There must be other spiritual systems that help humans advance. Sahaj Marg is safe, easy, and efficient. We develop a natural state within -- which transports us beyond.

The natural state of our soul is a state of universal love and ultimate joy. Don't wait to be "up there" to be happy. With the Sahaj Marg cleaning system, and through meditation, we learn to develop this condition within ourselves, now.

I feel that my spiritual quest has been the biggest asset to my financial and material success. I can honestly testify that my life came together when I took spirituality seriously. Somehow, I'm in tune with nature and thus money comes to me rather than me having to run after it. I have a higher goal and a higher purpose, thus all my lower needs are met. Spirituality is definitely a plus and never a minus.

I can only wholeheartedly encourage you to please, "wake up." Both the material and the spiritual wings of our being need attention and care. If nothing else, you will benefit by feeling less fragile and reduce your anxiety and stress.

At 9 p.m., for 15 minutes, in conjunction with approval given by the UN (United Nations), many of us pray for world peace - a specific prayer is sent from our heart 'that every human being realizes that we are all sisters and brothers, and that a true faith develops in every heart.'

We all have the same needs and, on a higher level, the same goal. We must all become one with God. Religion is speaking to God (prayer) and meditation is learning to listen to HIM. Religion has divided humanity but spirituality is here to unite our <u>hearts</u>. This will have a tremendous social impact. Regardless of the name we use to call God, we must overcome our differences and focus on our similarities instead.

God is not outside. He is in a safe place, in our heart. He awaits us there. Close your eyes and seek Him. He waits for you within.

Sadly, in many countries, money has become the new religion. As the world economic situation declines and nature takes its toll on earth, a higher purpose for our being here is Growing. We are currently in the third dimension, the world of duality. If we wish to graduate to a higher dimension, to the fifth dimension of Love, Sahaj Marg is the key. It is the vehicle which will help us to sail through the storm, the tool to help us feel what is right and what is wrong and, most of all, the inner wisdom to know the difference. We are refining our inner compass.

I once asked my mum why she always refers everything back to 'Master' and she told me He was the transformer of universal energy that transforms this Ultimate Source for the transformation of our soul. As a prefect (meditation teacher), I feel how Masters' work is specifically tailored to each person. No [meditation] sitting is ever the same. His powers are Infinite and we are ever so fortunate to benefit from them. God is love. Master helps us to vibrate an essence of pure love.

THE JOURNEY WITHIN

Please share this book with all those you love. And read <u>Whispers from a Brighter World</u> (Chandra, 2010, 2012, 2013). We have so much knowledge to learn from above. Sahaj Marg (the Natural Path) is a gateway for the soul's journey.

Shared with gratitude for being part of this divine plan.

THE JOURNEY WITHIN

Chapter 8   Once There is a Bridge, There is No Need to Swim

Jean Baptiste

20 years old, French living in India, permaculture worker & student in Australia

Preface: It is somewhat amazing that I even got to interview Jean Baptiste. He, his mother and sister were resting in the garden near the ashram (remember the one with the mosquitoes and cats?) when I arrived to conduct an interview. They very kindly and graciously allowed us to encroach on the patio space and eventually became interested in the interview to the point of wanting to be involved. Jean Baptiste's mother Virginia gave a wonderful interview, highlighted in the second book of this series, and encouraged Jean Baptiste to agree to an interview, as well. What a goldmine, so to speak! You will find some serious gems in both their interviews.

Jean Baptiste is only 20 years old, but clearly a deep thinker and well-spoken. He shares some of his experiences as a person who is new to meditation despite playing around the ashram "since I was a baby." He also shares his real concerns about young people today feeling lost, really lost. He hopes we all can stop thinking about how to control (money, power, profits) and instead really concentrate on the spiritual world. Once we find the first step, the others follow.

Kim: Could you tell us a little bit about yourself?

I'm 20 years old and I did my first [meditation] sitting a month ago. I've lived in India most of my life and, [although I am French], I have only lived in France for two and half years during my studies. I feel more comfortable in India than in France.

THE JOURNEY WITHIN

Kim: Were you interested before you had your first sitting?

I've been playing around the ashram since I was a baby. I used to see them meditating and when they had satsanghs [group meditations], we had to be quiet and were not allowed to run around or to be around or talk to them. It was pretty hard for kids. We were often in the playground with no parents around us.

Growing up, my parents used to talk to me a lot about Master and Babuji and his Master. I was interested because religion was very complicated for me. However, I liked religion, liked Zeus and Greek mythology, and even Indian religion like Ganesh -- and Christianity with my grandmother. I found it very interesting.

I feel that the Mission is not a religion, but a way of life. In a way, it is a religion because we follow a way of life that connects us with a higher spirit that helps us, guides us and shows us many things.

What I like about the Mission is they say that life is sometimes unfair, sometimes very fair and it has joy, hate and everything. I really like it because they say, "Do your best." They don't say, "If you do this, it's bad." or "You have to come and repent your sins, and God will forgive you." Instead, you need to try better next time and not say, "I'm sorry, I won't do it again." You don't need to say it; you just need to try to do it.

For me, it's very free, open and I really like it.

Kim: What's it like being an abhyasi kid?

When I was younger I had a lot of problems, psychologically. I didn't like school; I didn't like living in the city. I was actually fairly lost.

I always wanted to do something to make the Earth a better place but I didn't have the drive that I do now. I knew I could do it and I had to do it, but I always felt lost when I thought about it. Where should I start? Am I really capable of doing it?

THE JOURNEY WITHIN

Now I don't need to ask myself these questions. All I need to do is to say I'm going to do something either big or small and it's going to be something, and I just need to focus on it. I don't need to be the center of the world by helping the world. I just need to be someone who is bringing something to the world.

My first sittings were clean and I felt a strength that entered me and at the same time a lot of emotions went out. When I finished my sittings, I felt much more grounded, more centered and confident. For me, it's just about myself, knowing what I will be as I grow older. Even though I always knew it when I was young, now I really know that Chariji is always going to be there to help me.

Mother: How did you feel being the child of two parents who are abhyasi?

Mother explains: His father and I are a little different abhyasi, in the sense that we never, never asked our children to become abhyasi. We never gave them "ready-made" thoughts. We wanted them to think for themselves and if one day they feel ready, it should come from them and not from us trying to mold them, like what is done in religion.

Jean Baptiste's father was very respectful of all of this because he was brought up as a Christian and he did not like it at all. I was brought up with a lot of freedom, with no religion at all. I was searching for it, so it's actually a good balance between us.

The children are taking their own time. Jean Baptiste started at the age of 20 although he could have started at 16 or 17, but it took time for him to be ready. If our second son will be ready, he will most probably indicate it.

Mother: Would you agree, Jean Baptiste?

Yeah, I do. When I finished my sittings, he (the meditation brother) asked me how it was and we talked about it. I found out that he also had some of the same thoughts and feelings I had.

Especially in France during my two and a half years there, I saw that many young people were and are very lost. It doesn't mean that they go out and drink all night or do bad things, although that is a factor because they're looking for a good time... They don't know what to be, what to become and they are just really lost. I would say that you should try and meditate. I believe it would be good for you. I would say try it and see for yourself.

Kim: That's good advice. I really like what you said about coming out with inner strength. I hadn't really thought of it that way.

After my third sitting, I met Chariji. I was about to leave for Australia to learn organic agriculture and when I told him this, he said it was very interesting and he told me to return to India. I believe he wants me to do something, to help. That gave me a lot of strength because I knew I wanted to do something, but I didn't know where to start... It's like when you climb stairs, you want to be at the top without thinking about how you're going to get there. The first step is the most important because this first step will lead you to the next one. So once you find your first step, the others just follow. Climbing up the stairs can be tiring and sometimes you just want to stop. It is easier to climb down than up, but I know that Chariji will always be there to encourage us to continue our efforts.

Kim: That's a good way to describe it. You have a gift with words. Have you been to Australia or are you going soon?

I really like animals and nature and I used to watch Animal Planet and there was this amazing show by Steve Irwin. He would do shows on crocodiles and he also did [investigated] all kinds of animals. I thought Australia looked amazing with all the animals, so since then I always wanted to go to Australia.

I stopped school when I was 16 and I entered a re-forestation project, did long-term voluntary work and studied permaculture for a few months. My teacher was Australian from the College of Permaculture. He talked a bit about Australia and I met many Australians there. Permaculture was my favorite subject that I ever learned, because it was so "concrete." It's what you see when you go out in nature or what you feel; it's not just 2 plus 2 equals 4. I really put myself into it and when I heard it was an active area of study in Australia, I felt I had to go there. My mother kept pushing and pushing me -- and now, I'm going there in two weeks.

I'm not actually going to the college. I am going to work there for a while to earn a bit of money and meet people who do permaculture. My mom put me in touch with Xxx who knows many people that do permaculture.

Kim: Would you have any advice for somebody who is new to spirituality and is just starting to look around beyond a materialist focus?

I would say the spiritual world is the inner world. We are so much into what we see and what we feel, even though the spiritual world can be felt from the inside. We watch movies and we are taught that if you don't see it, it doesn't exist. It's like when science started. People thought it was very bad and people were burned or hanged.

Spirituality has always been there but we are so much into the material world that we live in a mostly scientific world. The scientific world cannot really prove anything about the spiritual world, so if you are looking for answers from the material world for spiritual questions, I don't think you will find them.

It's very hard to find your inner self. I had parents who would always answer questions and try to help me. To find the spiritual world is not only to accept it, but to believe it and believe in yourself. I would say you don't even need to accept it. All you need to do is believe it and open yourself to it and it is there all around you.

When I talk like this to young people, they look at me wide-eyed and say, "Where are you from? Mars?" I get it -- that it's very hard to understand for some people.

Kim: Can you comment on the benefits of Sahaj Marg as a social movement, as a way to improve and change the world, to help people, pollution, climate change, and politics?

Yes, in a way, because it helps people understand themselves and the essential things in life. But we need someone to help us to connect the physical world to the spiritual world, a link. Once there is a "bridge," people will not need to swim to get to the other side; they will just walk on it.

So once people stop thinking about how to control -- money, power, profits -- and once you put all of that aside, you can really concentrate on the spiritual world. So for now I would say we should help the physical world. The spiritual world has been helping us to understand the important things in life, but not all people are willing to get out of their bubble (comfort zone) and see what is really happening on our planet.

Chapter 9 It's Not Just Everything Wonderful. It's Hard Work!

Joseph

European, male, late 30's, social worker

Preface: Joseph was a bit reluctant to speak with me, seeming to feel there are others perhaps more qualified or appropriate as interviewees. However, I had heard of Joseph's altruistic work, unusual in both length and intensity considering his young age. He not only did a lot of volunteer work for SRCM but also worked with refugees, especially children. He finally agreed to an interview and, over time, began to warm up. I especially appreciate that he eventually shared a little about his relationship with Master.

Joseph discusses the hard work involved in spirituality, emphasizing the importance of prioritizing and using will power to make progress. He describes meditation as a tool used in daily life with an awareness that we are meditating to <u>become</u> something, we are meditating to change. The focus should be on what we are becoming. Joseph shares valuable advice with those getting started and also shares insights about his relationship with and understanding of the role of a Master as he experiences the subtlety and sacredness of the practice.

Kim: We've never met, so could you tell me what might be pertinent about yourself?

My name is Joseph and I was brought up with my family and my uncle's family, so it was one big family. I went to an alternative school that gave a lot of space for creativity. It gave a lot of space for learning to take care of the smaller ones because you're in big groups with all ages. You had no homework. You had to take responsibility of your own teaching and things like that and you have to evaluate [yourself] each week, even from a young age. Of course, it is also about having a lot of freedom and having to do everything yourself, without having strict discipline. That was the balance. It was a very good school. That was to 10th grade and was a good thing.

In the early 1970s, my parents, uncle and aunt all started meditating in Sahaj Marg. Slowly, other people started following this system, as well. There were a few people in the beginning but slowly it was growing. Our current spiritual guide – Chari – his Master, Babuji, came to Europe along with Chariji three times. That had an impact on people starting [meditation] and on the growth of the Mission.

In the beginning, I was not even born. I was born in 1977. Of course, I'd been to the seminars when I was small, in and around Europe, and also later when our current Master became the spiritual head of Shri Ram Chandra Mission.

Kim: You were not an abhyasi at that time; you were just kind of along because your parents were involved?

Yes, because I was a child. There were a lot of children around from all over Europe.

Kim: Did you really have a choice? Do you feel like you had a choice?

THE JOURNEY WITHIN

Yes, because in Sahaj Marg, you cannot force anything. A choice, in terms of choice connecting to what your heart is telling you – that's another thing; but when you're asking like that, I presume you're guessing, "Oh, since the family's in it, were you forced to then start?" No, I wasn't forced, by any means, because the Sahaj Marg system is based not so much on knowledge and lectures and teaching and rituals. Not at all. Actually it's based very much on a practice, on a method, and to change and become something.

Anyway, all I know from my childhood is just the atmosphere. Now we have meditation centers and ashrams in Europe. In the beginning, we didn't have those because we were not so many. It was just in private homes, people coming for group meditations and things like that. I was brought up in that whole network. But what I want to say is what my Master had said later on, that children growing up and coming - not necessarily being brought up their entire lives - but children coming to the ashram and experiencing that atmosphere (and young people also), they can see how the world can be, how the atmosphere can be, how you can create a society. [They can see] how love and non-judgmental nature and how empathy and all these kinds of things that we speak about very often but do not really practice - we can experience that when we go to the ashram. We can bring that into society and see how it's actually possible.

When you're a child, you're not conscious of all these things. Later on, you reflect on your life and see all this. As a child and a teenager, like everybody else, you see all the negative things. You get fed up with your parents and you're angry because of this and that and you're blaming them for this and that and all these things – but there are all the good things also and my life has been wonderful in that context, being brought up in Sahaj Marg. It doesn't mean that life is easy and you can just sit back and you are just in this spiritual atmosphere. Not at all. Not at all. You are maybe more aware…We are just doing something here that everybody is trying to do and we have a practical method.

THE JOURNEY WITHIN

What happened for me was, when I became a teen, I realized my own behavior, my own character, whatever -- I felt something was not right. I didn't feel alive inside. I was a normal teenager. I was a political activist very early. From 11 years old, I wanted to save the world from all the wrongdoings and pollution and racism and whatever. I was using a lot of time on that and I was going to drinking parties, concerts – I would say, a normal Western cultural upbringing. By the age of 18, I started realizing I needed something else. My heart was somehow lacking air or something. I was not so conscious of it like that; it was more a feeling.

So I went to my aunt and she gave me [meditation] sittings. I asked her, "Why are all these people meditating for so many years? Why are they still having this and this?" As a child, you see everything. I pointed out all the wrong things. She said to me that we have so many layers. There are so many impressions – samskaras – impressions from past lives, if you believe in that, or just impressions from wherever it comes, that we need to get rid of to reveal what is inside. Everybody has that. Some people use other tools; they take a walk in the forest and they are connected. Here, we have a meditation system.

I started that when I was 18 – to go inside. So when I asked my aunt the question, "Why are all these wrong things still there when people are meditating so long?" She said, "We are not even aware. Sometimes we have to surrender or sacrifice things we are holding onto deep inside and slowly -- as we meditate and do our cleaning, and we are meeting with the Master, we are going to seminars, for group meditations -- slowly things are coming up. The more you develop and the more you are working on yourself, the more things will come up, and the more subtle things. She was trying to explain to me that it's a process. I was a little bit like, "I'm not interested in the whole thing. I want to change completely and I want to get rid of everything and I just want to be reborn," I told her. Then she looked at me and she said, "Okay, good" and gave me my introduction sittings.

THE JOURNEY WITHIN

In Sahaj Marg, we need a minimum of three introductory individual sittings from a prefect. She gave me those and then I slowly started. There are so-called guidelines given in the system; if you want to progress fast or if you want to progress, there are a lot of guidelines. We have the Ten Maxims (see references), we have our method, how it's prescribed, how to do it, so I knew all the rules. They are not rules, they are guidelines; but as a child, letting go of non-veg, not drinking – all this is important but has nothing to do with the meditation system. I was very focused: "Oh, I want to do everything right from the beginning."

But as I started, I realized, like my aunt told me, it's a process and you really have to make an effort and you have to have willpower. You have to apply the will and really work hard on it. It's not a weekend cause and ding, ding, ding [done!]. It's a tool you can use in your daily life. We are not meditating to meditate, we are meditating to <u>become</u> something, we are meditating to <u>change</u>. Meditation itself is a tool. We are focusing on what we are becoming.

So I started that when I was 18. It was not like everything was right from the beginning and it's still not right, but what I'm trying to say is I realized that this process needs what I was saying before - effort, willpower, all this. There are different tools. For me, what helped me was I went to many seminars where there were a lot of people. It's like an intense cause, like you're going for some school trip. I also went to India a lot. I have been in India many times and I helped work in the Mission.

It's all voluntary, what we are doing – arranging seminars, weekends, whatever – and for me, that means a lot because while you're working, focusing on these things, it helps you also to develop. Also, I was brought up with our Master, so I had a social bond to him as a child -

THE JOURNEY WITHIN

knowing him, talking to him - but once you start meditating, of course it changes.

It's difficult to speak about the concept of Master and loving the Master and you have to love the Master. Again, in this system, you have to start meditating and experience things yourself, not from what somebody is telling you - so I don't want to go too much into that, but it helped me a lot. It's the essence of everything: my connection to Master and what I experience in the seminars.

Kim: I'd just like to pick up on something you mentioned because I'm pretty new to all this and it does help if you have a lifestyle change. I live in a kind of Portuguese place. A lot of people drink wine. I know Scandinavia's or Western Europe's reputation with more freedom with drugs and sex and all that kind of stuff. How important is it to be clean? I'm interested to talk to you about that because you're the first person I've talked to who's started at such a young age. Were there any conflicts between fitting in with your cohort group and doing this? Was it ever really an issue for you - giving up meat, stopping drinking alcohol - all the things that a young person would normally be exploring?

What is happening in Sahaj Marg is that you can stop such things with the advice from seniors who know you or somebody who you look up to and you can say, "Okay, this person is telling me to try to stop doing this and this." You can try for some time, but if you don't really want to, it'll not last. That is one thing. Another thing is, when you start meditating, you're not told, "This and this - you're not allowed to do." You're told, "There are some guidelines. If you want to benefit from this… it's a very good idea not to put poison inside yourself. It's just a waste of time. Have a go at it, try, find out why you're here, what it is you want to do, and you make the effort. Once you ruin your own condition with bad thoughts, with screaming from anger, with being hostile, with judging people, or by drinking or whatever, you can feel in yourself. Do you want to progress? Then you have to sacrifice and stop doing all this nonsense."

THE JOURNEY WITHIN

But it is not easy. People are so different. For me, it was very easy to stop drinking; but for me, other things may be very difficult. So it all depends. Of course, it is expected after some time that people at least try to work on themselves. If there was a new person, I would say if I introduced them and they come and ask, "Oh, I'm feeling... my condition is... I'm drinking and drinking... This meditation system doesn't take me anywhere." Then I'll tell them, "It's because you're drinking." All this about 'Oh, you're not allowed to' depends on what it is you want to do. Put your will to it, and then you have to sacrifice.

For me, I sacrificed – actually, it's the wrong word that I'm using because I didn't sacrifice anything. I prioritized things - that's the word I wanted before. I'm prioritizing. Instead of going and drinking [Saturday night], I'm going for Sunday satsangh - Sunday morning meditation. Also, to tell you the truth, I've not been drinking for more than 18 years or --I don't know how long – I don't even think about these things because they're useless – but I understand in society for young people, it's a social tool and you will maybe feel left out. But what do they feel when they wake up on a Saturday [morning]? Why that loneliness? What are they looking for? What do they want to achieve in life?

Kim: I know that early on in the Mission, in terms of overseas, Europe was important... Why Europe? Do you have any idea?

I have no idea, but there were also people in Italy and in Germany and in France and in Denmark and seeds are sown, hearts are heard. I have no idea. I cannot tell you why. I know that all humans are the same and I know that all hearts are there, but I also know cultures and respect cultures and religions and peoples' practices and uniqueness, which is the beauty of humanity. But why are some hearts reaching out and being heard and why did Babuji come and bless Europe and help Europe? I don't know.

THE JOURNEY WITHIN

Kim: What are your goals? What are your dreams? You started out in social activism. Have you continued with that?

I like to work together with people, in groups. I work in the Mission and am a prefect now. I'm also a photographer and I studied film. I have worked with children, refugees, in all different kinds of suffering. Babuji once said that social service is not giving clothes and money to the poor; that is human dignity. You don't really need a big brain to do these kinds of things. He said, "Real social service is to bring calmness to other people's minds." So I've been thinking a lot about that. In order to do that, I have to bring calmness to my own mind, so I have to do that to myself. It's maybe helping me; I have no idea.

[In] the context [of] the work environment, my main goal is to try to bring that calmness to myself and work on myself and try not to give too much advice to other people in what to do. But it's up and down and here and there and it's not just everything wonderful; it's hard work.

Kim: Have you ever thought about giving up the practice?

For me, it's not fragmented like that; it's like one whole, so I cannot give up my life. What we can say in Sahaj Marg is that we're trying. People are not saints here. Maybe there are some. There are beautiful human beings all over the world and in Sahaj Marg, you have beautiful human beings. [In fact], it's lovely to be associated with this Mission because we practice love and brotherhood and you can actually see it in numbers and statistics and in the atmosphere when all these people from all over the world are gathered. I've seen so many NGOs and all these people and even democracies preaching love and brotherhood and not practicing it, but here I see it practiced. I'm not saying it's the only place but I see it here and I like that.

THE JOURNEY WITHIN

That doesn't mean that people are all perfect here. They're trying - try the abhyas, try the meditation, see what change it does. Apply your will and try. It's a method and it's free and it's available for everybody.

We have this saying in Sahaj Marg, 'One lion is better than a thousand sheep.' What is a lion? A lion takes a step and goes for what it wants. So I am taught here, from this system, to take charge of my own life. I'm not some small little being following some big herd, no. I'm connected to my heart and I make the decision. I should be able to do it and take charge of my own life and take action.

But I have to say, I'm not totally there. I'm trying, and then my Master can help me. He's emphasizing family life. I'm not yet married. I don't have a family, but he's emphasizing family life. It's good for spiritual growth. I think basically you develop love in a family and sacrifice for other people and all these things and it's all about children being brought up in this world - to a better world, to become better.

The reason why I use the word 'love' a lot is because it's very difficult to define. We're meditating on divine light in the heart and it's always very difficult to find words for these things. People have to experience and then apply their own words because I don't want to tell them what to feel. When I say 'love,' it's because I have love, I feel love in Master's presence; but we're trying to <u>become</u> love. What is love? We have to reflect on it ourselves. So in this process, Master can help.

Here we are taught to believe in ourselves and take action. We also need help. So people are in different places. It's emphasized that you create your own character. You take charge of your life and connect with your heart and then our Master can help you in your heart. We all know what to do and we're supposed to do that. It can be very difficult but you can get help and we have a lot of tapes and books and a lot of good people to speak with -- but if you're ill, you need to go to the doctor or psychologist.

Kim: Sahaj Marg really tells you to connect with your heart, that the center of your being is your heart — but we've kind of been socialized and raised to think of the power of the brain, the power of the intellect. Might you want to comment on that?

I think in recent years, everybody knows that it's not enough with the head. So there comes the heart, there comes love. I mean, I have never been in doubt. For me, I've never wondered, "Oh, is it the brain or is it the heart?" and "How?" and "What?" No. Because I feel it. How it's working, I have no clue at all. Do I need to know? I don't think so. For me, it's about my Master – my spiritual guide, Chariji - that I have seen [since childhood]. He was just a grandfather to everybody. That has been amazing.

The thing is, to emphasize for people who are not practicing yet or just starting or new abhyasis: it's all about meditating and going for the group meditation and therein lies the path. At the same time, I have to also reveal my own path, [which is] to go and be with Master, to go and be in the meditation hall and be in satsangh, to be with him. He's on another spiritual level and he can work wonders. How he does it, I don't know; but sit and try and feel and you will see very well for yourself.

Coming back to my own life -- yes, I have travelled a lot with Master, both in Europe and also in India. I've been in India so many times. Maybe I could talk about how you feel when you're with your Master. You know, when the meditation is feeling good. We're not supposed to feel good, actually, because we're working like hell. So it's like big machinery going 'grrr' inside. We want to feel peace. Of course, you will feel peace but you need hard work also. After sometimes cleaning or whatever, it's going on in your system and you're freaking out. There are moments where you feel so relaxed and at peace and feel

THE JOURNEY WITHIN

[instead of say] whatever words you want to use. I had those moments, especially with Master. Whether I was really in a good condition – I don't know – but I felt bliss and all these things. That also happened in the meditation hall when he was not there, but what I can say is that some of these moments are sacred. Some of these moments are subtle. To explain them is somehow a little bit useless and there are people that are better in explaining these things.

Kim: What about the term 'Master'? It seems like there should be a better term-- when I talk to people who aren't part of it and haven't read anything about it, that word makes them very uncomfortable and I remember when I first started, too, I was like, 'Master'?! I know he's told people, "Oh, it's more like 'Mother' – like a mother – but that doesn't do it, either."

No, no, no. Master has mastered himself and he is an example and we can actually all become like him. What is he? Go and find out. The word 'master' is not a name that he gave himself; other people are giving him that. In this interview, you have heard me saying 'spiritual guide' also. It's because I'm aware when I speak with people that we all have different vocabulary, we all react differently to words, but I also cannot be responsible for what people are feeling. I hope that if I have love and I show my character, people will somehow understand. It is very important to look at the people in front of you when you're speaking with them and to try and relate to them…

Another thing is, this kind of growing up in a Christian country where Christianity was used for creating fear and dogma; all this kind of blame and punishment, rules and feeling guilt and all that – that is their kind of background. So when you're trying the system, just give it a try for three months. If you really make an effort, you will feel the benefit and, when you feel that benefit, I don't think anybody would want to stop unless they have some other wonderful system. Are they able to sit by themselves and attain this enlightenment? I've not met anyone [who could]. People are totally free to leave and everybody's welcome; but what I'm saying is, try to keep your prejudices a little bit on the side.

THE JOURNEY WITHIN

Try to wait with your evaluation. Try to just sit and feel and see what is happening and don't listen to all the nonsense that others are telling you. Try to practice and see what comes.

Kim: I was just talking with a friend, an abhyasi, and she's convinced the world is going to change cataclysmically. Even in Tiruppur for Babuji's birthday, Brother Kamlesh talked about Babuji mentioning, I think back in the '70s, changing the DNA of human beings.... I don't know if you want to comment on any of that, but both that and Sahaj Marg as sort of a social movement. 'The future of the world' kind of an idea.

First of all, I have no idea about this changing DNA, but what I can say is that the world has always changed. The world is not static. It's the same with cultures. They are never static but always changing. We know that everything that is static will die. It's like water becoming rotten [if left to stagnate]. The world is changing – yes. How? I think it's up to us. Are we putting oil in the water or are we giving it a nice loving thought? What is the effect of that? I have no idea, but if I sit and meditate upon it, I think I know what to do. So, just be very basic with these things and then the world will become better. It's not easy for me, either. I'm also struggling.

Kim: If we all work on ourselves, will that change the world?

Yes, of course, but what do you want to change into? What do you want to become? Do you want to develop more?

Kim: I personally would just like for people to get along. The divisiveness – your country, my country – I've always felt like we all live on the same world and sphere, why can't we think of it that way? Why can't we just love each other and be good to each other?

THE JOURNEY WITHIN

So you start with the one you hate. That's what you can do.

Kim: I don't know if I'm big enough.

No, no, but you can try.

You were speaking about this change of DNA and then you were asking about social movement. Let's say that here in Sahaj Marg, we are practicing loving, brotherhood, meditation for human integration – these things. Not only within Sahaj Marg, but everybody. If that is there to some degree, then you're speaking about social movement that should reflect in the world. There you have your social movement. It's not a club only for Sahaj Marg. Not at all. It's for everybody. We are not the only ones who want things to change.

Kim: Some people say 'you can only change yourself and you never even know the impact.'

No, but you can try. So if you want someone to change, don't go with some pamphlet from Sahaj Marg and hit them on the head. Maybe you try to change and see. Maybe they will think, "What happened to her?" That is the best thing you can do. Then, of course, when it is the right time, you can give them a pamphlet and show. It all depends on your relationship to the person and what you are feeling. Be alert and see the people in front of you and don't force other people to do what you are not doing yourself; they will totally know that you are. But when we are experiencing something good, we want to share. We want people to feel what we have felt – that moment of bliss – but we have to remember people are in different places [spiritually]. So we are taught in the Mission that prayer is actually a very good tool, a very subtle tool. I think that's a good place to conclude.

Part IV: **Living in the Heart**

In this section we hear from four people who are really "walking the walk," so to speak. They have made the spiritual life a full-time pursuit and a priority in their lives, while continuing to contribute meaningfully and significantly to society. You will meet a homesteader, a university translation professor, a recently-graduated university student, and an agricultural researcher, all dedicated to Sahaj Marg as a lifestyle.

One thing we heard from Joseph was that this way of life is "hard work." I agree with that and often feel I am unsuccessful. When one is working on trying to learn patience, tolerance, and forgiveness it is easy to often feel a failure. As I explained earlier in the "Lifestyles" section, I have been struggling mightily with putting goals into action. It is even harder when trying to live a Sahaj Marg way of life in every aspect possible. While not even close, I do realize that the lessons are in the journey.

Going down a busy city street in Macau or nearby Hong Kong, I often chant silently to remind myself of "patience, tolerance and love." And then I turn right around and am impatient or unkind to someone (!). I find it so very frustrating and hard to make behavioral change and even harder to make lasting inner change. It is hard to put principles into practice -- and that is exactly the focus of this section of the book.

Leslie advises us that "Western mind, Eastern heart" is what we're after. We want a strong mind but need to know how to set it aside to "let your heart take the fore," as she puts it. Leslie goes on to talk about the joy and changes that will come from "having our souls directly fed with divine essence." She touchingly describes how she and her husband have raised their children to be likewise connected to divine energy and to nature, truly living a land-based life of simplicity and self-

THE JOURNEY WITHIN

sustainability. She advises you to let the practice into your life: "Then there's not one single thing that will not be transformed, every single thing -- and that is fantastic. It's an adventure you never run out of." Leslie describes herself as passionate about living a life 100% in service to the spiritual goal and goes on to describe how she has operationalized that in her life, especially within her main roles as wife and mother. Her dedication, clarity of purpose, and ability to explain difficult aspects of the practice are remarkable, as is she herself. I know you will enjoy hearing her thoughts in this interesting and somewhat poignant chapter. Make sure to read the update she sent as a message at the end.

Next you will finally hear from Hari, whom I have mentioned several times already. The preceptor in Macau, he is also a Chinese-English translation professor. He tells the story of his family's introduction to meditation and traces his and his mother's pathways to increasing involvement and service. His was the first interview I conducted and I asked him to respond to my question about leading a pure lifestyle. His response is interesting in understanding various stages of life development people go through, as taught traditionally in his (Indian) culture. He talks candidly about early experiences, his discrimination between Master and the Ultimate Master (God), then goes on to explain concepts important to spiritual development including surrender and constant remembrance.

When I was interviewing Hari, I was very new to the idea of reincarnation, not really sure what I thought of it but, nevertheless, the whole package began to make sense to me. I had struggled my entire life to make sense of religion and finally decided to follow my own idea that we are all made up of positive and negative "energy" (for lack of a better word) and our life experiences and reactions hopefully will contribute to adding positive energy to the cosmos as a whole. So when we discard our physical form here on Earth, we still are somehow "alive" in the sense of energy. I have always believed deep down that our goal is to merge somehow with our origins, our maker/creator or the energy of creation. My experiences to date with this meditation practice lead me to firmly believe that is true and also

THE JOURNEY WITHIN

that there are methods such as this one whereby it can happen in this lifetime, given enough faith, love, help and will power. Hari talks about becoming one with the Ultimate and the importance of being one with the true Self: "So, to return to the Essence, the Ultimate, is what I think we <u>really</u> aim at -- where the lower self merges with the higher Self and is one. That ends all duality. It ends the separation which is the cause of all misery." Take your time reading this rather long and complicated chapter. I anticipate it will give you a lot to think about.

Likewise, I think you will learn a lot from and enjoy meeting Jules, from Detroit, Michigan (U.S.A.) who also gives a long, fascinating interview. His story will hit home with many young adults as he describes a "life in the fast lane" while an exchange student in Shanghai, P.R.C. Popular with his cohort group, a talented athlete, and educated in psychology, religion and philosophy, Jules tried various yoga and meditation practices before his introduction to Sahaj Marg. He is quite forthright in saying, at that point: "So my first feeling was that this was a crazy cult, but I'm digging what they're putting out there. I'm okay with it. So I did it for four and a half months and I came home." Although his way of learning about the world had always been through reading, Jules decided to not read any of the literature but rather dedicate himself to the practice. He explains, "I don't want to be critical and I don't want to be overly intellectual. I just want to try. By the end of two months, I knew this was for me. So I stopped looking elsewhere..." Jules went on to become a preceptor and is very involved in helping others to better understand and develop their spiritual practice. He advises us to "make time to invest in yourself, nothing else. <u>Make</u> that time and adhere to it with love and kindness." If we want to change, we have to be intentional and just get started, he explains.

Next you will meet someone who has been involved in Sahaj Marg since 1974, when he met Babuji Maharaj in India as a young man in the Peace Corps. As he puts it, "I got to meet Babuji and he was very open and brought me in with open arms. I have to say that the experience is so surreal, it's essentially to me just the best Hollywood movie out there: California surfer boy goes to India, meets his guru,

THE JOURNEY WITHIN

and lives happily ever after." Now helping to supervise mission work throughout the Americas, Bill travels widely as a volunteer while also running a successful agricultural research company to create a better food supply for the planet. Bill shares several important ideas with us, including his take on vegetarianism, indulgences vs. the simple life, use of the word "Master," and samskaras. His discussion of samskaras is particularly interesting. As part of the explanation he presents, when individual souls were created, "the first real samskara or impression that was created at that point was fear – because we were now separate from the whole and so what could we possibly do but worry that we were separate?" He sees how much of his life was oriented around the fear "of just getting life done." As he puts it, "I was pretty much a prisoner to my own creation and it was not easy to be able to exist in that environment. Meditation has unlocked the door and now I'm free." He says he left that prison behind and never looks back. I think you will also enjoy Bill's comments on Sahaj Marg as a social movement and the possible impacts on humankind's future. He concludes by asking us to find self-fulfillment because "then you've made it, you're on cloud nine... if we can reach that stage of human development, I think all of our problems will go away." I leave you to the words of these four people who are really living in the heart.

Chapter 10   The Hidden Beauty of Living Simply

Leslie

U.S.A. American, late 50's, female, homesteader

Preface: My friend Claire recommended I contact Leslie and interview her, partly because she knew I was interested in homesteading and partly because she thought I would be fascinated by Leslie's story of actually "walking the walk." After some email correspondence and the realization that we were in completely opposite time zones, Leslie and I finally meet via Skype. It is early morning for her and early evening for me. It was a delightful interview, even though Leslie was coming off an illness and still very tired.

In this touching and intimate chapter, we meet a woman who, despite an Ivy-league education, has homesteaded, home-schooled, and made an art of living simply the last 20 years of her life. She believes in putting principles into practice and is an example of how devotion and love can help us decide priorities, thereby transforming our lives. She describes spiritual education as "luscious" and shares with us some of her wonder that, despite sufferings, she has such contentment and joy now as a human being, wife and mother. She and her husband are raising six children, focusing on creating a loving, supportive environment in which spirituality is their life. A proponent of landbased communities, Leslie shares with us her hopes for the future.

Kim: I'm particularly interested to learn you are homesteading. I wonder how that fits with your and your husband's emphasis on a spiritual life. Could you comment?

Neither my husband nor I were raised to this. He grew up in Hartford Connecticut, the insurance capital of the world. I was raised in corporate America. There was none of this, "get your hands dirty" stuff like washing our laundry by hand and hanging it on the line, none of that. It's hard. The skills you need are generations old.

I want to encourage you to please get my husband's book, <u>The Choice</u> (Romano, 2013), and read it. It's a story, an analysis of why the world is the way it is, and there's a lot of Sahaj Marg in it. It's based on research we have done and was like channeling, so we were receptive to this kind of storyline. He tried to take a lot of what has come up in research and put it into a narrative in a way people could digest it. It's the first of three so I really would like you to read it.

Kim: Could you just give a little bit about your background? Your approximate age, where you're from, occupation and as part of that, maybe talk about formative experiences? Is there anything from your early years that encouraged you to lead the life that you lead now, and to have the priorities in your life that you have now?

Let's see. I'll be 55 in a few weeks. Childhood, education? Where do I start? My parents were very much corporate-climbing, social climbing materialists. I was raised Catholic, sort of. We went to Catholic Church every week. My father took us, but they were clearly not religious at all. That bewildered me. When I was in church, I was often aware that what was being said was not true -- but I still preferred being there than anywhere else.

I could say that growing up encouraged my native tendencies in wanting the truth -- seeking the truth and living the truth. It's also a

THE JOURNEY WITHIN

tendency of mine to want things to be consistent, and to have a way of life that is consistent with professed beliefs. These things were very important to me, so I could say that living with the total lack of those things was very much an encouragement not to repeat that myself.

I have an Ivy League-ish sort of education. I went to Wellesley and studied philosophy. With philosophy, I got irritated lots of times. I studied Western philosophy quite a bit and the philosophers would try to fix the structure they were trying to create. They would throw God out of it, and throw God in it to fix it. I thought that was just ridiculous, just dishonest.

Some years later, I went on to graduate school and got a Master's degree in Social Policy. My particular area was health care, education and social policy. Doing that was a stepping-stone for me to get to India because I was a research assistant for a person who was Greek and ended up going to Greece. He paid my way from Greece to India, which is a trip not everybody takes, by the way. It was very weird getting from Greece to India. It was an airline that only flew three times a week. That was in 1988.

I'm very clear that it was a soul decision to become an abhyasi before I came into this life. It was a decision already made. Listening to the stuff I did in the Catholic Church, I thought, "Why do they say this stuff?" I know this isn't so; it isn't what God is." Then in college, studying philosophy, I felt that wasn't it either.

I had only been out of college for a couple of months and then I literally bumped into somebody on the street. I felt somebody behind me. It turned out to be an abhyasi and I got my first sitting a couple of months after that.

THE JOURNEY WITHIN

One thing that was interesting to me when I started was, I was also very academic. When I was graduating from Wellesley I even had people angry at me, mainly students, that I wasn't going to get a PhD in Philosophy. Getting a PhD in Philosophy never even crossed my mind. To sit around reading incredible books, talk about it and write about it? Oh, come on! This is only a nice way to spend time.

But I was very academic. When I started the [Sahaj Marg] practice, I would read the books and couldn't remember anything. I would just be affected by reading the books; I couldn't be "mental" with the books. I couldn't even talk about them. I was very aware that a muzzle was put on me. It was there for years and I was grateful. An abhyasi who was my preceptor at the time said, "Just wait until that muzzle is taken off." I was very grateful. I couldn't ricochet; I was prevented from ricocheting. All I could do was to absorb.

Kim: For me it's really hard to shut that darn head off and stay connected with the heart.

It's probably better not to put energy into trying to shut your mind off. The pressure makes it worse and you're putting mind energy into something you want to soften. What's needed is for your heart to be strengthened and to take the lead role. Then you're going to be grateful that your mind is that way.

Western mind, Eastern heart is what we're after. We don't want a weakened Western mind. You want your mind strong -- it's just that your heart has to be boss, that's all. Don't put your mind down. You just have to set it aside and let your heart take the fore. It's a balance thing.

THE JOURNEY WITHIN

Kim: What advice would you have for somebody who is starting to question what's going on in our world, the purpose of life?

I would say this. People are aware that a lot of what we're eating now that we call "food", isn't. What comes out of a factory isn't food. We've been trained to call it that, but it's just really stuff we put in our mouths. Our minds call it food, but our bodies know that it's not. We are walking around in a state of deficiency so even our physical bodies are starving. We live in a time of tremendous deficiency because of the state of the Earth. If soils are deficient, food is deficient and we come up with this bizarre definition of food that includes chemical products. So the body is the way it was designed and the body is starving. As much as the body is starving, how much more are the heart and soul starving at the soul level?

What is unique about Sahaj Marg at this time and indeed over the last 10,000 years of human history is the *pranahuti*, the transmission. Transmission is the food that goes directly to the soul. I can only say that what awaits you is wonder beyond wonder and adventures you could never imagine. Things in yourself that you thought were hard-wired and could not change turn out to be "soft-ware," and you become Yourself.

You cannot even imagine. For instance, for we English language speakers there are no words to designate the joy, the love and the subtle change that will come from having our souls directly fed with divine essence, divine grace. So I would just say to anybody who's hungry -- try. Be open and be aware. For anybody who's got any inkling that the story we are told, the history that we are taught, the politics we are subjected to, the social mores we're raised in – if there's any sense of hollowness there, or if there's anything that veers away just a little bit from the truth, from the overall design, the "operating manual" -- dig deeper.

THE JOURNEY WITHIN

There is only one way to dig deeper and that's on a spiritual path. This is the connection to truth and reality. It's only as we travel farther and farther down that path that we begin to look at ourselves and the world around us and say "Oh. I see." Only then do we begin to start to become freer to make real choices about how we live, about how we spend time, about how we raise our children, about how we love, about how we feel about everything.

Once you step into the spiritual path, once you get fed from the inside out, apply the cleaning process (which is very important to Sahaj Marg) and, once the baggage gets cleaned off, the old heaviness and the misconceptions get cleaned off. Only then does some clarity come when you can start to make actual decisions. Then real life can begin. Really.

There are many unique and magnanimous qualities in the characteristics of Sahaj Marg. One of them is the only quality you need to start, and it is willingness. That's the only visible quality. You don't have to have purity to start it, but there has to be purity to become it. That's what these lifestyle changes are and that's what these thought changes are – to evolve.

That's what all of this is -- The Master calls you --because he is a Master of such capability and because of the *pranahuti* which creates change in such a very natural manner. Purity has to be there to experience and to maintain what's given. You don't have to have purity to start, but you are going to go through changes to create purity; which is to say that the bondage is going to fall away. But you have to create a way of life so that the purity becomes more and more. That's why Master talks so much about character development, sometimes using the image of a bird flying with two wings. Character development and spiritual development go hand in hand.

THE JOURNEY WITHIN

My daughter is an abhyasi and she wrote an essay [in which] I thought the main metaphor was wonderful. She said character is not a wall, it's a staircase. Good character is not a wall you put up to keep out negative influences. It's a stairway you climb to get to higher levels of consciousness and awareness, and the ability to reach out to brothers and sisters.

What I want to say is, the most important thing is to let the practice into your life. Practice is not some separate thing that you do in the morning and a little bit in the night, and then you live a regular life. We have this idea that we live this material life and then we have this spiritual life that we gradually integrate into it. I say no; that's not what's happening. What's happening is that we live this material life where layer upon layer has been glued on top of spirituality and on top of who we really are. We are peeling away those layers and what we're left with is a healthy, natural life with divine light beaming out of our hearts.

That's why you let your practice into your life. Then there's not one single thing that will not be transformed; how you dress, what you eat, who you're with, what you read, what [media] you watch and how you interact in all of your relationships, what your priorities are. Every thing -- every single thing -- and that is fantastic. It's an adventure you never run out of. I've been doing this for over 30 years and I'm still discovering things all the time.

For at least 20 years, I have been obsessed with living simply. It's a purity thing. Sahaj Marg is different because it comes from inside. This desire for living purely? It just becomes a joy to live morally, it's a joy. It's not a restraint; it's a relief.

Kim: Frankly, this is one of the reasons I was interested in interviewing you. You are the only person I've met who's really walking the walk. I have just so much admiration. Some people see it as dropping out of society. I see it as building a new

THE JOURNEY WITHIN

vision of society. I think about doing it. But how does one go about that? How did you do that? I mean, who washes their own clothes anymore? Who makes their own soap? Who actually milks a cow? So if you could talk just a little bit about how you "put your money where your mouth is"? (laughs)

That's a very good question. I'm very interested in trying to understand what is natural law, the natural law that governs the Earth and human life. I'm very interested in coming to understand what the original operating instructions were. I am very passionate about living a life that is 100% in service to the spiritual goal.

I live this way in the interest of the future. I live this way to be in connection with brothers and sisters all over this planet. It's one of the reasons I don't have a washing machine -- because hardly anybody does. I'm American but I don't subscribe to that. Years ago, I eventually realized that anything this modern day society tells you to do and how you're supposed to live is going to be 180 degrees wrong. I don't go by that because that's going by a negative; it's just something I realized.

There's societal programming which is fuelled by economic and political interests. Then there's the spiritual truth that's always been there... Being an abhyasi for me has meant to be willing to satisfy social messages and seek the truth of what it means to be a wife, what it means to be a mother, what it means to be a spiritual person, what it means to be a human on the earth at this time, of what it means to relate to all living things. All of it. There's this willingness and then doing it. As I said, I have this real thing about consistency so I'm not interested in talking about things I'm not willing to do, and that's just how it is.

You go to your edge; you feel Master's hand at your back. You have no idea what grace is there waiting for you -- to support you to move towards what's natural -- until you take these steps.

THE JOURNEY WITHIN

So I have learned things about being a wife, for instance, about leading from behind and being there as a support to my husband. I'm not trying to push forward my own agenda. I take myself as a support to him. Loudly politically incorrect; wonderful transformation in my marriage. I have a happy husband, which makes me a happy wife.

We've done everything we've done by ourselves, just the two of us and the children. The system doesn't want it. It's almost illegal to live as simply as is appropriate. We're there for our children and they can be there for each other. I wasn't raised like that. I was smart, and that's how you get points. Your mind is the way you get points. Right? But I have been rescued from that. The Master creates amazing women. There is nothing higher than a woman's natural role. I'm not saying a woman can't work in a career outside the home; I'm saying it's an inner thing. Over the years, I learned that being a woman is a good thing. It's a critical thing. Morality and the future rest on our shoulders.

You have only two roles for this. One is your behavior, the atmosphere that you have around you, and the other is prayer. Pray, pray, pray. That's where you pray for your role as wife and mother, where you lead from behind through your chastity, your inner prayer life, your discipline and all that kind of stuff. You have your eye on the future... [others] don't have the wit to know what's coming in the world, but you do.

I've long thought (because probably I didn't have it) that having a life that was land-based, somewhere in the country and natural, was really important. So we have gone through different phases of cows and all of this. We don't have the livestock right now because we're trying to move, but that's how the kids have been raised -- to milk cows, to make cheese and butter.

THE JOURNEY WITHIN

Kim: *Can you talk a little bit more about raising your children, about raising a family in this alternative, natural way?*

Okay. We have taken having children in the most natural way from the very start. We have never used birth control. They've all been breast-fed, they've all been cloth-diapered and all this happy stuff. I have six children and four of them are basically one a year. I say to people, it's not how many you have because once you're in over your head, it doesn't matter how deep the water is. Having one a year is tough.

So out of whatever naturalness we had as husband and wife, came the children. These children chose to come to us. They chose to come into a Sahaj Marg household and it is on this basis that we raised them. We have done as much as we can to protect family relationships, the mother-baby dyad, if you will, and we have protected them from this rapacious economic system.

The two oldest went to school and that was for separate legal reasons, but we have otherwise homeschooled our children and we live quietly at home for the most part. I have created a Sahaj Marg- oriented curriculum as best I can. I think about education every single day and have done so for decades.

We have purposely raised them to milk cows, grow tomatoes, forage and all these kinds of things, partly because that's a healthy, natural way to live and partly for self-reliance. In that way [self-reliance] it's important, but also partly because we know the world's going to change and it's going to be important to have people around who know how to milk a cow and who know what lamb's quarters [a wild plant] are, and that you can eat them.

It is Master's wish that these children become the torchbearers for society. So we are raising them in a way that is best to create the right orientation towards spiritual life and strength of character now. At the same time, we have an eye towards the future and what they perhaps are going to be called upon to provide, with all the changes and uncertainty that are coming.

Education is trying to have a balance so as to not get all academic, which is my tendency. I tend to want to load them up with a lot of great books to read, but I need to pull myself back. To have a balance between what people call education and life skills, being able to cook and grow into their roles as husbands and wives and fathers and mothers, this is really critical.

I wanted to try and raise them according to what I have always thought are the qualities of an abhyasi. One of the important qualities is imagination. Master once said that Babuji had the greatest imagination of all because he imagined a whole new world. So you better believe we read <u>The Lord of the Ring</u> (Tolkien, 1954) and C. S. Lewis. It's not some dry thing. Spiritual education for adults and spiritually-based education for children is luscious. This is what we try to do.

As for the Sahaj Marg aspect, I started reading Sahaj Marg literature to them when the eldest was around six. I've read to them a little bit every day for years, and for a long time I read twice a day, all of us together. We read <u>Down Memory Lane</u> (Ragagopalachari, 1993) and <u>In His Footsteps</u>, both volumes (Rajagopalachari, 1988, 1993) and <u>Reality at Dawn</u> (Chandra, 1954 reprinted 2010). I'm reading <u>Whispers</u> (Chandra, 2010, 2012, 2013) now. They have heard a lot of Sahaj Marg literature, and we pray and sit silently for a few minutes. It used to be twice a day but we are doing it once a day now. We have always done that. When the babies were born, my husband scooped up that baby and whispered the prayer in the baby's ear.

So Sahaj Marg is our life, it is our passion, it is our love. It is our saving grace, so every aspect of it that we can, we share. It is for them; it isn't for us. These children are His. Everything He gives us, we give them that they may go into this great mission of raising the vibratory level of Earth for humanity, for restoring to Earth the peace and harmony, for the devotion that is meant to be Earth's for every human being.

Let me just say one thing that popped into my mind... Speaking for the people I know and I can certainly speak for the West, I think people are starved for intimacy -- blessed, sweet intimacy. What I can say from experience is that the spiritual path and Sahaj Marg, in particular -- a close-knit family -- provide that intimacy.

Here's an anecdote that has nothing to do with Sahaj Marg. When my oldest one was first born (a week old or something), my parents came to visit for a few days. They're not the kind that would roll up their sleeves and help. They needed to be entertained. I had to find out what the best restaurants were. They're fancy people and they do fancy things. I had my little baby in my arms every minute and, by the end of three days, I realized my attention had been pulled away and that had created a slight ripple in the intimacy. That was not okay with me. That was a real realization. That feeling of intimacy and that state of awareness are very delicate.

This is why we have to live in a pure and simple way -- because it's very easy for that to be jarred and we lose that which we treasure, which is the reflection on a still mind. The thing that causes a ripple you really notice, and you want that beautiful unmarked reflection. This is a real discipline of life and I noticed that with my little baby.

It's the same thing with Master. The things that we do create waves, like tsunamis, so there's no opportunity to see the reflection at all. You

THE JOURNEY WITHIN

want to clear all that away so you have this smooth surface as a reflecting pool.

My visual image of a family is of a wheel because Master is the hub, the spokes being the family members. No one spoke is more important than another. All are spokes equally in this wheel and this wheel as a whole is moving in the right direction towards the spiritual goal. That's the way I think of it.

My joke about homeschooling is that it's a way of preserving that intimacy. We are all living together. So my joke is -- and if you've ever engaged in homeschooling, it's a massive undertaking but it's a way to be together. You want to be together but you have to do something all day, so we homeschool.

Kim: And milk cows and make cheese and wash clothes.

Exactly. But that's what meditation is; it is the most intimate thing. This thing that you always reached for outside yourself, whether it's a relationship or it's a material thing or money or beauty. All these are things that we reach for outside of ourselves. When we have it, it's great for a moment and then it's gone. Then you're left feeling, "Ugh" and then you reach some more.

[But we have to realize] that intimacy is always there 100% of the time. If you turn your attention in(wards) and build that relationship, it's always there and it nourishes you. It's just always there. Then your whole life is on a different footing.

Our life right now? We don't have any livestock right now so we're not milking or anything like that. Our life right now is that we all get up early in the morning, we say the prayer, I read from *Whispers* and three of the children can work pretty much on their own with their studies, so they go do that. I work with the youngest and then I cook.

We recently shifted the way we eat, now eating only two meals a day, one at ten and one at four. It's unbelievable, like I've been let out of jail. What I've learned is that your body goes through a cleansing cycle until about 10 o'clock in the morning, and so it's really better to have hours [of not eating] before you go to bed while your body is digesting. Now we'll have an apple or something, and the kids are instructed to have snacks because they need to keep their calorie level up.

So basically, we work together outside. We study together and I read to the family a lot. There are a lot of books that we share reading aloud. We spend time cooking. It's very simple what we do. We don't go out much. We go out and buy food. We go out and go hiking. That's it. There's not much to tell. I wash clothes outside under the sky. I'm very aware of weather. I started washing everything by hand some years ago, and then my intuition about weather improved because I had to guess whether to hang the stuff out on the line or not. I've found that any of these little changes that you make in your lifestyle can open up levels of awareness that you had no idea were there.

I ended up writing a series of blog posts about washing laundry by hand because I realized so many things just from doing that simple thing. For one of my [Pockets of the Future] blog posts, I pulled YouTube videos of people washing clothes by hand from all over the world. They have beautiful hand movements.

Everything is about consciousness. It's possible to change any little thing that you do to increase consciousness. Wow, what a reward that is! If you pay cash instead of using a credit card there will be things you realize that you wouldn't otherwise. Anything you do by hand you'll realize things you wouldn't otherwise have [understood]. Doing

THE JOURNEY WITHIN

something naturally, doing something that takes some time – all these things increase the possibility of awareness and increased consciousness. Then you discover stuff that you have no idea! It's amazing.

What I have found and I always say is: there is a path, there are stepping stones waiting for you, in front of you at your feet. Take the first step and go ahead. Have the courage and it is guaranteed that the next stepping stone will become visible. It goes on forever and up and up and up. You just have to make that movement. As Master says, if you make a ten percent movement towards him, he'll make a 90% move towards you.

There are so many beings in the hierarchy, there are Masters reaching down to us, showering us with encouragement and transmission, and so-called coincidences, all to give us a chance. All you have to do is make some effort and to set your will. "I will discover this thing called spirituality. I will allow my soul and my heart to be fed directly. I will allow myself to change. I will improve my character. I will hit the pause button before I speak. I will really learn what it is to be a woman or a man or a spiritual person or someone of the future instead of the past or whatever it is. I will become what it means to be a wife and in all of its manifestations." Whatever it is; it's so many things. We have to exert ourselves a bit, and it all just opens up.

I've always wanted to share with people living morally, living according to the maxim of natural law, whatever you want to call it. It's not some onerous thing. That's the big joke. It's an adventure; it's a discovery. You're discovering things every minute. You're discovering new strengths in yourself, you're discovering new aspects to the created world that you had no idea of. It's an adventure! It's the best thing! You can do this. People just need to have a thread to pull.

THE JOURNEY WITHIN

There are a lot of people who want to live the way we do. They want to spend time with their children, they want to have things they know how to grow, and they want to not have jobs that divide the family so much. They want to be intimate and natural. A lot of people want this. They feel this pull inside them. They're attracted to it, but they don't know how to even take that first step.

Just take a step and then things will become more obvious. Just pick some area in life and experiment finding whatever feels to you more simple and natural; then watch how you feel as you do that. It's a natural process just waiting there for you.

Kim: You talked about intimacy and Sahaj Marg as a social movement and a hope for the future. What about the sense of community? Do you feel a sense of community and in what ways can it be nurtured?

I feel a sense of community internally, but I think there's a very strong need for the future -- a community living together. Families living together, a sort of land-based village life where you share resources and you share strengths and weaknesses. There's so much to be gained. I wish so much that we were in a community. We wanted to create a community for a long, long time. We are waiting, I don't know, for the time or for some kind of critical mass, but there are other people who wish for this, too. I wish that we were in a kind of a land-based village situation where the kids can be running around with each other and there are other adults to go to than just us. There are so many advantages. I think community-based is just natural. I don't think that living alone in an isolated life is natural at all.

My husband and I are very aware of being a transition generation, being a swing generation. [It would help if] our children were automatically part of a community and had more people to share a life with, to share the work and the joys with. We would really want that. I would like to see an actual spiritual-based, land-based educational

THE JOURNEY WITHIN

system for children. It could have boarding students, but I wouldn't focus on that particularly. I would want to see families sharing this together and adults sharing together their expertise. They teach each other and they teach the children; I think that's what is natural.

This needs to start happening more in the West. My mind is on it, and has been on it for 20 years. So I live in full faith that it will happen -- but whether it will happen for me personally, I don't know. It's critical and I think it has to happen, especially with the changes that are going to be coming for the Earth. People are going to have to pool what little they have to make it. We also need to come together for inspiration as well as just shared elbow grease [hard work]; and to laugh, just laugh together.

Kim: Make music?

Music? Absolutely! All those things that are some of the genius of human beings, of our species. In the West especially, people have no clue how to conduct nourishing and fulfilling relationships. So communities become these scenes of drama and pain. This is not what we want. We want people who are on a spiritual path together who are becoming finer and finer in their vibrations, and stronger and stronger in their character so that it can be successful. Having communities would be much, much easier with people who are on a spiritual path together -- especially with this path that is so very effective, based on cleaning and transmission.

The community, then, is that same wheel with divinity at its hub, with all those members as spokes (whether they're biologically related or not). Ultimately, it is humanity that we are and this where we need to get to. This is my image that I have had for a long time. I see the Earth from a distance. Human beings have been healed and raised up. At a distance, Earth emanates songs of devotion and peace. (This is the image I hold.) I am convinced this is the distant future and this is why we're putting our shoulders to the wheel. In that image, the wheel becomes a clumsy metaphor, but life on Earth's all one. Humanity is one aspect, so graciously created. It's all there to give thanks to the Creator, just to be in devotion. Then all things are possible.

The logo that my husband made for our website http://www.pocketsofthefuture.com/ is an earth with little lights. Each light is a pocket of the future. We have to try; some movement has to happen here in the West, where people are willing to put aside their individual agendas for His agenda. That's the thing. People have to be willing to do that. I think that material life here is just so addictive. People aren't able to let go of the addiction long enough to try this new thing, and that's why our kids do not have the choice of going out, they don't have the choice of having a cell phone or going to the mall. We don't give them those particular choices. They are shielded from that until they are strong enough to sustain the subliminal "blech" that's out there. This idea that you can throw your kids to the system and expect them to undo all that it puts into them when they are 18 so that they can magically become abhyasi is unfortunate.

Kim: I look at global warming and other predictions. Where is there a place that's safe? Especially if you're concerned about your children, which I know you are. What can you set up for them? How can you do it?

We have to start learning to depend on each other.

I've tried on and off for years here and somehow nothing in the West has taken off. I don't know what the block is, whether it's this obsession in this country with individualism or the materialism. I really don't know what it is making it so hard to do the obvious, which is to create a community and create a land-based life.

THE JOURNEY WITHIN

It's basically already too late to be practical and raising these skills this is a message that my husband and I have had for years. We can't get abhyasi to listen to for some reason. Others have experienced the same thing. Somebody tried in the south of France to start a community.

We come with so many scars anyway, and to add this whole modern way doesn't make sense to us. So I don't know why it takes longer in the West that we know, the wealthy West. It just makes it so difficult to create simple lives and community. It seems crazy to do this but we're wired to do this. We are hard-wired for community. This is so obvious to me. Why is it taking so long?

I haven't given up. I'll never give up. I can't. I was very conscious as a child of having a mission; I've always known I had a mission. I get really stressed out if I feel like I'm not going to get the mission accomplished. In that way I am driven. I've always experienced myself that way. I had a vision when I was 12 that my life's work was with the earth as a whole. I had no idea what that meant, but there's no giving up. I'm just standing here in a state of "yes," waiting to be used. That's all.

The following was sent as an addendum via email message a week or so later and is being included with the writer's permission:

As you may have surmised, I was raised in a loveless household -- a cold, cruel household characterized by intelligence, isolation, sarcasm and competition and narcissism, borderline personality disorder and physical and sexual abuse. Marriage and children were looked down upon. Anything related to the Divine was nowhere in the picture. Food was used as a weapon. Clothing was a way to be fashionable and spend money, etc.

THE JOURNEY WITHIN

Life with my "family of origin" was not the only difficulty I encountered in this life. Fast forward in my life quite a few decades. I was stalked and nearly killed in my early 20s. I was married before to someone who also turned out to be mentally ill, and those are just a few highlights.

But now here I am married to an actual husband with beautiful children living in a very humble farmhouse on just a few acres in the mountains of southwest Virginia. Our place became what I called a tourist attraction for Indian brothers and sisters from the D.C. center. A prefect would drive down to give sittings and bring someone with him. Abhyasis there took turns coming down. Without an exception [after] they landed here, their faces would soften and they would start mooning about their village childhoods back in India or the lives of their grandparents in villages back in India. That was fun. One couple came towards the end of the time when that prefect was coming down. The gentleman walked into the large farmhouse kitchen we have and went into a state. I could see it but didn't know what was happening. After a few minutes, he kind of shook himself, looked at me and very softly said, "I feel like I am in India here. I don't even know why." That brought tears to my eyes.

But there was one comment even better that came which is the point of this anecdote. Another prefect used to come here some years ago who was very devoted and hard working. He used to be on the ashram management committee. He gave loads of sittings all over the place and was really into it, if you know what I mean. How we enjoyed his visits. Anyway, some time ago, he mentioned to me in an email that he had told his wife after returning from one of his visits here that he had never felt such great love in an environment, outside of an ashram, as he felt at our place.

See that? Master could take a woman who had been battered and beaten, who had been raised to be intellectual and cold and competitive and so utterly transform her through her years of association with him

THE JOURNEY WITHIN

that she could grow into managing a home where brothers and sisters might be startled into remembering a way of life that was more simple and intimate and, even more importantly, feel waves upon waves of the Master's love. What a miracle. Why pursue a spiritual way of life? Because that is what we are designed to do. Why step onto the path of Sahaj Marg in particular? In order to experience that the word "miracle" just means what happens when you and your life are touched by His Divine love and guided by His far-reaching vision.

With affection,
L

THE JOURNEY WITHIN

Chapter 11   See What It Is That You Have Found

Hari

Indian living in Macao (S.A.R. China), male, age 35, university professor

Preface: Hari is the first person I interviewed and actually had to suffer through being interviewed twice due to technical failure (and, yes, some stupidity on my part). We meet around the coffee table in his home and I enjoy the hot cup of chai provided by his wife. He helps me make sure both recording machines are running and we begin. We both know it will be a long interview, but I look forward to having some rather basic and, for me, pressing questions answered about the meditation practice. At this point, I had been meditating only about 18 months, long enough to feel I had grasped some fundamentals but really only starting to see what could lie ahead, given enough dedication.

In this chapter, Hari leads us through some basic and difficult principles of the practice, including the idea of "balance" so as not to feel or experience extremes that create impressions. As we go through this life, we are working to "clean" ourselves of past impressions while avoiding the creation of new ones – thus the importance of daily cleaning and 1:1 "sittings" with prefectors to help us work through and rid ourselves of our samskaras (loosely thought of as "grossness" or impressions from past lives, if you will). He also explains the differences between wants and needs and between religion vs. spirituality. Hari will impress you with his mastery of words and his ability to explain fundamental concepts related to spirituality, including "surrender" and "constant remembrance."

My parents are both Tamil and I was born and raised in Delhi, which is in the north of India. Tamil speakers are predominately located in South India. Tamil is one of the longest surviving classical languages of the world (Stein, 1977). My father moved to Delhi when he was quite young, around 16. So we had pretty much an immigrant kind of upbringing, because we were distinctly different from the place that we were born.

My father's father and his family were some of the earliest people who took to learning English. Much of the latter half of his life, my father was working with the Australian high commission in Delhi, where he was at quite a senior position. At home, we spoke exclusively in Tamil and in English and as we went to school, we picked up Hindi. [Our parents were] traditional and quite religious, but not orthodox or conservative. We used to have a lot of friends from every conceivable part of India.

Typically, as would be expected of a South Indian Tamil Brahmin family, there was a lot of religious ritualism around us. Nothing was regular or fixed but you grew up hearing devotional music and looking at your mom lighting up lamps every evening at six o'clock… anything that's new, anything that's bought and brought home (be it food, be it clothes), you would first offer it to the Lord and then start using it, so things of that sort. On birthdays, you go to the temple and make an offering … there was this constant undercurrent of devotion and prayer.

Kim: Sometimes it seems the Indian people I've met have an advantage when it comes to being spiritual or leading a "pure" life. Many don't drink alcohol, for example, and there seems to be a values-based system already established. I know that's a huge overgeneralization, but I wonder if you want to comment?

I think one of the reasons why you would see that is because society is so extremely stratified in India. Most of the people that I knew were

THE JOURNEY WITHIN

quite similar to what we were like, but as I've traveled outside India and met other Indians, I do realize that it's a society that is divided not just by languages, not just by class, by affluence -- it's [divided] by caste, by region -- there are so many things that come into it. The kinds of people that you meet are mostly middle-class and upper-middle-class who have the means to get what we call public school education (which refers to privately-run schools), who travel outside. But, if you consider India, they comprise 200, maybe 300 million. The best estimate puts them at 30% of the [Indian] population, so there's still a huge bit of India which is very different, which doesn't speak in English, which doesn't do things the way we do. So I guess that would be part of not just language but all these things such as drinking.

There has been a very strong movement toward asceticism, particularly [among] the Brahmins. I'm talking about the traditional way of life before India meets the West or India meets Islam. So there was emphasis on restraint and learning to remember. Sanskrit verses would be committed to memory and recited over and over again. They had mnemonic devices built-in like pitch which would help (the idea being that you might not understand much of what is happening now). So the emphasis is on discipline and restraint.

The traditional way of life was divided into four phases (Asramas). The first phase, lasting from birth till about roughly 14 or 15 years of age, was called Brahmacharya and was supposed to be a phase where you were taken to a guru who would train you and there would be extreme emphasis on discipline -- when do you wake up, when do you go to sleep, what things you do. Then there's the second phase of life, which is called Grihastha which is the life of the householder, which begins essentially when you are married and settled down. The texts say that this is the phase where you fulfill all of the desires that you have. Eat meat if you want to; have sex if you want to have sex. Do whatever it is that you want to do. This is a phase that will continue until the time that your children are coming-of-age. So, in the previous phase of life, the strict emphasis is on no alcohol, no indulgence, celibacy, rigorous discipline, waking early in the morning before sunrise, doing your daily worship, and all of that. In the householder phase of life, it's like, "Okay, fulfill whatever desires that you have."

Then, when your children grow up, when you're roughly 45 or 50, you're expected to enter the next phase, which is called Vanaprastha, which literally means living in the jungle, living in the forest. This means you now have to start working on curtailing desire again, reducing desires, becoming more simple [and] in tune with nature -- to prepare for the final stage, which is called Sanyasa, which is renunciation. So you renounce everything and you recede away from worldly life.

Now this system has existed for thousands of years and, particularly among the chief proponents of that way of life (which would be the Brahmins), it was pretty much taken as a fact -- so much so that, even today in Indian society, if you see someone who is approaching 50 or 50+ with a lot of zeal for life and doing things and going places, people would typically feel that, "Oh, you've still not given it up." So, that bit is still there.

Although there are a lot of parents now who would indulge their children, the traditional way of bringing them up would be [so as to teach] restraint. You will eat this, though you don't like it, because that teaches you restraint. There was a lot of emphasis on discipline and a framework within which you are free to do what you want, but there's no freedom beyond that. And then there's a period where you're free to do what you want, fulfill whatever desires you have, go where you want to go -- but which I think is easier said than done because you have responsibilities, you have a spouse, you have children and you have to raise a family, and all that is going to kick in.

In terms of diet, the Vedas (which is considered the holy text for Hindus) say that, except for the period of Grihastha, you have to eschew things like meat and alcohol. So, if you have an emphasis on staying away from all of that when you're a kid, do it if you want to do it when you're enjoying your adult life, but then finally you [renounce it]. So in some ways, yes, people who have been brought up with tradition in a relatively conservative family, you would see that. We have prohibition in most states, except for a few. So you wouldn't see alcohol consumption in public; it would be a very private affair. You would buy whatever you want to buy from government-authorized agencies and probably just drink at home; you didn't have places to drink. But all of that is changing. And with that change, lifestyles are also changing. There are a lot of people who do consume meat. But yes, there remains an overwhelming discourse in society that tends to look down upon people who drink, looks down upon people who eat meat, looks down upon people who have divorced for whatever reason there might have been.

So there's a lot of emphasis on restraint and, where there is no restraint, people would feel very much at liberty to judge. For instance, one of my earliest memories is, if you took an Air India flight, the air hostess would ask you (and typically they were people who have jobs for life, so they would be aunties) -- and they would ask, "veg or non-veg?" That's the way we ask the question in India -- it's "veg or non-veg." We don't say you eat meat. We say you are a non-vegetarian. And those people who would want to say non-veg would need to muster up a little bit of courage to say non-veg and they'll be like, "O--K..."and they'll give you that look like, "You're on <u>that</u> side." You're a minority and, you're not supposed to do this, but you are doing this. That discourse, although in an attenuated form, still exists. So there is that emphasis.

Kim: When and how did you become involved in spirituality, in Sahaj Marg, in particular?

My brother was the first one who got involved; this was in Bangalore in 1994. After my 10th grade, we moved to Bangalore, where I did my 11th and 12th [grades]. My father had passed away in an accident and it

THE JOURNEY WITHIN

was decided my mother should be in Bangalore near her elder sister. My brother was interested in improving concentration, because he was going to take some competitive exams to get into business school, so he was looking and experimenting with transcendental meditation at that time. We (myself and my mother) never got interested in any of that, but then we started hearing about prefectors and sittings and it was all quite mysterious and was also making us a bit wary. There was this talk about prefectors who could see what you are thinking and all of that. My brother was the first to join. I can't recall under what circumstances we agreed to go, my mom and me, and get the sittings. One by one, we kind of joined, not knowing much about the system initially. We would just occasionally meditate or do the cleaning. We started getting regular with sittings and satsanghs fairly early, but practice was by no means regular.

I wasn't an abhyasi, in any sense of the term, until about five years later. If my memory serves me right, it happened in China when I was there as a student studying Chinese. Everything seemed to be coming together. It seemed like I left a lot of chaos behind. Things were getting clearer in the mind and in every other way and, there is this feeling overall that you are getting smarter in a more penetrating way. It kind of dawned on me that it was probably because of this practice that I was doing (and not doing quite well), and that made me get more into it. Starting with cleaning, it got regular and then with meditation it got regular and then we were quite regular with practice. But even at that time, we (me and my mom) did have a very big problem with accepting this figure of Master. So, my brother, I think, was one of the fortunate ones, who actually had no problem whatsoever from very early which is quite strange because, before coming to this system, he was much less involved in all the religious rituals and all of those things that me and my mom were otherwise involved in. He was a lot more like my dad who was there but rather aloof and not really that involved.

To talk about Master again, we had a big problem because we would look at all these crowds trying to go close to him, say something to him, touch his feet, garland him, and all sorts of things which all seemed quite theatrical to us. We would have these discussions about how it's

THE JOURNEY WITHIN

all the same; you talk about idol worship elsewhere and here you have person worship… But what helped all throughout is we had prefectors and prefects who told us that the real Master is the Master inside and, even in the prayer when we say "Oh Master…" it refers to the Ultimate Master which is God. It helped at that stage to kind of bifurcate it into the real Master is that Master [God] and these people are calling this person who's the president of the mission, [Master]. In my mind, yes, for a very long time, I did have this problem of "can't really accept it." The good thing is, my prefectors told me, and what Master says in one of his talks is, your relationship to begin with is with the practice. Each and every one of us has to prove the practice in him or herself first before we can talk about becoming an abhyasi or becoming a disciple. I mean, Master doesn't even come into the picture before you've actually practiced sufficiently enough to know what the practice can do for you.

The point where I started getting involved more was when it became more and more evident to me that the way my life was now unfolding had a lot to do with this practice that I was doing. Then a sense of gratitude developed and I wanted to know what it is that I could do. All of this kind of happened to me when I was in Singapore.

The earliest point where I started getting drawn a little more into the mission was at university in Delhi, where I moved after graduating from high school. I was doing my Master's (degree) in Chinese [there] and the prefects in Delhi were telling me, "Oh, Master would be interested in meeting you because he's been making these trips to Singapore and there's no one in China." And so it started that way, that maybe there was a role for me to play.

But it really happened in Singapore. There was a sister in Macao who had dreamt about (seen) Lalaji in a dream, not knowing who he was. She went to India, spending time looking for the person [but] she didn't find anyone. On her way back she transited via Singapore and found a listing for Shri Ram Chandra mission in the Yellow Pages and, according to her, she decided to call because it said we charge nothing. She thought, "Okay, so that must be something genuine." She was put into touch with the headquarters and Master sent two senior prefectors to Macao. On their way to Macao, they passed through Singapore. I am a translator, so I passed on a lot of Chinese materials that we had translated for use in Macao. One of them recommended me to Master to be made a prefect.

There was an episode before this which happened in Perth, Australia. Master was sitting on the porch, we were talking about Chinese or China and, for 30 or 40 minutes it was like a dialogue between just the two of us. That was one of the closest and most intimate contacts that I had with Master that I really cherish. In Perth, he spent a lot of time with me. He took me in his car when he went into the city to buy gifts for the volunteers, I had a couple of lunches and dinners with him -- and again back in Singapore, I was trying to hurriedly go out to get some books for him and he would call me and say, "No, first have lunch with me and have dinner with me" and all of that. So that's how I kind of got drawn in. It started in Singapore.

Kim: Have you ever regretted joining?

No, not at all, why would I, why would I? If anything, I've regretted not being regular right at the beginning. In some ways, it was too early because I was not even 18 and I had no idea what I was doing. So it was more of a fun thing that I was doing on the side. And I wouldn't have made a lot of stupid mistakes that I did make in my personal life -- and some choices that I made at that time which I probably would have done differently -- if I had been regular right from the beginning…

Kim: I wonder how Sahaj Marg has had an influence on your interactions with other people, how you run your life, your scholarship? So I'm asking you basically to comment on your reputation and how has Sahaj Marg influenced that?

THE JOURNEY WITHIN

I can only say this; that there are times when I almost feel like -- prior to Sahaj Marg practice, I would've probably been a little more courteous. I often find that, if anything, the expressions on my face are quite blank when people indulge in general niceties... I think there's a strange kind of focus on addressing what seems to be most important. [It is] not something that I do consciously, but I think that is quite a direct result of this practice. There is a certain amount of clarity as to what is important in a conversation or in a discussion and you can quite easily cut through the rest of it. But that sometimes might not be particularly polite.

As for the rest of it, I can definitely say that I was always an extremely average student, particularly with mathematics. I was almost on the verge of failing every time but would just somehow manage to pass. Chinese was something I could start from scratch. I also believe quite strongly that it was part of Him making best use of my *samskaras* [tendencies] that I got into this and then I managed to do well. And strangely, after that, I would take economics and I get an A in economics. I would take history and I get an A in history -- all because I think there was a certain sense of clarity as to what I was doing. And I think that is attributable quite clearly to Sahaj Marg.

Kim: Could you share with us any best, interesting, funny, etc. memories related to spirituality and Sahaj Marg?

Lots of them. In fact, one memory that always kind of accompanies me is that, each time we went and attended these large gatherings, we were utterly miserable. The first couple of times, when I was not married, me and my mom would repeatedly ask each other, "Why do we have to do this?" and "Why does he do this -- put all of these people through all of this pain?" It's uncomfortable. It's dusty. It's messy. It's a huge exercise in organizing. You've got people who have to cook and people complaining and fighting about all sorts of things.

THE JOURNEY WITHIN

And each time we would still go back, which is quite difficult to explain. The more we did it, the more we found that there was a certain atmosphere created there which couldn't be felt through what it is that the eye met or that the senses felt; there was something else. There was a <u>drenching</u> of sorts, coming out of which you felt like fish out of water. And we were going back for that. And then it made sense, why the rest of it is kept to the minimum. In fact, the amount of comfort that's provided is probably more than what Master would like or is good for us...

There was this one time we decided that it was just too much of a bother to go and live in those tents and we decided to take a hotel outside. We really ended up regretting it because it just wasn't the same. We spent a lot of time in taxis, shuttling between the hotel and the ashram. Each time you left the ashram to come back it was like something was just missing. And every single time you came out of these gatherings [bhandaras] or you returned from being in Master's presence, there was this distinct feeling of alienation from everything around you. It's like you didn't see people, you didn't see things, you didn't see these buildings or anything you're going through. It's just like you are safely tucked away somewhere -- very blissfully -- away from all of this. And then <u>slowly</u> all of it came back to catch you. That's something that I've always felt.

In terms of episodes, we've had a number of very interesting episodes with Master dropping hints as to what we need to do, telling us stories. [Once] I just wanted to say something to catch his attention so I kept talking about how we could do something in Hong Kong and how we could do something in Taiwan and he told me this story. There's this guru and he sent all of his disciples out into the world and said, "Go in all different directions and see what you find." They came back and told him about all the problems that were there and said, "You really have to do something because people are suffering." And then he said, "You fools, why do you think I sent you out in the first place?" He was narrating this to everyone and then he turned towards me and he said, "Do you understand?" So, things like this kind of pointed you in the direction you needed to go. But even now I think, what impedes

THE JOURNEY WITHIN

us is really <u>us</u>. A lot of us are waiting for personalized instructions to be given to us and he's clarified that he cannot add to our problems by adding the sin of disobeying. So he will never give you a direct command that you might then disobey. He says, "I have to address it at you generally and there the problem is that people think it's not for me." Particularly with people who are fairly regular with the practice, they might feel that there's nothing else [more] to do. But there is. The 10 maxims (see references) are something that you need to tick off.

This morning we were watching a talk where he's repeatedly told people [in India] to drop their last names because they serve to separate people from one another. That was really the strongest statement I've ever heard. He also said, "I'm again making this request and how many of you are going to listen?"

There was also a speech where he actually changed satsangh all over the world from nine o'clock to 7:30 a.m. because he said that would show a certain degree of commitment. Do this first. Previously it was at nine o'clock and people were still having problems, saying, "I have to commute, I need to travel so nine is too early, and can we do it at ten?"

So, is it all like, yeah, I'm an abhyasi and I'm cleaning and meditating and attending satsangh. Or are you really getting into it to make sure that your cooperation is maximum and <u>then</u> we can talk about progress and elevation. I'm kind of jumping forward but one message that I personally found very, very useful was, we're not here for niceties. We're not here for you to compliment me and me to compliment you. We're here for us to work upon each other." Another very important point, at least to me, that he made was, why should nature bestow you with anything or raise you a level? Why should you be granted a higher level of evolution than where you are, if not for the sake of nature's work?

THE JOURNEY WITHIN

And then he said there's all this talk of love and constant remembrance and everything but it's really impossible for people to love each other. It's only for the chosen few who have that heart and they can love each other. So the best way to really secure both an intimate relationship with the inner Master and evolution would be through service. As you work, you start working for Him and then it becomes incumbent upon Him to make you a better worker. So therefore you're given the ability to do higher work -- and in that process your evolution happens, if at all. Even then, I'm conscious as I'm saying this that in the end, somewhere, if the goal remains climbing higher, being more evolved, or anything, you will still stop short of that goal because there has to come a stage where you're doing it just out of <u>love</u>. So unless that dawns, I think we still kind of stop short of spirituality. It's still something like going to the gym and you're looking at your biceps and you're hoping every day that they will finally make that mark.

Kim: I wonder if you could talk a little about balance and surrender and constant remembrance? What if you could start with balance because I remember fairly early on when you were trying to help me to get started with the practice, I was kind of alarmed to hear that I wouldn't feel as much. Master talks about feelings versus emotions. Sometimes it kind of bothers me that, now when I get a hug from one of the boys, I don't feel it -- that piercing love way deep in my heart anymore -- and I worry sometimes that that's lost. At the same time, I don't feel anger or frustration to the degree that I used to either and I'm slowly, just through learning and living, understanding the importance of balance, the importance of keeping the pendulum from swinging too far.

There was someone who actually asked Master, saying, "I don't enjoy the company of my friends as I used to anymore. I can't enjoy food the way I used to enjoy it anymore. What has Sahaj Marg done to me?" And Master said, "Well congratulations, that's exactly what we wanted." I think, to some extent, there are these phases we go through and, to the best of my understanding, it's like you've spiritually gotten there but your system is still catching up. So, in these in-between times, you have the problem of -- you have internalized a certain state, but it has not yet fully sunk in -- so that's where you feel like you're in two places. But eventually it does catch up. Because, as Master has said, every

THE JOURNEY WITHIN

single atom of your body is being changed, divinized, by this act of stopping yourself and looking at yourself squarely, every day -- by which act your true essential nature gets revealed to you progressively. As that happens, you realize all the filth and all the unnecessary redundant things that you piled up on top of it [and they] start falling away. A lot of those things include emotions that limit. [Emotions] that might be celebrated in the world generally, but are not particularly constructive.

I would very boldly make the statement that, it would probably bother me less outwardly if somebody has passed away, probably because I think that, well, they have been relieved from the toil of the world. [This] would be quite inhuman to many people who would feel that, "Oh, come on, you can't grieve anymore for people, is that it?" On the other hand, I also feel that I'm in a better position to love and do what is necessary when it has to be done. Other considerations do not come and dilute it.

Going back to balance, I think, like you just said, it's really the swing of the pendulum, and if it goes up to a certain point to the left, it has to go to the same point to the right – and that's the choice. If you want to continue feeling that immense happiness in the core of your heart, you can be assured you will feel immense grief in the same place in your heart every time you get hurt. We are in the business of narrowing down this range gradually – in the wisdom that, in the end, you can only do so much as what you can do. You can do the best that you can do to address any situation today to the best of your abilities. Beyond that, to think of the consequences in different permutations and combinations doesn't really help the problem in any way. So, in that sense, (I'm now merging balance to surrender) balance comes because you are no longer so happy that you jump for joy and therefore you're no longer capable of being so aggrieved that you drop everything and you lose a day because you just can't work anymore. So, increasingly, it's like you're on a train or you're in a bus and all of these are but passing scenes and you're just watching them go past. Some of them [are] nice and some not so nice. but you're not really going to get

THE JOURNEY WITHIN

out of the bus to take a closer look. You just keep going because you're going elsewhere.

The true sense of surrender is not to say, "Okay, I have surrendered and you do whatever it is. I'm not going to eat. I'm not going to get up from the sofa. I'm just going to sit here and let happen whatever's going to happen." I think surrender is really (to the best of what I understand), it's surrendering results to him. I'm going to do my level best with whatever understanding I have, whatever capability I have, at this moment. Beyond that, it's wisdom that says, there are simply so many human beings, factors, things involved in determining the end result of anything, that you cannot possibly control all of those things. So, humility dawns when you realize that, in every so-called success of mine there were numerous people, numerous factors -- none of which necessarily had to act the way they did. So, same way, surrender comes when you know that, if this thing in the end doesn't work out, there's absolutely nothing I can do about it except for what I have done. "Okay, I've done what I had to do and whatever's going to happen is going to be good. Because that is what's supposed to happen."

For me, particularly, I know increasingly (initially with a little bit of doubt, later with one eye closed and one eye opened), increasingly, much to my delight, I feel that, if this is what my Master wants me to have, I'm happy. I'm the child who doesn't have to worry about what to make for dinner because my mom made something for me and I don't have to deal with what to make, where to get it from, where to order it from, and I'm happy. That's it.

Constant remembrance, yes. I think the way Master says it is, we are charging ourselves every day by getting sittings and by satsangh and by meditation and all of this – only to lose charge and then be charged again. If there could be a way where we don't lose this charge, where we can remain constantly in touch with the higher being, then the need for these things would drop off. A more important point here would be: The chief reason why we accumulate impressions is because we are

THE JOURNEY WITHIN

self-conscious (as in conscious of the ego doing things). "I am doing this. I don't like this. I like this. I wish this hadn't happened. I really wish this will work out." Each of these creates an imprint upon ourselves because we know that it's me who is functioning. So, if you want to congratulate yourself, pat yourself on the back for a job well done, you're going to curse yourself for something that didn't work out. If instead, we could understand that it's not you who's doing everything. You dedicate everything that you do to the Master and say, "It's not me who's getting up; it's he who's getting up. It's not me who's working; it's he who's working." So it's his work, and then we are constantly in that remembrance that he is doing it and then you kind of forget yourself, this lower self. You don't even know who is "I" when you say "I" when you're speaking to someone. Then you no longer make impressions. Then all that remains to be done is for him to clean you of all the impressions you have. Keep that minimum required to still keep you anchored here in this world so that you can do whatever work you have to do, get through life, and be there with Him.

Kim: And so the ultimate goal is liberation and evolvement to the brighter world and in order to do that we need to remove the samskaras from our past lives... I've heard people refer to them as karma. Do you see that as the same as karma?

Karma is a simplified way of looking at it where you do good and then, what goes around comes around -- as you sow you shall reap. It's more of a formulaic version of the same thing. Here we don't make a distinction between good and bad. We don't say, "Do a lot of good and therefore you come back as king" because that's as bad as do[ing] a lot of bad and you come back as a beggar, just in a different way. You're still stuck with the duality. Instead, we're talking about impressions that become tendencies which are then compulsive and dominate you. Instead of you choosing to act a certain way, you're forced to act a certain way -- which you then mistake for your character, your personality, or your nature.

THE JOURNEY WITHIN

The goal of practice? Yes. Master has said that liberation is really something of a preliminary basic minimum kind of stage that we need to reach which is reached fairly early in the practice. In fact, he goes ahead and says that all abhyasis who are sincere in our practicing will be liberated and liberation is nothing but <u>ending</u> the cycle of birth and death. It is really very basic.

We need to go much farther where we become one with the Ultimate. The problem is (although it's not distance), when something is so far away that you cannot see it, how do you have the desire or the willingness or the need to want it? So, I think, a lot of us start with some intermediary goals like peace of mind, etc. And then we need to get piece of mind to realize that peace of mind doesn't cut it. And then you need the next thing, and then you need the next thing, and I think gradually you are led on -- and then, at one stage, it becomes important for you to be one with the <u>true</u> self of which we are all a part. Just like different things drawn on a piece of paper – each one of which represents a different item -- an object, a ball, a baby, a tree -- but all of which, it remains true, are on that piece of paper. So, to return to the Essence, the Ultimate, is what I think we <u>really</u> aim at -- where the lower self merges with the higher self and is one. That ends all duality. It ends the separation which is the cause of all misery.

Kim: Just to maybe clarify a little… The idea is that we all have, for lack of a better term, a divine spark inside of us and once our ego has taken over and our mind, our intellect, has taken over…we've kind of lost touch with that connection with the divine. I've only been involved for a little over a year but that's what I see as just a huge shift in how to run my life and what the purpose of life is in general that, we've kind of been taught it's the intellect, it's materialism, it's power…all of which are driven by the individual ego, and now the realization is that, what we really need to do is subsume the ego and let the heart take over because the heart is the home of divinity.

Yes. Absolutely. Dead on. That's what it is.

THE JOURNEY WITHIN

Kim: From some of the stories I've heard there clearly seems to be an all knowing, higher-level of Being at work here. And some of the stories are somewhat fantastical involving cross-dimensional communication, possibly time travel or space travel and even the ability to manipulate the DNA of human beings. I wonder if you could speak to that?

I can only say what it is that I have experienced and what I have understood. I think somewhere, at some level, all of us, when we think about something spiritual or something like a religious revelation, we do imagine some kind of an event, something out of the ordinary, something miraculous to happen. There's this emphasis on miracles. Whereas, I think, true spirituality happens rather naturally, rather boringly. It's like a seed you're looking at and you're looking at and it doesn't turn into a tree. You go away and you come back in 10 days and it's a sapling. You go away again for some time and come back and there's a tree and you think, "Oh my goodness, how did that happen?" But that's not a miracle because we know it takes that much time. So I think anything that violates nature to exhibit itself, to my mind, is not spirituality. That is magic, that's a show off. That's some kind of need to impress you. The great Masters of the world who have done these things have done them rather naturally. I think it's something like -- suppose you are in a water body and there's a pebble thrown in it which creates ripples. You are, by virtue of being in that water body (like say, a pond), immediately in touch with those ripples. So now, there is this space between each other and all the objects; therefore, there's this assumption that we are separate. But let's say the space that is between us actually connects us; it fills the space that is there between us. Then, technically, it should be possible (if you're very sensitive) that, when there's a bird chirping 10 miles away, you could still feel it. It's just like elephants can feel animals walking from really far away. We don't feel it. It doesn't mean it doesn't exist.

So I think you become what you meditate. And what we're meditating on is God -- not limiting it by imagining it in terms of male or female or big or small or powerful or not powerful and not giving it any

THE JOURNEY WITHIN

appearance of any sort -- but meditating on the Essence of the Divine. Progressively we should be closer to that and, if we are closer to that, looking at divinity right now, you would be looking at what you would see if I was not here. In which case, and if I can be in touch with that, it's not that I can appear in any place I wish but I <u>am</u> everywhere. I am in everything. If nature so requires that I exert myself to listen to what is happening [somewhere else], then I can have access to it. Some of us have had this experience of meditating really deeply and then you hear some sound and you might come out of meditation and say, "Did you hear that? There was a loud cracking and..." Nobody else heard it. So what was that? How did you hear that? Sometimes when you're meditating and it's relatively quiet you hear something happening really far away and probably, in normal circumstances, you never would've heard it. So I think it's a lot to do with sensitivity -- particularly with Master... he can feel everything else happening. So if there is someone in his presence who is troubled by hunger, I think he can feel it at a certain level because you are sending out a signal -- just like you're really scared and you have these dogs and they can sense the fear in you. Not [that it's] any miracle but you can sense it because you are sensitive. I think that is basically what it is.

As for the DNA... If you are not transmitting simply carbon copies of the DNA that your mom and dad gave you, if you're also creating something of your own in between – otherwise it should be just the same. And we should be able to isolate it in terms [such as] 50% from dad, 40% from mom and the rest of it is mine. So, based on how we choose to act and react and mold ourselves, <u>we</u> form our DNA. Suppose now you've stopped doing that and you are instead meditating. As you meditate, you are more in touch with the real you. You're facing all the things you would otherwise escape from. Progressively, you start simplifying things, sorting things and (sort of) changing your DNA. I think that's basically the way I look at it. At his level, he's doing something that is much finer. What I just described is probably a lot grosser, a lot external, but what he's doing is at a much finer level. But it's none of that voodoo stuff where I sit and I look at you and I make a gesture and you transform into a monkey or something of that sort. I think that's -- that's just not spirituality; all that is hogwash.

THE JOURNEY WITHIN

Kim: I wonder if you could comment on Sahaj Marg as a social movement? I feel there is a sense of hope for the future of human beings which I know I didn't have before and I think a very interesting idea is that the way to change fighting and war and things like that is to give people peace of mind and calm and interest in not creating hostility in other people. In fact, some of the strongest language I've heard Master use has been talking about religion and the problems with religion and religion versus spirituality. So if you could comment on Sahaj Marg as a social movement and this idea of a big difference between religion and spirituality.

I'll take the second question first and the way I understand it and the way Master explains it is that anything, if you make the best possible use of it, can be a positive force. I think what we talk about as religion is essentially organized "clubs" that are exclusive. I think that that is where the problem is because you cannot have a God who is exclusive to a people… I think all religions that we have today <u>were</u> spiritual and they <u>ceased</u> to be spiritual and <u>degenerated</u> into religions as the Fountainhead disappeared. The way I look at it is, I mean, Jesus brought change. He brought a break from dogma, from obstinacy, from a stolid involvement in the things that were no longer helping anyone – for which he was crucified. But, to now have Lutherans and Presbyterians and Anglicans and Protestants and Catholics and all of this, I think, would just only pain him because his message was one of love, very simple. The problem is, practically speaking, that guy's not here, [so] who is the authority? Who is the ultimate authority on what should be done and should not be done? Each one of us is standing on a different floor looking at a different version of the same reality and saying, "This is the true version." So who's to say that there are not going to be 100 more churches in the next 100 years to come because each person is evolving and none of us know on which ladder we stand? In that sense, I think religion has a part to play but it runs out.

Just like, taking the example of India (and I'm sure this is true elsewhere), there was a Congress party that won independence. There is a Congress party today which bears the same name but the people are no longer the same. They no longer have the same sense of idealism, the same sense of urgency, the same sense of dedication as the founding fathers would have had. So it's always that, I think, which is the problem. The people who are today propagating religion or who champion the cause of religion -- unlike the people who generally do service and quietly win quite a few hearts -- these people insisting on swelling the ranks at all costs are making it into a political force that can be harnessed. They have another agenda, and I think that is what causes much of the disillusionment.

Going back now to talking about spirituality and the role of Sahaj Marg as a social movement. We start by saying that we are open to absolutely everyone, not making any distinction of class or caste or education or culture or nationality, ethnicity -- any such distinction -- number one. Number two, I think you just pointed out -- if each person could be at peace inside him or herself, then much of the strife that we see in the world wouldn't exist. I'd like to think of it this way; there're always bad guys and good guys and we're usually the good guys and there is some bad guy working against us. But I'm pretty sure no bad guy (who we think is a bad guy) thinks he is the bad guy. Nobody probably thinks, "I'm doing something wrong to this person and therefore I'm going to go ahead and do it." For some reason they feel justified in doing what they do and we perceive it as something that's wrong or unjust. So, in that sense, everyone is tired and trying to carve out a space for themselves in this world and achieve whatever their goals are and they feel justified in whatever they're doing. Otherwise, they wouldn't do that.

So then the question is, "Why then do you have wars?" and "Why then do you have arguments and fights and problems?" Simply because, I think at some level, we are not able to face ourselves and know what it is that we truly need, which is nothing. I mean, in terms of need, need as in physical need, yes -- you need something to eat, you need something to wear, you need somewhere to stay. But beyond that, you really need much less -- although you might want more.

THE JOURNEY WITHIN

Now the problem is all with <u>wants</u> then. Suppose you have a country which has a few hundred square kilometers and you have a million people there. It's fine, fine. But, what if you had a bigger piece of land? Better. Who says so? How is it better? How are you going to manage it? Well, it will be better because we have more space to do more things and there will be more resources. But to do what with? The question gets lost and then we have these big spaces, coming not out of need but out of desire. We could work on telling people that what you need is what you need and let the river flow. You take all the water that you need, all the water that you need to quench your thirst, and then let the river flow -- and there would be enough for everyone because God has made enough for everyone. I went through this phase when I was feeling like not wanting to buy anything at all so I asked Master in Perth, "If all of us became contented with whatever we have, then what's going to happen to all these people who are providing these services and who get employed because of that?" And he said, "That is His job. He has made enough for everyone."

The problem is, enough is not enough for us and we need more. And the reason we need more is not because we need more in general but because we have our lower selves fooled that we need more – and <u>with</u> that "more" we shall be better off. And when you have that 'more' you'll see it's not good enough because it comes with its own set of problems -- and you need something else. So it is a social movement in that, if we can help people find contentment within themselves, then a lot of unnecessary fighting for what is really not required <u>should</u> stop. And you would automatically have world peace. But I am again tempted to make the same point I made before that, if you do have perfect equilibrium and world peace, that's the end of the story. There's nothing more to do. This is paradise. It cannot be that way... Only by working upon yourself can you make sure some of that rubs off into the environment that you're in. People who are tired of this rat race finally know that there is a choice and could choose that instead. But there shall always be some strife, there shall always be something to remind you of how good your peace is and how valuable it is. If we all were peaceful and all had plenty and all had whatever we wanted, I think there is nothing more to do.

THE JOURNEY WITHIN

There's a fantastic story that Master once told in one of his talks. Krishna used to have a couple of devotees who he really loved. So there was one of these disciples who felt (I'm not sure I'm getting the story right but in spirit), so one of these disciples came and said, "Why is it that you like <u>him</u> so much? I mean, I can do everything that he can do. What is it that he can do?" Krishna said, "Are you sure you can do that?" He said, "Yes." So Krishna said "Okay, I want you to give away gold. Here are three mountains of gold. Give them away." So he sat down with a scale and everything. He had people form queues and he started giving it away and giving it away, and he found it really tough. At the end of the day, he was really tired and the mountain -- there was not even a dent in the mountain because there was so much gold. And then Krishna said, "Okay let me call my disciple." "Come and give it away." And the disciple came and said, "You. You. You. This mountain's for you. This mountain for you. This mountain for you." And the disciple got up and was ready to leave. And Krishna said, "That makes all the difference. You were still counting, isn't it? You thought you could distribute it to everyone."

And there's another story which is similar which is part of Hindu mythology that, out of these three main gods there is this god Shiva who told his two sons to go and circle the world and come back and whoever comes back first will get the prize. So the elder one started off immediately and went to circle the world. The younger one was a clever one and he basically folded his hands and he circled his mom and dad and said, "That's the world for me." And he got the prize. The story goes that the elder one came back and was very angry and went on to a mountaintop and sat there for some time. But it also shows you something: There was the statement that, "For me the world is this. I don't care about the rest of the world." In the end, you don't <u>get</u> anywhere. You just realize a fundamental truth that you might've heard a number of times, but you finally get it -- and that's the moment when you are enlightened.

THE JOURNEY WITHIN

Kim: It's like people telling you there is no point in worrying because worrying doesn't change anything, so you might as well save your energy. But it's awfully hard to do....

It's hard to do because our lower self, which needs to propagate its own life, has us fooled into thinking that if you let go of this mentally, something bad might happen – or, you might not be prepared for the bad that happens. So we are trying to prepare ourselves for the worst, hoping for the best, getting really tired in the process. Again, the beauty with this system is all of these things are not things that you need to impose upon yourself (which never sticks), but instead something that comes from within and you wonder," Oh! How am I able to do this today? How am I able to not worry about this today? How am I able to just not bother about this today?" That is something which happens because of internalization, which can only happen through practice.

Kim: So the idea is that the divine is always radiating love but it's up to us to be able to access it?

Imagine a large space out in the open, with the sun shining -- and you have really fine sheets of glass, totally transparent, not a speck of dirt on them. When you look out there they are all of different shapes and sizes, you can almost not see them as they are so fine. Because it's glass, it's completely transparent. You can almost not see them – the light just goes through them. We are that. Only now, we are the same sheets of glass with soot on them and black on them and graffiti on them. Then, the individuality of each of those sheets becomes prominent. Earlier, you had to really look hard to see the borders, to make out a sheet of glass out there -- and now, you can immediately see that, "Oh, there's one here, one here, one here, one here and all of these." Once you're covered with that much dirt, when the sun hits you, it's blocked. Nothing goes through, and there is shadow. That's what we are. So, we're basically cleaning, to become that again -- what we originally were. I think we become really fine, clean sheets of glass, and

THE JOURNEY WITHIN

then we chisel away at this leftover mass of the glass until we are almost fiber-thin. And then there's that final leap -- where there's still a little bit of you left, almost imperceptible -- and when that is gone, you're done. You're one with the Everything.

Kim: Considering again the purpose of this book, the target audience are people who maybe haven't even started looking at spirituality or being serious about spirituality. So I wonder if you have any advice for someone who is new to the concept of spirituality and still pretty firmly entrenched in the everyday world, the physical world. And I know even my family has trouble with the concept of multiple lives, something which seems to me an essential concept to accept before you can move on, in a way. So, basically, just any advice or anything to add for this target audience -- not people who are practicing but who might be wondering, "Isn't there more to life? And what should I be doing about it?"

The first thing is, whenever people think that way, when they start feeling that there should be more to life or when they think, "What is this?," they immediately send bells ringing up there which are naturally responded to, and then nature will hold out these signs to them. Take a left here, take a right there, offering them ways to further this quest. It's kind of like a homing device; you've just got to go back home --all leads to the same thing, in a sense. What I mean is, as soon as you have that thought, immediately you send into motion forces that have to then set about showing you the way. So in that sense, it's true that, as Master says, "A path will come and knock on your door." The Master then comes and looks for you -- but not literally so. What happens is, you will be presented with an opportunity.

The question then comes whether we can find the courage to go and experiment (and of course there shall be this fear of whether this is something bad or something will harm me), whether I'm going to walk half the way and then realize I regret it and this is not what I wanted. But you would never know if you don't try -- it would always be the road not taken.

THE JOURNEY WITHIN

So if you have the courage, spend some time practicing the method. If anyone offers you a shortcut and says, "This is all you need to do and you can get there," that should be taken with a pinch of salt. If you can find it in yourself to try something with an open mind – not accepting anything you cannot believe. I, for instance, have had a problem with believing about past life. I don't know a past life, I don't see a past life, so why should I have a past life? But it seems like a damn good theory when you think about -- okay, I started off in a good family with good financial resources and somebody starts out as a beggar or starts off with one limb short. What explains that? It's a good theory to say, "Well, probably you left it there – in your past life."

Okay, suppose you are Christian or Muslim and you are forbidden from thinking of a past life. There is no past life. So how do you explain that your life sucks and somebody else's life is better? No, God is testing you. He has given you this position to see what it is that you do with it. So I think it really doesn't matter and that is what Master said. It's not a prerequisite to practice Sahaj Marg that you believe in past life or past something. It's just easy for him to strike a chord with someone who believes in past life by talking about past life, by somebody who believes in Christianity by talking about Jesus. It's just that. What Babuji has said is, the only life we can know about is the one we are living. This is in the book Reality at Dawn (Chandra, 2010).

So the point is to do whatever we can now to get wherever we need to get. The rest of it might help you or might not help you, who knows? Who knows if there's a past life? Nobody has gone and come back to tell us that this is what happened. And even if somebody has had access to his past life, it still doesn't mean you would have access just by virtue of knowing it. There is no method or portal that you can go through and see it. If truly there is a past life, then God has been immensely merciful that we don't have the memory of all the past lives. Imagine living to 60 and then remembering how you lived to 70 -- 70 times before – that would be so tiring you'd probably commit suicide.

THE JOURNEY WITHIN

So I think it's an ultimate wisdom [to] wash it all away and make a fresh start so that you can then work upon yourself.

The only suggestion I would have is, try it with an open mind. Make your relationship with the <u>practice</u> rather than with anything else. You don't need to read anything. You don't need to believe in anything. Practice the way you are asked to practice and then see what it is that you find. Base your continuation of the practice on what it is that you find. And be very strict with not saying anything or being coerced into saying or agreeing to anything that you have not felt. That's important. That's where true faith differs from blind faith. When we talk about faith here, it's faith that is tested, that comes out of your experience. And then of course you might have a skeptical mind still saying, "Well maybe that was luck; let's try it and see what happens again." But when you have experienced it again and again and this is something that stays with you, it's subtle -- it happens almost naturally -- so much so that your ego is tempted to feel, "Well, I just got smarter." It's probably something that's making you better.

I think the best way to approach any of these things would be, "Let me try the practice and, after I've tried the practice for a decent length of time – three months, six months – review. See what it is that you have found." If you have not found anything, you can be sure (at least in this life) that this path doesn't lead to anything particularly good, and you can continue your search. Thank you.

THE JOURNEY WITHIN

Chapter 12 **The Graduate**

Jules

USA American, male, early 20's, IT and People Development

Preface: Jules and I meet at the canteen, having made an appointment. We're both on time, but 10-15 minutes go by in chatting. Proficient in Chinese, Jules talks easily with a woman from China on her way to graduate school in the U.S.A., whom I had just interviewed. I chat with his uncle and marvel that they are both dressed nearly alike and all in white (T-shirt, light cotton pants, and a belt). From the U.S.A. Midwest myself (Indiana), I consider myself a neighbor knowing Jules is from Michigan, the next state north and only a few hours from my father's farm. Excusing ourselves from the others, Jules and I find a concrete bench near the lotus pond at the back of the ashram.

As a young adult, Jules brings his interest in psychology and in philosophy to emerging experiences with spirituality, which he discusses candidly, even jokingly telling his parents he joined a "cult" when he joined Sahaj Marg. He discusses his lifestyle as a university student and the pressures on young people today as they try to find their way in a world increasingly oriented toward materialism. He encourages young people to get off Facebook, to stop looking around and to start looking within oneself. You'll enjoy his explorations as he shares his experiences as a "cool guy" who went from success as a soccer player and successful (A) student to success and contentment when he "graduated" to a life focused on spirituality.

Kim: Could you tell a little about yourself?

My name is Jules and I'm 24 years old. I was born in 1989 in a suburb of Detroit, Michigan, and spent my whole life there. My parents are Reform Jews, which means we did not practice a lot of the dogmatic rules of Judaism. For example, we did not eat kosher but we kept Shabbat (which is saying a prayer and eating a meal together). So we grew up secular Jews. [We] went to the synagogue very rarely but I can read Hebrew and I was barmitzvahed. My parents are extremely hard working, incredibly kind, compassionate people.

Growing up I read a lot and was a good student. I was also a pretty good athlete, a soccer player. I graduated in 2012 from the University of Michigan (Ann Arbor) with a degree in Asian Studies. I actually travelled for three months for Sahaj Marg in China from June through August in the summer of 2012, and now I've been working in Ann Arbor for about a year.

Kim: How did you become interested in spirituality and Sahaj Marg in particular?

I was in the seventh grade when the Twin Towers went down, and we had a teacher who was a first year teacher. He was a very nice sweet teacher, a young guy. I was playing in a band at the time and he'd let us rehearse and play the drums in his room after school and give us lessons, etcetera. He was a punk rocker himself.

He had decided it was less important for us to learn about geography than to learn about the world (I give him a lot of credit for this because this was a very bold move). His exact words were, "It really doesn't matter to the world if you learn geography while you're in my class. What matters now is if you learn about other parts of the world and what they believe." So he really went against the grain with our curriculum. He taught us world religions (Jainism, Buddhism, Islam, Judaism, Christianity), and really made our class important. When we started going through Buddhism and Jainism, my interest was piqued. He gave me the Tao of Pooh and said, "Here, read this. You might like this." And really, it began with that book. Throughout the year,

THE JOURNEY WITHIN

I'd ask him questions and he would give me more books and I owe him a lot.

So through that I actually had a therapist when I was younger. When I learned what psychology was, I realized that there were adults out there who weren't coaches, who weren't parents and who weren't teachers, but were rather adults trained to help people learn who they were -- and I wanted to meet one of them. So I told my parents and they said okay. I sat down with a therapist who is skilled in working not only with adolescent and young adult males, but he also approaches everything from an Eastern perspective. He himself is a black belt in several different types of Aikido and different Samurai arts from Japan and he has his own meditative practice. So sitting with him basically throughout middle school and high school, we were reading Buddhist parables, Taoist parables and really just talking about life. Quite frankly, I didn't have a lot of struggles growing up but was still figuring out who I was in the world, feeling the outside pressures of sex, of money, finding a job, of the rat race; I was very much plugged into these. I felt I was a part of but also a part away from all that. I always said that he was actually my first guru.

Kim: Very cool. Did people think you were weird?

No, I was one of the cool guys of my high school/ middle school. I had a lot of friends, a lot of followers. I was the leader of my friend group.

I was embarrassed for some time to say that I had a therapist and then I realized that things only make you weak if you try to hide them. By owning it, I realized it was having a more salubrious effect on those around me for them to see that: a) I had a therapist with whom I was working on myself to "be"; and b) it would encourage them to do the same.

THE JOURNEY WITHIN

Kim: Sometimes I feel like our Indian brothers and sisters have a little bit of an advantage when they come to spirituality because they've been raised perhaps more conservatively and they don't have some of the expectations about drugs, alcohol, and early sex that Americans, particularly North Americans and Europeans have. I wonder if you might want to comment on that in any way?

I would say – maybe -- it is an advantage not to have these pressures, but at the same time, I wouldn't be who I am had I not undergone those things. So yes, it would be nice if my mind has not been saturated with the sexual imagery, the constant pressure, all of that. You know, I experimented with drugs when I was younger -- nothing heavy, but marijuana and alcohol. But at the same time, I can't say it was a disadvantage because I had to lose myself in order to find myself -- and I didn't even really lose myself, but I had to undergo those things.

I think we tend, including myself, especially when I first began -- to see the Indian brothers and sisters, the souls who were born in India -- as having some sort of advantage. But if that were the case, then we'd be seeing saints for them and nothing for us. What I have seen is that there is a lot more emphasis in the culture in India and an easier acceptance of the role of the guru, but I've noticed a lot harder time to motivate towards practice. This is me speaking of my experience as a prefect and I'm not trying to make generalizations, but there is a higher uptake and a quicker uptake of the role of the guru and the love of the Master, but there's a slower uptake of the actual practice.

What I'm finding with our brothers and sisters born in the Occident is there is an immediate aversion to any idea of the Master, but there's a willingness to at least try the practice. So yes, maybe no disadvantage with sex and alcohol, but materialism is still all-pervading and just because you find a guru does not mean the path is over. So what's important is to get over that hurdle, actually sit down, and practice from either side, whether born in the Occident or born in India.

THE JOURNEY WITHIN

Kim: Did you experiment with other methods? What is your involvement with Sahaj Marg, in particular?

During high school, there was a series of events that made me want to take a year off after high school. My brother and sister are both elder to me and they were very much encouraging me to take time off after high school. My brother took a year and a half and my sister two years. I was at the time looking at different soccer scholarships as well as just going into university. I stopped playing soccer late in my senior year due to health reasons and then I decided to travel. At that time, I had been, in some ways, really "living the life." I was very liked in school, had a close group of friends who I'm still close with (there are few guys at 24-years-old who can say they have had close friends for over 20 years but I'm one of those few people). So I was never wanting for friends or familial love, respect from peers, respect from teachers, good grades, a girlfriend at the time, and I went through that checklist I just went through with you, and I realized I had everything I was supposed to want or need, and it wasn't enough; it just wasn't enough. I was 17 at the time. I realized I could see in that moment, down the line: a good soccer scholarship or good scholarship, good college life, good job, happy wife, happy kids -- and that not being enough. It took me about a year to unpack that emotion and really try to start figuring that out, what that was -- and that brings me to my senior year when I decided to take a year off and travel.

So I decided on China; I moved to China in September by myself, lived with a Chinese family and attended intensive Mandarin courses in Shanghai. While there, my goals for the year were as such: number one, to grow. I wrote it down. I wrote, "to grow spiritually," but spiritually then meant to understand myself more. So that was my first goal. My second goal for the year was to meet as many people from around the world as possible and learn their stories; who they are, where they come from, what makes them tick, why they think the way they think. My third goal for the year was to learn Mandarin and by the end of the year that was a far third goal because I learned a lot that year.

Kim: It's harder than it sounds.

THE JOURNEY WITHIN

Yeah. It sounds hard, too. My Chinese now is fine, so many years later -- I'm a fluent speaker.

[So I] landed in Shanghai but I hit the ground running. For example, before I landed, I looked up a bunch of yoga studios, looking for a teacher. I had done enough yoga at that point to know it wasn't about the asana – the place or posture when doing yoga -- it was about the teacher you find. I found a really great teacher from Canada who had been travelling and living in Asia for a number of years in South East Asia and East Asia. We clicked. I found a studio right near my school and, when I first walked in, we sat talking in the studio for two hours. It made sense.

So I started studying under him and, for three months, I honestly was living three lives, or two lives. Two of them were connected so I'll put those two together – my school life, where I was one of only two Americans in the school with people from all over Europe and South America, ages 17 through 25. With that crowd I would study during the day and we would go out partying in the evenings; honestly, five to seven days a week. Before I'd go out in the evenings, I'd tuck over to the yoga studio for class or else spend the night out and, early in the morning, drag myself to yoga class. So I was living both [lives] full on.

On top of that, I was working with this teacher who had given me a variety of meditation techniques to start practicing. My way to spiritual thinking came first through psychology, which I spoke about earlier. My psychologist is brilliant and so understanding. He helped me understand how I was feeling moment to moment. That made me socially smarter in some ways and more self-aware -- it gave me situational knowledge. But it didn't bridge the gap between me and who I am; it just gave me tools with where I was already at -- indispensable tools, but not the deeper work.

THE JOURNEY WITHIN

In 2006, going into my senior year of high school, I quite literally discovered philosophy. I was at the bookstore and I found this wall that said "Philosophy" and I bought a bunch of introductory books and I read them all within a few days. I thought philosophy was the *sub bonum* {the "highest good"} of psychology. I very quickly realized that it was making me smarter, so I took a critical literary theory class in my senior year of high school and continued with my reading. I studied philosophy in college, as well. I found that philosophy was making my intellect keener and sharper and thus gave me a stronger faculty of discernment, but it didn't bridge that 'gap' anymore. Psychology made me calmer, more open and more tactile, I'd say, in my ways of being -- and philosophy made me smarter. But again, that deeper work (which I can now style as the opening of the heart or the feeling of the heart) wasn't there. Because both of those [psychology and philosophy] don't have love. So the sub-bonum of those two is love, which comes with spirituality.

During this year in China, I was building upon that edifice. I was still reading a lot, but I wanted to get in tune with who I was. So I took a look at history and the philosophers that I liked the most, the writers, the people we venerate: Buddha, Jesus, etcetera; they all meditated. It just made sense to me. While I was enjoying the idea of asana practice, the parts I enjoyed the most were the contemplative practices that came with them. So, working with this teacher, he gave me different practices that he tried in India while he was travelling with different teachers and I bought some books. The results were there but they were unsettling.

I had two experiences whereby, after a day of meditating, I had woken up in the middle of the night in what I'll call a full-blown spiritual state. At the time, I was also experimenting with lucid dreaming. I was trying too much -- that was evident -- but I was looking for something. I woke up on a different plane of existence... The first time it happened, I was absolutely terrified but it was exciting. It was a feeling unlike anything I have ever felt. When it happened the second time, a few weeks later (again after a full day of trying this meditation practice that had been given to me), I realized that it was time I stopped dabbling

THE JOURNEY WITHIN

with people who were dabblers. I respected the teacher whom I was working with, but he was a career dabbler -- you know, a little bit of this from this teacher, a little bit of that from that teacher. I think he was a serious yogi in the sense of his peripatetic lifestyle (travelling and just wanting to live that kind of life) but I don't think he was a serious yogi in some other ways. I am not trying to be judgmental, but there was a hankering for the lifestyle and not necessarily for the goal; or, to say it differently, we have different goals and I respect his thus. That's completely reasonable and good for him but I wanted something more than that. So I told myself, "I need to find a group of people and a teacher who are dedicated to only meditation and immerse myself in them; and figure out what it is that they are doing, learn from them and then really evaluate what meditation can bring."

Every Sunday morning, I went to a yoga class at 11:30. I went in early one morning to meet with the teacher as we were going to grab an espresso before yoga class – but he left his wallet in the studio. So we went to the studio and, unbeknownst to either of us, there was a satsangh, a group meditation meeting, happening [there]. At first, he was alarmed; he thought he left the door unlocked. It turns out the owner had been renting the place out. They weren't on the schedule because they weren't directly affiliated with the studio.

So he and I asked what they were doing and we were told they were practicing Sahaj Marg. They also explained that the preceptor was out of town and that we should wait for him to come back the following week and he'd explain the practice to us. I could hardly wait all that week; I was really excited for this. I got up extra early and didn't go out that Saturday night and made sure I was down in time and got there about half way through the satsangh and waited. The preceptor was a French gentleman (very, very intelligent) and he came out and gave a very quick exposition to what the practice was, what it's called, etcetera.

He was living with another preceptor at the time. They weren't boyfriend or girlfriend or anything, but they were keeping the center in

THE JOURNEY WITHIN

one apartment. He very openly invited me to their home the following day to take my sittings. Really, that was it for me. After my first three sittings, I just knew that this was it for me.

Kim: Did you feel anything?

Yeah, I did. I don't want to go into specifics because I don't want to cloud anyone else's experience but I'll say this: What impressed me was my yoga teacher had started at the same time I did and he told me he was really excited for me to finish my three sittings. He finished a day before I did. He asked me once after yoga class how my third sitting was. I told him and he said, "You know, I experienced a feeling during my second and third sittings, Jules, that I had only even *touched* upon after day ten of intensive meditation in India for five to seven hours a day." He said," I only touched that feeling, but, in these sittings, very quickly and for the entire duration for both of them, I was there and beyond." That for me was impressive because again, he was somebody who was really trying different systems. So that piqued my interest. For me, however, the most important feeling was not those initial sittings and satsanghs, but it was the natural way in which my preceptors interacted with each other and with myself.

It's worth noting, I was 18 years old at the time and, as I said earlier, I was sort of living two lives. On the one side was an over-sexualized, alcohol-oriented fast-paced life with a bunch of people my age who were really down on destroying themselves and those around them. I don't think everybody who drinks is like this, not everybody who parties is like this; but the particular crowd I was with was extremely wealthy from all over the world -- and they were not there in China to learn and study. They were there to get away from Mom and Dad for eight months. We're talking about the top one percent of countries where the top one percent there are billionaires. I know people of that economic range too, who are wonderful people, but this particular group of people really just wanted to drink away their days and nights.

THE JOURNEY WITHIN

But I was hanging out with them; they were my friends. It was just vis-à-vis proximity; and with them, I just never felt like I belonged. This is a feeling from high school, as well (the partying and the being cool in high school): I was always saying things that are the right thing to say (but nobody had ever taught me what to say). I was doing things that were the right things to do that nobody had ever said were the right things to do (but somehow I just knew how to do them). So they were put inside me through culture but I just never felt I belonged with those people.

With the preceptors, every third word out of their mouth was "Master." In fact, the male preceptor giving me a copy of My Master and it freaked me out. Yet at the same time I could not deny how loving and caring they were; they genuinely felt well of me and cared for. They had nothing invested in me staying in Sahaj Marg; I wasn't paying anything… but they were just always quick to call me and see how I was doing. When I was with them, they would cook food and just listen to me. They just felt nice. To me, that was more important than any of the feelings I had during meditation. When I was with this group of people, I just felt I was with a group of normal, loving people. I was able to be myself. I didn't even know who I was in life -- but when I was with them, I felt like the person who was me.

Kim: So that was the beginning of your involvement?

Yes, and this went on for about five months… I want to say this too, especially if this is for a general audience: My way of learning about the world has always been through reading and writing. I read a lot, particularly fiction. (Most people read fiction for enjoyment and non-fiction to learn about the world. I read non-fiction for enjoyment and fiction to learn about the world.) As I said, about a week and half into Sahaj Marg, I was given a copy of My Master, read it in about four hours and freaked out. I realized that I wanted to change my way of thinking. It did not behoove me to use my old way of thinking to evaluate this new way of being.

THE JOURNEY WITHIN

Looking back, I think this was one of the most sophisticated decisions I could ever have made. And I don't think it was the 18-year-old me making this decision; this was a decision that came from somewhere else and it was," I'm not going to read any of the books; I'm just going to dedicate myself to the practice. That's all I really want to learn. I don't want to be critical and I don't want to be overly intellectual. I just want to try." By the end of two months, I knew this was for me. So I stopped looking elsewhere and I dedicated myself fully to this -- two satsanghs a week, a sitting every week.

I want to say this, too. When I was in Shanghai, I was just convinced that I had joined a cult. I mean, I told my parents, my siblings, and my friends that I had joined a cult but it was okay [not to worry]. Quite frankly, I said to myself, "These people are nuts. They're nice [but] they're crazy. I'm going to do Sahaj Marg for four and a half months. When I go home, I'll take the lessons learned here and I'm going to apply it to something else and try to find something else." This was my ignorance of an Eastern practice (of what it means to have a Master, or a practice of any type). We have master carpenters back in the U.S.; I didn't understand the significance of a teacher -- but also [I had] a visceral reaction to belonging to a group. So my first feeling was that this was a crazy cult, but I'm digging what they're putting out there. I'm okay with it. So I did it for four and a half months and I came home.

When I came home and walked into satsangh in Detroit I was the only Occidental -- and basically to this day I still am. Most people, my friends included, who started the practice, have a very difficult time interacting with our Indian brothers and sisters back home. But really, the differences are only what we perceive. People are people and there are human connections. Any time you're up here (that's in the head) it's individual, but once you start moving to the heart, that's universal. I'm not trying to be deliberately philosophical here but, over time, you realize that everything else is nominal. It's not important. But I did feel a sense of peace and calm knowing that this was an Indian practice.

THE JOURNEY WITHIN

To say it more perfectly and correctly, Indians were practicing this practice. I felt much more calm and rooted once I came home and saw the all-Indian satsangh in Detroit. I'm not saying that's a sophisticated emotion but it's the way I felt.

I had already started doing some writing for the Mission (before I came home). I deliberately cut my trip short by a couple of weeks because Master was going to be in the U.S. for the international seminar in Cleveland, so I wanted to come home for that. So I came home.

Kim: Had you met him?

Never met him, no. Of course, there were already profound experiences beginning to happen, but I never met him, no. When I came home, I got all prepped to go to Cleveland. I contacted the center here and met some people who were driving down from Detroit. Master cancelled due to health reasons. But I still went to that seminar; it was an interesting experience seeing how large the Mission was.

I was disappointed that Master couldn't come to Cleveland and then I told my parents, "I know, Mom and Dad, you just helped me with this great year abroad. Nevertheless, I want to go to India for this meditation Master's birthday and I have to meet him and this is important for me." So I was thinking about taking another year off at that point so as to live in India for the year. I was exploring those options with my parents.

I have amazingly understanding and open parents. My last name means "man of the world" in German and my Dad has always said you need to honor your last name. They have always pushed my brother and sister and me to travel. For these two people who are my parents, who never really traveled and have always lived within the same 15-mile square radius, that's amazing. I want to give my children the gift of travel, as well.

THE JOURNEY WITHIN

So we were prepping for me to go to India. I had gotten into Michigan and was deciding what I should do. We were exploring some options. My sister was in France at the time and she fell ill so we sort of re-oriented our plans and brought her home and that was that; I started school in the fall.

Kim: You didn't go to India?

Didn't go to India. The day I decided I wasn't going to India, when we decided that it was important to get my sister home, et cetera, that was the beginning of my true practice of Sahaj Marg. I had a dream (I shouldn't even call it a dream because it didn't happen in the evening -- but something happened). It was like a vision-come-meditation special moment in my life. Saying it differently, when I came out of that state, I knew that this was it for me. I had finally accepted Master on a subconscious level, but in a way I did not know how to verbalize. As a result, I spent the next three years in school studying Eastern philosophy and Western philosophy -- but for me I think a lot of that was me trying to find a better vocabulary for what was going on with me.

In school, I meditated every day and never broke my practice but of course, [I was also] going to bed at four in the morning after writing papers. I always tell students, "All you have to do is to get to your meditation chair. Get out of bed. Go to your chair, say the prayer and whatever happens, happens. Just sit in the chair for an hour. If you say the prayer, you let him do the work. Of course, the best-case scenario is that you're conscious of the work as it's happening, but at least be obedient and get to the chair. Everything else that happens is in his hands." So I'm talking nights going to bed at five in the morning, up at six, out of the chair at seven and on to my day. To be frank, there are not too many 18-year-olds who took to the practice the way I took to the practice and were serious about the practice the way I was about the practice. I still am.

THE JOURNEY WITHIN

There was another brother there and we used to drive an hour for satsangh twice a week, an hour each way. My preceptor is in Detroit. Every other week that third hour would be for sittings. He's a brother of mine; I feel he's like a natural brother. He patiently answered every question, was so loving with me and never stern. I slept through Sunday once and was so embarrassed. He didn't call me and let me call him and then he said, "You know I didn't want to call you; I figured you were embarrassed" … so loving and generous. My prefects are my mentors and I have spent more time around them than I have many other people. They're just so loving and kind, always giving me the support I needed.

So I studied for a couple of years. Then, in the summer of 2010, I was in Shanghai working at the 2010 World Expo. At the end of that trip, I came to Master's birthday gathering for the first time and I met Master. That was very special. I met him on the day of his birthday. I would call that day number two of my serious practice beginning.

Kim: Did you actually talk to him? I'm not sure anybody can talk to him the very first time you meet him.

How can I say this? We had robust communication [but] there were no words that passed between us; it was pretty phenomenal.

After the birthday gathering, I traveled by myself to Chennai [the headquarters]. I can't even believe that first trip -- babe in the woods, words cannot describe it. By his grace, I came back to Chennai and then I got hellaciously ill here at the ashram with shigella, a lower intestinal virus. It's common in refugee camps where there's bad sanitation. So essentially, I spent that first day by myself with 104-degree fever. I thought I was going to die. I mean I was delusional, the whole thing.

THE JOURNEY WITHIN

A couple of Canadian brothers found me and took me to the clinic. They put me in the hospital for five days, but this was an absolute turning point for me. You know, I was working in Shanghai sometimes 15-18-hour-days for four months straight. My first seven days in India were manic – at the birthday gathering in Lucknow there were 50,000 to 60,000 people, combined with the traveling and the heat. I had not taken any time in so long just to calm down. Also, because of my work situation in Shanghai, I was having a hard time getting healthy vegetarian food so I resigned myself to putting on some weight, knowing India was coming and my diet would stabilize.

Being in the hospital for those five days, I told the brothers and sisters not to come visit me because I was fine; I was stable. I told them to stay at the ashram and that I'd call if I needed anything. As a result, I spent five days in silence; I didn't turn on the TV. I'm not saying this for vanity, but I also lost all of the weight I'd gained. I lost a lot of emotional weight along with the physical weight, and I came out of there cleansed and quiet. When I finally came back to the ashram, I was able to deepen my practice. I had about 20 days until the North American seminar started; I spent all day meditating and reading in the library. I wanted to deepen my relationship with Lalaji so I read all his writing and meditated on him. That was a very, very important time.

The day before I left, I had been asked to speak and had given a talk. Later, I was approached by a brother who asked me a series of questions like, "Who are you? Where are from? Where do you go to school? What's your GPA?" and all of that. Then he said, "Have you met Master?" I said, "Yeah, in a way." He said, "Have you *really* met him?" and I said, "Well, no" and he said," You're going to meet him. Come with me." I put on a nice shirt and I went. I sat with Master for a half hour and we spoke about physics, languages, philosophy and then Master asked if I wanted to come for the international training scholarship program (ITSP) that was happening in December or January and I said yes. So I went home, and for that whole semester, I read the complete works of Ram Chandra and I was doing my practice as diligently as possible.

THE JOURNEY WITHIN

Later, when I told my friends, they said, "Be aware that ITSP is a training program for preceptors. So you're going to be made a prefect." To be honest, I sort of assumed that was going to happen, but I figured down the line [much later]. That really shocked me. Number one, I had never heard of somebody my age or even close being made a prefect. I thought, "This means so much to me but how dare you, Jules? You're going to be a progenitor of this system without having fully internalized being a good abhyasi?" I was really afraid I was going to be asked to be a prefect -- and I would say yes, obviously, but I would be a sham.

Secondly, at that time, I was in school so I didn't know what my schedule back in Michigan would be like. But I said yes and figured I would take two months off if I had to. Soon after returning home, I won a fellowship through the Chinese government. Their semesters follow the lunar - not solar - calendar. Since their second semester didn't start until March, I could do my first semester in Ann Arbor, go to India, then go to China. Fancy that!

So it happened. I went to ITSP, was made a prefect, and I feel the day I was made a prefect was the day I grew up. That was January 4, 2011. Since then, just to wrap it up, I've been giving sittings and have traveled quite a bit in China to give sittings and put on seminars. Back home, we have been having satsangh in my apartment in Ann Arbor since the summer of 2011. It's an amazing path and I'm going to be doing this for the rest of my life.

Kim: Do you see that as a natural step? That people who are serious about the method will naturally become prefects?

No. Number one, I don't think everybody has the skill set to be a preceptor. I'm not saying I'm special, but there has to be a willingness of time and also a sensitivity to others -- a desire to be sensitive to

THE JOURNEY WITHIN

others. It's not easy work. I always say that ten percent of what I do as a prefect is meditate; the other ninety percent is prayer and listening. You have to want to do that and be capable of doing that. It's a very secure way of serving because the path is laid out; you give sittings, etcetera, but it's not the only way. Most people have the desire to be a prefect in order to serve, but they don't have the aptitude.

The biggest lie in Sahaj Marg is that you have to be a prefect. You know, Babuji was not a prefect; he wasn't -- so if that tells you anything, it's not necessary to be a preceptor. I think people who aren't preceptors oftentimes feel that they don't have an avenue to serve, but really, whatever you do in your professional life can absolutely be applied to the Mission. There are a million different ways to serve and being a prefect is not the only one.

Kim: Do you feel or do your relatives feel that you've changed since starting the practice?

To quote a friend of mine since pre-school, he said, "I was trying to tell my girlfriend the other day *what* you've become." We laughed. "It's not a 'who,' it's a 'what.'" He said, "You are who you have always been, but you've become a 'what.' It's that you're dedicated to self-development." I mean, just by virtue of the fact that I don't drink or smoke, it's a paragon of weird. To my friends and family, though, they don't find it weird. In fact, for my parents this has all been extremely digestible because I don't drink, I don't smoke, I go to bed early and I get great grades in college.

Kim: Dream kid.

Yeah, in some ways, maybe; but interview them and you'll get the full scoop! Haha. But this is a natural path. I haven't changed how I dress, I haven't changed how I speak and I haven't been forced to do

THE JOURNEY WITHIN

anything that's unnatural. That includes when I'm with my friends.
I'm a 24-year-old guy. We talk about what 24 year-old guys talk about.

I often find (mostly with women who come for sittings, especially
when they begin), they think about things in terms of exclusion. Again,
natural path. What I mean is that, if I'm spending so much time on
myself, it comes to the exclusion of spending time with others.
However, I think that's only selfish if your end goal is to only serve
yourself; it's self-less and inclusive if your goals are to positively impact
those around you. To get on my soapbox for a second... Change is a
very difficult thing to bring about in the world the way it is right now,
with the systems [currently] in place. There's no just changing the
system now. No, it's small changes now; that's very insular, local,
intense change... I use the practice as a metaphor for the way I
approach everything; with us it begins in the innermost part of the
heart, percolates out to the rest of us and reaches the mind, the body --
and the ripples move out. As a result, it has an impact on those closest
to us. We impact them and then they impact those around them. All
these things begin to change and begin to work as one. It's a very
subtle, interiorized vibrational change. With my own practice and my
way of being with the people around me, I've changed in that way over
the last five years. It's been subtle, it's been gradual, it's been over time
-- and, as a result, our relationships have changed.

In today's era, the pressures of choosing the life you want to live,
etcetera, can lead to depression or anxiety. I think that's part of being
this age, regardless of what time frame you live... Every single person
that I know (and this is not abnormal) -- at some point over the last
couple of years, nearly every single person that I know in my age range,
call it 18 to 30, has gone through an intense, deep stage of depression
and anxiety. But I didn't go through that. That's partly due to my
psychological training previously as well as the year off I took and then
the meditation training. Because I didn't have to go through it and I
have other tools, I've been able to assist every single one of my friends
who has gone through it in ways that I otherwise would not have been
able to [assist]. Most of them have started the practice and attribute
getting through it to the practice -- or at least in part to their friendship

with me. I don't believe it's me, necessarily. It's just the tools I've been given – a higher awareness -- with the real effect of an ability to navigate those dark parts.

Kim: You seem to be the perfect person to answer this question. What advice would you give somebody who's just beginning to look around and becoming disenchanted with the focus on materialism, and maybe starting to look for something else?

My first advice is to get off Facebook. To be quite honest, that's probably where their highest sense of dissatisfaction is, just because they're spending too much time looking around. Stop looking around. Start looking at yourself.

You were going to ask a question about social impact, and I'll jump to that with this answer. Sahaj Marg is a human movement, but it's not for everyone; but it could be for someone. So whatever you try, try something. Like, have the audacity to try something and stick through it. Don't try two things at once. It could actually start with just going to the gym four days a week. Do that. Don't try to meditate and learn French and at the same time go to the gym. Just go the gym and try to get yourself to do that. Put all your force and energy into it. Sit down with your calendar and try to make yourself do one positive thing that you think is positive, and stick it through for a few weeks and see how you feel.

If it's a real spiritual bent, if somebody wants to find something meditative, try. A lot of people want to go to meditation class and tell their friends later they went to a meditation class. That might feel good and it might be what somebody's looking for -- in which case, good for them -- but if you want something deeper, you have to make time for it. There's a book by a Tibetan (I never know how to say it) Rinpoche. I read it for my Asia Studies degree. He said there's no good time for spirituality. When you're too young, you don't understand the value of it, so you don't make the time to sit and meditate; you're too busy having fun and playing games. Honestly, your brain is not developed enough to understand it; you lack the wisdom. In your high school and college years, your focus is on school and getting good grades, so you say, "Well, okay, I'll do it later." In your young adult years, your focus is on find a family, establish career, etcetera. Then kids come, so the focus is on kids. Then old age comes, and you no longer have the actual physical faculties to meditate. There's never a good time, particularly in today's world, to invest time in yourself -- unless you make the time to do it. I would recommend that everyone read <u>Words Of My Perfect Teacher</u> by Patrul Rinpoche (2003).

You've got to make time to invest in yourself, nothing else. Your job is not going to give you that time; they are not going to put it on your schedule. Your kids are not going to give you that time. Your wife or husband is not going to give you that time, and your family is not going to give you that time. You have to <u>make</u> that time and adhere to it with love and kindness; but [it requires] strict discipline and [you must] make the time every day.

That's what I tell people when they come for the first time [for meditation]. I say, "Listen, if you don't want to make the time, we can sit and talk and I'll give you sittings. We'll feel good when we're together, but it's not going to change you in any fundamental way. If you really want to change, I can show you some ways of doing that, but you have to want to put in the time to do that; otherwise it's not going to happen." The root of what I'm saying is, just be intentional. If you want to change, be intentional about finding something that will help you change and then be even <u>more</u> intentional about actually doing it because there's a million different things you can do. There are so many different types of meditation, there're so many different types of religious practices or religious communities that people get a lot out of. There are many different things that one can do.

I happen to think this is an excellent path, which is why I do it, but it's certainly not the only one and you'll find something. Just take responsibility. Anything that's wrong in your life is your fault; it's your fault with the meaning that you've made choices along the way. Of

THE JOURNEY WITHIN

course, I'm speaking outside of systems like poverty and sexisms that have created barriers for others. What I mean is most people – despite their situation – still retain autonomy over how they feel. And, if they're willing to look back with discernment, will see that in their past there were forks in the road, and each time they came upon one they either knowingly or unknowingly made a decision of which way to go. That is the responsibility I'm referring to. What the spiritual journey has taught me, and what I think it teaches all of us, is that nothing happens that is outside of our control. You can't control whether or not your spouse passes away or your kid gets sick or you get a promotion, but you can actually control how you feel about it.

Most people who are at the stage in their life when they start becoming dispassioned with life and disquieted with the material world is when they realize they've made a bunch of decisions but they didn't realize they were making choices. They sort of slid into the next thing, which sort of slid into the next thing. I tell people they can start making choices now. Just because they didn't make, or felt like they didn't make, the choices then doesn't mean they can't start making choices now.

Kim: You started to comment a little bit on Sahaj Marg as a social movement. A way, one of many maybe to change our world sphere. Some people have said that the twentieth century was the century of the mind. The twenty-first century will be the century of the heart.

It could very easily be the century of the atom bomb -- either one of those two, or a host of others.

Kim: Basically, there are some people who strongly believe that Babuji can travel through time. We have "The Whispers," where he's speaking from a brighter world. We hear mention of mutation of human DNA and special "rainbow" children being born. Might you comment? Are these signals of hope for the future?

THE JOURNEY WITHIN

So I said something this morning that I'll say now: One of the biggest mistakes somebody in Sahaj Marg can make is to see Master as only a man. He's much more than that and he has certainly achieved something fantastic, but the even graver mistake somebody can make is to see Master as more than a man. He's a human being. He's just a completely normalized human being, moderated.

I bring this up because these so-called sophisticated "Indigo" or "Rainbow Children" might be; we have no idea. You see, I spend no time worrying about or thinking about these things because they are really not important to me. Again, my focus is vigorously focused on my own self-development insofar as I'm having a positive effect on those around me.

These "Indigo Children" may exist (and I don't want to sound like a conspiracy theorist here), but if we're feeding them terrible food with all this crazy pesticides and hormones -- and we're giving them a Game Boy before they can even talk and all of this, then we're squandering any sort of spiritual potential that they have anyway. They're coming here with potential. We lack the awareness, though, to create an atmosphere for them for their spiritual life to flower.

What I think you're driving at, though, is there seems to be a collective awakening right now that's going beyond occult and New Age and hippie, which is moving more towards mainstream science. Science is becoming fed up with itself. What's the point of just studying things in and of themselves? We have scientists who have spiritual inclinations, be they spiritual or religious, who say, "You know what? I've been practicing these things for many years. I now want to cast my learned scientific eye on what happens when I'm in meditation -- or why do people venerate these lamas or these gurus, etc.? Why do I feel like, sometimes, I get my best inspiration in the middle of the night when I don't feel like it's coming from the mind; it's coming from the heart or from dreams?" I believe in this collective awakening. At the same time, there's still a lot of work to be done.

THE JOURNEY WITHIN

I don't worry myself with that so much. There's so much happening now. I pray for the future obviously, but there's way too much happening in the present to be distracted by the future.

Secondly, I just want to comment on this idea of Babuji traveling through time. Again, this is taking the Master and turning him into something more than a man. I would never question Babuji's faculties, but when one sits in meditation and if you've been practicing for some time, nobody in Sahaj Marg -- no matter their length of practice -- can say that they've never had a meditation of 40 minutes or an hour but it felt like it was two minutes. That's traveling through time. Or, when you're sitting in your apartment but you somehow feel like you're sitting in a meditation hall in Manapakkam, or you feel like you're in your preceptor's home or the train where you did your cleaning one evening -- that's changing space. So by meditating anywhere our relationship to space and time changes. To say, "travels through time" -- I think as we go further on this path those two things become less and less relevant.

There's a great talk by the Master called "The Fruit of the Tree" about Invertendo where he begins to talk about how the body becomes a vessel and how one becomes less encumbered by space and time. So it's not so much a traveling, in my opinion; it's more of a relationship change.

I'm a little stern on these facts because there's nothing that the Masters can do that we do not have the potential to do; this doesn't mean we can do it. But to call it time travel or to talk about changes in DNA or mutations -- it takes a science fiction approach and a fantasy approach to something that's very real and muted, so I hesitate to use those terms.

Kim: Could you share with us, and just pick what you like, are there any particular memories that are either funny or even tragic or poignant from your time as an abhyasi or as a prefect? It doesn't have to be about Master. It could be anything you'd like to share, any good stories.

I've only really lived this life. My entire adult life has been in Sahaj Marg. I think one only becomes a person at the age of 18 when you start making your own decisions. I've been an abhyasi my entire adult life, so all my poignant, fond experiences have all been colored by Sahaj Marg; I can't just choose a Sahaj Marg memory.

That said, I like talking about my first preceptors both because it's important for new people to understand a preceptor but also I like to talk about this so prefects understand. (I guess I'm also a little didactic and I do have a sense of how prefects should act.) I will never forget I was at my prefect's house and I was asked, after a sitting, if I wanted some tea and food and I agreed. He was in the kitchen making something and she was in a spot in their apartment where they make tea.

I just remember watching her make tea. There's a passage in Siddhartha (Hesse, 1922) where Siddhartha's in the mango grove and he sees the Buddha for the first time. He's never been introduced to the Buddha but, upon seeing him, he knows who he is. He can see the gracefulness, the ease and the peace in which this individual is moving through the disciples and walking. I'll never forget my preceptor make tea. She was calm. There was something from watching her from behind. She dropped something at one point, and there was an ease of movement and a fluidity of being. I'd never seen that in anybody before. That was just the epitome of how I felt around them. I think that's all I have to say. Thank you.

Chapter 13　**The Best Hollywood Movie Out There**

Bill

American (U.S.A.), male, 60's, agricultural researcher

Preface:　Bill had been pointed out to me as someone I "really should interview." Jules, in particular, was adamant that I try to catch him if I can, saying he had been an important mentor and really did a lot to promote Sahaj Marg meditation, especially in North America. I was interested to learn that Bill had a doctorate and ran an agricultural research company, yet also found time to travel and volunteer for the mission. That's about all I knew as I met and walked with him to the apartment he and his wife had rented while in India for a few weeks. As we settled at the kitchen table and they offered me a cold drink, I had no idea I would be hearing an amazing story of spiritual searching and discovery.

It would make a great Hollywood movie but it's instead real life – California surfer boy meets his guru in the early 1970's in India. Told with a factual tone and self-deprecating honesty, Bill shares his search for spirituality, something which goes well beyond religion. He describes early experiences as a Peace Corp volunteer in a remote region of Karnataka and his relief and contentment when finally finding a guru and practice that "fit" for him. He emphasizes the benefits of meditation, which are to be happy and feel good. If we can achieve that, then everything else can fall into place, including a brighter future for humankind.

Kim: Could you tell us a little about your background and how you became interested in spirituality?

I grew up in California the first of four children in a fairly religious setting. I was sent to parochial [church] school as a youngster and we attended the Episcopalian, Anglican church every morning except for Saturday, so I had a very strong connection with the church. As far back as I can remember, I had interest in an esoteric existence. I can remember, when not even in high school, being fascinated with the Oriental cultures - Buddhism was something that really caught my interest. Even though it was superficial, I definitely had an orientation that maybe most of my peers didn't have at the time.

As I went through high school and college, I began to acquire writings of the alternative culture that was growing in the United States, and a lot of that had to do with an Eastern philosophic connection. I graduated from high school in 1967 and from University in 1971, so I rode the [hippie] wave right through with everybody else. There were a lot of different options in those days and everything led me toward a spiritual discovery. I was always looking in that direction. The first major opportunity came when I was in my senior year in college and one of my roommate's brother's became an instructor for transcendental meditation (TM). I'd seen his experience and it looked interesting to me so I went ahead and started TM, but within six months to a year, I felt that I had figured it out, pretty much, and I was continuing to search for something more profound.

Superimposed on all of that was the late 1960's and early 1970's, which meant that all able-bodied males and many able–bodied females were to be drafted into the U.S. military and sent to a war that had no real purpose. At that point, I applied for a conscientious objector status and tried to prove the fact that I was not interested in serving, but to no avail. Another option came up at the time, which was not a deferment but rather alternate service, so I applied to the American Peace Corps and was accepted. Of all places, they sent me to India.

THE JOURNEY WITHIN

So in 1971, out of college only three or four months, age 21 or 22, I was on an airplane to India and very unprepared for what was about to happen -- just a huge, complete change in my life. There were 23 of us in our batch and we were trained for three months and then sent out to villages in the state of Karnataka (in southwest India), which at that time was called Mysore. We had separate village assignments and I was in an area which was quite remote, very rural. [There was] no running water and no electricity and it was five miles to the nearest transport.

I was unprepared for the experience but up to the challenge and wanted to make it work, regardless. So I stuck with it, made it through the first hot season, which was nearly unbearable, and learned how to make commitments and follow through with them. The commitment at that point was to see this through and make it work.

On weekends and when I had extra time, I went to different locations in India and tried to figure out what meditation system really suited me. Most of them, it seemed to me, seemed to be extensions of religion and not truly spiritual practice (apart from religion); so, eventually, I was feeling a bit disillusioned. There was a fellow in our group who was an Indian gentleman who overheard me discussing this with some other volunteers from the U.S. and he said, "Well, it just so happens I am practicing a system of meditation and it's called Sahaj Marg." So I ended up finding entry to this practice with it right under my nose, so to speak, in a rural village in India.

He lent me a book which is written by Babuji, I went through it, and it really appealed to me because the simplicity that it presented was what I had been looking for all along. I'd spent so much time in churches and was pretty much fed up with religion. This seemed to be the call that I was looking for because it was simple, it was natural, and it didn't have any associated practices that appeared to me to be ritualistic. At that point, I tried to find out how to pursue it. There was a prefect living about four hours from where I was serving, so I finally got up the courage to go see him, was introduced to the practice and started practicing. That would have been January of 1973.

My tour of duty in India was to end in the early months of 1974, so I had another year in India to practice, to meet people, to visit some of the other locations and to really get an honest experience. It just so happened that the return to the U.S. was from New Delhi and the guru at the time, Babuji, was living in Shahjahanpur, which was located pretty close to New Delhi. So I traveled north from Karnataka to Delhi, which took about two days on the train, then took a side trip over to Shahjahanpur for about 10 days. I was able to meet Babuji and really get a full taste of what the mission had to offer. It happened to be the time of year when we celebrate the birthday of Lalaji [Babuji's master or guru], so I attended the gathering there, which was a fairly small group of people at that time as the mission was fairly young. I got to meet Babuji and he was very open and brought me in with open arms. I have to say that the experience is so surreal, it's essentially to me just the best Hollywood movie out there: California surfer boy goes to India, meets his guru, and lives happily ever after.

So I met Babuji in that ten day period, early 1974, and then pretty much was asked to go back and serve the [Sahaj Marg] mission in the States. In the Peace Corps, I worked in agriculture; I had studied botany in college. So I came back, was married within six months of coming back and then did a Master's in agronomy and later a PhD in genetics, so I've been working in agricultural research ever since -- and that all came from the Peace Corp experience. I wanted to help create a better food supply and to help disadvantaged people get a better diet.

Kim: How would you say you have changed since starting the practice?

I think we all come to this planet with certain baggage that we need to deal with and, as a young adult, I wasn't any different than anybody

THE JOURNEY WITHIN

else. I had some good points and bad points. The bad points? I would say I was fairly pessimistic in my attitudes about life. I had low self-esteem and life was, in a way, a struggle because I couldn't get out of this chronic guilt-ridden point of view that I have. Part of it is because of the family I grew up in, but certainly most is because of the way I was, just <u>am</u>.

So the meditation -- not initially (I mean, it takes time because you learn the practice and there's a certain evolutionary process that occurs) -- but I began to see that things started to disappear, that some of these negative sides or darker sides of my life started to disappear. I was really impressed by that, by how I didn't really do anything but, "They're not there anymore!" I think that was probably the most important accomplishment, if you will, of having done the practice. It freed me from things that I thought were never going to change -- and without any real explanation of how that happened (pretty miraculous).

So my inward orientation of being a chronic complainer turned to a more outward orientation of being much more comfortable in my skin, being much more adaptable in situations, able to meet challenges and take care of them quickly -- being able to essentially work in a public setting talking to people without tying myself up in knots, and stuff like that. It pretty much turned things 180 degrees in my life, and I have to attribute that to the practice.

I understand it now. We believe that we come into this existence with impressions or samskaras, and that, through the practice, those are removed. Having gone through that, the soul is then less encumbered and so can really act in a way that's more natural. I believe that. I really believe that. I don't think that Sahaj Marg is the only way that can happen, but I can see how that process can change people in general. I think being put in adverse situations is certainly a way of also achieving this state where you realize that you have the ability to make things happen and you can overcome adversities. That's important.

THE JOURNEY WITHIN

I think Kamlesh [a very senior prefect and the Master's successor] said it very nicely, a couple of days ago. He was saying that, when the creation occurred, the idea is that we were all unified in one big human family, if you will, natural in the universe. Then there was the 'big bang' or whatever to create separateness, and so, in that separateness we as individual souls were created, which is something I believe, you know -- we all have a soul and it's infinite. But we're different; each one of us has our own identity. He was saying that when this separation occurred the first real samskara or impression that was created at that point was fear -- because we were now separate from the whole and so what could we possibly do but worry that we were separate and how were we going to deal with that? I see that in my own life as an adult now, and see how much of my life was oriented around the fear of just getting life <u>done</u> -- and how I felt that it was not something that I really could manage. I was pretty much a prisoner to my own creation and it was not easy to be able to exist in that environment. Meditation has unlocked the door and now I'm free. I left that prison behind and I never look back.

Kim: I think you might be fairly unusual in regard to your early interest in spirituality. What would you say to someone who is just starting to think about spirituality? Consider someone in an environment where a bigger car, more glamorous vacation, more prestigious address, and so on are viewed as the measurement of success. Maybe they're just starting to wonder, "Well, gee. Isn't there more to life?"

Good question. What you said is accurate. I don't think there was ever any inner resistance to my involvement in the spiritual realm. It flowed in a very natural way. I guess I could say that I've had that potential since the day I was born. Now I do know some other people (I happen to be married to one), where this situation was not at all the case. She can tell her story. There are certainly flip sides to this kind of thing where people struggle with everything from the general concept down to the details. It's not that I didn't have some reservations. I still struggle at times with the idea of a human being

THE JOURNEY WITHIN

representing God. I struggle with that; I don't find that it's an impossibility but I guess I feel that God has to be more than anything that we see or know in the physical realm.

Having said that, I have had the acquaintance of two spiritual guides in this spiritual path, Sahaj Marg, and in both cases, I found that their abilities to help and guide individuals along the path are almost supernatural. Their capacity to investigate individual needs of each of us and find the right solutions for each individual is something that works in every case -- and for that, I see that there is a superhuman capability, if you will. I don't want to see an organization that has undue adoration for these people and I try to keep that low profile because, I think especially for people in the West, it can easily be misinterpreted (very easily) and I can understand that.

So for Sahaj Marg to be ultimately of any value for an aspirant, it's a step-by-step process. You start with the very basic information and the basic practice and, through a process of evolution -- of single steps, if you will -- you reach a better understanding and a wider appreciation and perspective. At that point, you can make a better decision, I think. So it's not something that we can just <u>run</u> into (just like most everything in life). If I want to learn to speak Chinese, how am I and where am I even going to <u>start</u>? Obviously, I'm going to need the help of an accomplished linguist, because the sounds that occur in Mandarin and the sounds that occur in English have very little in common. So I can't even read a book and expect to know how to speak; I have to talk to somebody and have to learn. I have to practice. I have to spend time, energy, discipline myself and maybe in five years – or maybe in 20 years – I'll be able to communicate with a Chinese person. So, same thing: we have to dedicate ourselves to this part of our lives if we're so inclined and down the line, we'll reap the benefits, but it's something that takes time.

Kim: What do you think those benefits are? What are your personal goals (liberation, mergence with the Divine, not having to be reborn)?

THE JOURNEY WITHIN

I have to say that I've never really had those types of aspirations. For me, it's just been to live a life of peace and happiness and this, I feel, has done that for me. I did say that I have a sense that the soul is infinite so I can only deduce that there might be another existence, another incarnation or something, but I have no proof of that. I don't worry about it too much. I have done some reading, both within and outside the mission. There's a lot of literature out there right now with, I think, very interesting and informative content and I would recommend that people do their research, do their homework, and figure it out. They now have literature publications that point to the fact that there are other lives and there's even a period between those lives that has meaning. Sounds plausible, sounds plausible. But, as far as having a goal? Again, I just go back to trying to create a problem-free existence, if you will.

Kim: Do you feel you have to be pure to be spiritual (no meat, no alcohol)?

I guess again it comes back to the way you look at life, ok? If you look at life as a series of indulgences and sort of an opportunity to consume things, that's one way. I grew up in an era when we tried to be a little bit more self-conscious about things. It was the beginning of the environmental movement, things like that. I actually never had any real problem with letting go of meat-eating. It was not something I ever felt that strongly about. I was curious to know from a health standpoint, "What were the benefits of not eating meat?" So I tried it and I found I felt better. So, that was my plan: I tried 10 days with it and 10 days without, then the next 10 days with and the next 10 days without -- and I pretty much proved to myself that it was better. I was kind of my own patient. Then I read -- since I'm in agriculture, certainly, I read about what's going on in the environment and how much of the food that's produced is for animal consumption -- and now with the changing environment and whatnot, it just seems to be our responsibility to be more practical and more humane. So I don't really find that as a problem in my life.

THE JOURNEY WITHIN

I mean, there are things that I love to do that cost money and maybe aren't part of the simple life, but I try to put those in perspective. I try to ration that behavior at a level where I feel I'm not indulgent to a great extent. As we all have said, "everything in moderation" is a good thing. I would recommend to anybody who's struggling with the questions of how to keep your material life in balance with your spiritual life, to follow that rule of thumb: moderation. Don't cut anything out; just try it out in the context of your spiritual practice and see how you feel, and it will orient you. We believe that the heart has the messages that we need to follow and so, if the heart speaks to you and says, "this, but not this," check it out. See what happens. Don't do anything in a rash or fatalistic way. Just figure it out.

Kim: Some people talk about cataclysmic change coming to our world (volcano under London, magnetic shift of the Earth, etc.) and the role of the followers of Sahaj Marg to help humans evolve to a higher level. Do you have any comments on Sahaj Marg as a social movement, as hope for the future, or a way to change the world?

Regarding the predictions and things of that nature, I feel that those are metaphors more than actual events that are prognosticated. I feel that they are there to teach us to be more responsible. Again, the goal of my spiritual practice was to feel good and be happy. So if I feel good and am happy then I'm not going to worry too much about volcanoes. It might happen and it might not. If I am happy and I feel good when this volcano goes off, then I'm still happy and feel good.

Then there's this other question about ambassadors for good vibes and spiritual change in the human environment. Well, I'm not so sure about that. I feel that all human beings have a gift to give and something to offer to the universe. I try very much not to see distinctions between groups as one being more adept or more privileged than another. I do feel that, as people who have changed themselves through the practice, there is potential for helping others,

THE JOURNEY WITHIN

certainly; and that's a good thing. We have this project of creating ashrams in North America and throughout the world and that certainly is an opportunity for people who feel the need to look outside themselves for some kind of a solution -- to access that opportunity, to access that resource. Here in India, there's a school, there are hospitals -- all of which are doing good social work for the community. That's not necessarily the major goals of our organization, but it is a component and I think that it will continue to be there. We're using our resources to help the underprivileged, absolutely.

So, as far as the big picture down the line, I don't really know what's coming. I really don't have much of an idea. If these are nothing but metaphors, then hopefully, if we learn from them, we align ourselves in a more balanced fashion and so that takes some of the load off of nature and whatnot. You've seen enough Hollywood films about what's coming, and some of those have some realism there that might actually happen. I think that, because our nature as individuals is always changing, the outcome of our action is also going to be in flux.

We can, as the human family, alter the course of our destiny, if you will, through our actions today. We can make it a better place. We can take some of the burden off nature and maybe not have to face some kind of cataclysm down the road. Having said that, we can also see from history that there are some pretty crazy things that our family of humans can pull off -- World War II, for instance. I still just can hardly believe people can do that to themselves under any circumstance – or some of the things that are happening today. Yes, we need more love, we need more happiness, we need a perspective on life that gives us the ability to pause and reflect before we act. I think those are things that meditation, <u>definitely</u>, can contribute to.

Kim: Coming back to your idea of human family: How do you see the connection between Sahaj Marg and growing a human family? Growing brotherhood, sisterhood, Earthhood?

THE JOURNEY WITHIN

Well, it's interesting; being in agriculture, I work in a male-dominated industry, with a pretty rough bunch of men who do a lot crazy things. A lot of that doesn't fit into my interests in life, you know. I interact in that sphere, and I think that's one thing that meditation, Sahaj Marg, really helped with: that we can co-exist with our brothers and sisters under any circumstance... We are more adaptable. We are more flexible -- and we don't rush to judgment. I think that this is a thing that really comes with the meditation. We can pause and reflect and so we don't react quickly.

So when people ask me about the practice and why I don't eat meat, we joke -- and they enjoy the conversation. I'm a strong, healthy person so they can see that it's not about nutrition. We raised our family in that way and we have good, healthy kids. There is no nutritional doubt that it works... and in talking about that, everybody realizes and has to look at themselves in that context. So, everything we do in life has an impact on ourselves and other people. They know I'm going to India and so, you know, they're curious. And everybody respects that part of my life. They keep telling me what a great thing it is that I'm doing, in the sense of working in this realm [of a] nonprofit organization that has worldwide reach that believes that, through meditation, a better world can be created. They're very open to that and very interested to know more about it.

Kim: What exactly is your role in North America for Sahaj Marg? Or do you have one?

Yes. Well, we divided the world into regions and one of those is the Americas, North and South America, Central America, the Caribbean. I'm currently in the position of overseeing that responsibility so I do travel a lot to South America, travel a lot within the U.S. and Canada and, it's something that really I enjoy. I mean, traveling can always get a little bit old, after a while, but I've always enjoyed it and I <u>really</u> enjoy meeting people on their terms in their homes in cities and villages. Talking about the subject never gets old. There are always interesting angles to talk about. Having learned some foreign languages, it's even more fun because then you can joke and talk with them in their own languages, which is very satisfying.

Kim: Do you have any stories to share?

Stories about the Masters? Again, I go back to my comments, these are people that have the ability to help others and I've seen this in so many instances. I've been meditating now for 40 years and that's a long time; I've had a lot of time to reflect upon that.

Kim: Have you ever been tempted to quit?

No, no. There are times when I wonder if it's all worth it but I never thought about stopping, no. Never have. That's part of the beauty, I think, of this practice. One feels young pretty much all the time. You never feel like you've really achieved much. Chariji said this a few days ago on the porch; he still feels like he's a newcomer. If you really grasp the practice, you'll always feel that way.

I've seen how people work hard to spread the philosophy of the practice around the world. It's always the case of creating opportunities and this is what I love… we don't presume that anyone will actually start the practice but, if we can at least give the opportunity, then they can decide for themselves. I've been part of that process for practically all my life. When I came back from India in 1974, there were probably 20 people on the whole continent who were practicing at that time -- so it's been a very satisfying experience of meeting groups and individuals and sharing our stories and giving that opportunity a chance.

THE JOURNEY WITHIN

Kim: Do you have any idea how many are practicing now?

In the U.S.A., it's about 3000. Worldwide it might be even half a million.

Kim: Do you have anything else to add?

If people have an interest in spirituality, I encourage them to follow that interest. To me, as I said, the point of life is to find that self-fulfillment. It doesn't matter really what you do, or who you are, or where you came from or where you're going. If you are self-fulfilled, if you feel that self-fulfillment, then you've made it. You're on cloud nine. I challenge everybody to seek that out in their lives. Because if we can reach that stage of human development, I think all of our problems will go away.

Part V: **Hope for the Future**

When I first started working on this book, I didn't have a lot of hope for the future but now that has changed. This book is a personal effort to serve and promote change, in fact. Person by person, heart by heart, we can change the world by changing ourselves. "Change yourself, change the world" is a recurring theme mentioned by several of the interviewees in this and the next book in the series. There is no way to truly change society without changing individuals. The only way to combat hate and fear are through love.

As we all know, there was a great deal of worry about 12/12/12 being a date of, perhaps, the magnetic poles shifting on the Earth, resulting in cataclysm and chaos, with resultant suffering for most of humankind. Predictions included a volcano under London, tectonic plates shifting to the point where continents may disappear or reappear, and tragic consequences for human beings, which would require us to change and adapt. Among those adaptations would be a growth in spiritual capabilities and a greater acceptance of other worlds, other dimensions and other ways of being.

I mentioned traveling from Chennai to Tiruppur for a bhandara (special gathering of thousands of abhyasis in celebration of Babuji's birthday). Beloved Chariji was in very ill health at the time, so his chosen successor, Brother Kamlesh Patel, led the ceremonies. This included giving a talk in which he mentioned the DNA of human beings being altered slightly back in the mid-1970's. I later heard from Claire (whose chapter is upcoming) and from Jules (in the previous section) about Rainbow or Indigo children, and other people with amazing perceptive powers. In his 2003 book entitled <u>Living in the Heart</u>, Drunvalo Melchizedek devotes several chapters to superpsychic children and a woman named Mary Ann Schinfield, who can supposedly move through our solar system, able to "see" even though she technically has no eyes and is completely blind.

THE JOURNEY WITHIN

We are hearing more stories of people connected to other worlds or other dimensions, such as the mother whose two sons tragically died in a car crash. They "channeled" to her to reassure her that they are content and thriving in what they call "the spirit world" (Khorshed, 2009). In The Heart's Code (Pearsall, 1998), we hear from a heart transplant specialist who became convinced that the heart contains cellular memory. It thinks, remembers, communicates with other hearts, helps regulate immunity and contains stored information. In the final chapter of this book, Kali describes her NDE, likening it to one experienced and shared so well by Anita Moorjani in her 2012 autobiographical novel entitled Dying to be Me, which describes her journey from cancer, to near death, to true healing. In Many Lives, Many Masters (1988) and in Same Soul, Many Bodies (2004) psychiatrist Brian L. Weiss, M.D. shares his work with healing through past-life and progression therapy. Please see details, at the time of writing, of these and other references recommended or mentioned in this text. You will find them in the "Resources Referenced and Recommended" section toward the end of the book.

I started out reading some of this literature with a great deal of skepticism but am now taking a much more open-minded approach. I hope you will do the same as you read these final chapters in which Claire, Thomas and Kali talk about their involvement in meditation, its impact on their personal lives and their hopes for a brighter future for humanity. Claire focuses on alternative lifestyles and community-building, Tom (Thomas) talks about the need to fight our prejudices and his awareness that we all must be our brother's keeper. Kali talks about early encounters with Babuji when she was a young adult, now over 40 years ago, as well as her personal, vivid near-death experiences where she had first-hand contact with other worlds and dimensions.

Dear reader, please read with an open mind, envisioning a world where we live in kindness and tolerance of others, a world where humans are open to diversity and more loving and harmonious in our approach to others. Let us become united in our goals toward a spiritual rather

THE JOURNEY WITHIN

than a material focus to life, recognizing that we are on this Earth for only a short time and our ultimate purpose is to evolve.

THE JOURNEY WITHIN

Chapter 14   The Divine Spark

Claire

Irish, female, 40's, artist and author

Preface: Claire was part of the inspiration for this book. Ten months
after starting meditation, I visited India for the first time on a
meditation "retreat." My first time in India, alone and knowing
nobody, I stayed as a guest at the ashram headquarters before traveling
by train to Tiruppur (near Coimbatore) to attend a three-day bhandara
(spiritual gathering) of nearly 30,000 people. Claire befriended me the
very first night at the ashram and made all the difference in my
experiences both at the ashram and at the gathering.

At that time, Claire was in the last stages of writing a book about her
pathway to spirituality (please see The Divine Spark reference in the
final section of this book). An English professor, I was curious to read
Claire's book, and she kindly gave me a copy to read and help edit
before leaving the ashram. I was impressed by her story and by the
short stories of other brothers and sisters, which she included at the
end of her book. They reminded me of short stories about Christianity
I used to read at my grandmother's house along the Tippecanoe River
in Indiana. The germ of the idea for this book began then and, of
course, Claire was someone I wanted to interview. We met on Skype
one afternoon and had the interesting conversation which follows.

Claire first delves into her past, describing her emergence from
personal misery by tuning into the divine "spark" which she found
within. Also the title of her book, which describes her transformation,
The Divine Spark speaks through the heart. Increasingly, scientific and

THE JOURNEY WITHIN

other evidence indicate that humans need to evolve from reliance on the head (mind) to an improved understanding and connection with our hearts. The heart connection may even be necessary for humans to evolve and to survive in these and future times of change on our planet. Claire shares her vision of community and caring in the future. Please read, enjoy, and access the resources she has provided and which she herself has found so useful as you learn more about tuning into the divine spark in your heart.

Kim: The first couple of questions I have for people are about their background and formative experiences - family, religion, things like that. I know quite a lot of that already from your book The Divine Spark (2012), *including how you became interested in spirituality. So let's start with the question of why Sahaj Marg in particular? Did you try other types of things to help yourself?*

Well, I suppose there was nothing else presenting itself and I was in a very difficult space at the time. I had no hope -- or no faith -- in anything and, as I said in the book, I had just come from seeing a psychiatrist who prescribed a lot of medication. I couldn't cope with life at that point; I just was at a breaking point. I'd had several breaking points in my life, but this one [was especially serious]. As I said, I'd returned home to Ireland after years of living abroad and had nothing to do and no hope. I wasn't feeling much love in my life.

My dad had been doing this meditation practice, this Sahaj Marg, for 10 or 12 years but I had no interest in it because I thought it was beyond me or I didn't think it could help me or I didn't really know too much about it or meditation. I also felt I had an overactive mind and didn't think I could ever settle to be able to meditate. I somehow associated meditation with being a hippie, which I wasn't, and so felt it wasn't for me. But just the way he (my dad) spoke that day, which I describe in the book -- about chasing happiness outside of ourselves -- I knew I had to try it. So, I thought I'd go along and try it because I had absolutely nothing else.

THE JOURNEY WITHIN

Excerpt from <u>The Divine Spark</u>: His message was along the lines that, if we spend our lives being slaves to our desires and wishes, we will be eternally miserable. It hit me like a thunderbolt that I had spent years chasing something that was never really out there and it amounted to a life spent wishing for something else. (p. 36)

Kim: So you weren't looking for meditation but rather some way out of despair and hopelessness?

Yes, [otherwise] I was going to take the medication even though in my heart and soul I knew it didn't work before; I couldn't live with the anxiety. I hadn't tried Prozac so I thought maybe that would do the trick, even though I knew it could make people crazy. I thought I had to try something; I couldn't go on living the way I was living.

I got home that evening and called a preceptor who at the time was living [nearby] and he said, "We'll start tomorrow." And so I went to his house the next day and, after three days of sittings, the light came in and I had that amazing experience as I described in the book.

Excerpt from <u>The Divine Spark</u>: But on this third evening, while sitting there, a peculiar feeling arose. The cynicism lifted, and suddenly I had the sensation of freedom from thought, which was very liberating in itself. Then I felt an incredible lightness within, until I thought the light would explode through me. I recognized this same feeling from the "vision" experience I had in Istanbul. This was what I had been seeking all my life. I came out of the meditation session that February night and walked out into the cold, country air and looked up at a clear, starry sky. With a bewilderment of the highest form, looking up at those radiant stars, I saw for the first time that night the true beauty of this Universe. My soul had been stirred and awakened. (p. 37)

THE JOURNEY WITHIN

Kim: I think your case is especially interesting because you were grappling with a lot of things many people grapple with: family dissonance, difficulties and trauma in your formative years, drugs, alcohol, all of that. So it's pretty obvious to see why you would turn to spirituality but why Sahaj Marg in particular?

I recognized in that third sitting the same feeling that I got from the experience in Istanbul -- that first "wake up" experience [described briefly above] -- so I knew that it was somehow related, that there was something in this, and I had to keep going with it. It's like it opened this door into a whole new world that I never knew existed.

Kim: Did you feel that you sent a call out and it was answered?

I suppose, yes. I was in such a state of desperation, I did ask for help. I'm sure I've asked for help -- but I've asked for help at so many other times in my life. Maybe the time wasn't right [before] and I had to go through all that stuff.

I'm reading a book now by Drunvalo Melchizedek called Living in the Heart and it's all about being able to go into the sacred space in the heart; Babuji talks about it as well. He [Melchizedek] also talks about the super psychics, as they are called. They're children (all over the world now) but they can see without seeing; they have this inner vision. I can't recall how he describes it in the Living in the Heart book but it's fantastic stuff.

I know now from reading that book that's what happened to me in Istanbul. I had this inner vision being relayed to me. It was like I was watching a film. That night I had been lying in bed, feeling heartbroken and at my darkest hour. I was lying in a near-lifeless state looking out the window when I was drawn to looking at one particular

THE JOURNEY WITHIN

star that seemed to be burning extra brightly -- and then, this thing took off, this vision...

Excerpt from The Divine Spark: It [the vision] revealed many insights, one being how many women foolishly throw away their hearts to a man and get so engrossed or obsessed with this one man, that they miss out on their own journeys and the adventure of life. It showed me that I was now set free, like the butterfly emerging from its cocoon. The struggle that a butterfly goes through is necessary to send fluid into its wings; otherwise, it will never fly properly. My life of pain and struggle was necessary in some way. Now I had been released from the cocoon of struggle and a new journey was beginning... It was the most amazing experience, and during this vision my condition was turned from one of utter desperation to instant joy... What an incredible gift! p. 32

After that experience, I felt liberated. The next day that light energy was still there; I walked about the city and felt like I was floating with that sense of buoyancy. I was so incredibly grateful for it because I didn't think I'd ever come out of that pain I'd been in.

Maybe two years later I started Sahaj Marg [meditation]. The first two sittings I didn't really feel a whole lot but the third sitting -- again, it was like the doors to the universe opening up and being able to see clearly. It felt similar to my feeling after that magical experience I had in Istanbul. I went into another dimension. That was it. There was no way I'd take medication. I knew this spiritual path was what I needed to survive this journey through life.

Kim: How have you changed since starting meditation?

THE JOURNEY WITHIN

Well, now I have faith in God and I am able to feel love. I had absolutely zero faith in anything prior to it – not in the church, not in God, nothing. Now I understand that God is within us, not external (as is taught in most religions). Before, life had been pretty bleak, but now it is a wonderful journey of the soul, an adventure. And I feel like all these great things are coming along the path. I never understood what love was before, but now I know what a powerful force it is and how it can transform us and regenerate the subtle bodies of our entire being.

I also feel a lot more openness in my view of things, a sort of expansion of consciousness to all possibilities of both here and beyond, whereas in the past I would have been quite narrow- minded or limited. Even reading Drunvalo's book, I can see that he is being channeled to give more and more information about the higher truths and realities of the universe, the cosmos. We can always find more information. Doors are opening up to a much more incredible universe than we ever could have imagined. Apparently, we can only see about 5% of true reality. All of this new knowledge makes life so much more exciting to me.

The lives of these advanced souls, people like Drunvalo, they tell us what's happening and how we are moving into the higher dimensions so it may become easier for us spiritually after the transition that's going to happen in the coming years. In the future, we will hopefully be able to see more of the greater reality -- rather than this mundane or limited life that we're living at the moment.

Kim: And you're convinced that's going to happen in the next few years, in our lifetime?

Well, from what I have read in the various books from these awakened or advanced souls, they all seem to say more or less the same thing --

THE JOURNEY WITHIN

that we are waking up to the greater realities and will move to a higher vibration and state of consciousness. The more highly-evolved souls amongst us speak of the great changes in nature that will be necessary given the alarming imbalance of the world and the destruction that is being caused by us humans.

I view these changes with positivity in that it will help us to change our way and that we may go back to a more natural way of living, one which respects nature. I hope that we can become more spiritually-oriented as opposed to this overly materialistic society which has caused so much destruction and harm on so many levels.

Kim: That brings me to a new question, which is about Sahaj Marg as a social movement. What impact do you think it will have on our future and on our world sphere? And do you really think this is happening now?

Babuji refers in the <u>Whispers</u> (Chandra 2010, 2012, 2013) to the raising of our vibration, the mutating of our cells, so that we may rise up and move to the higher dimensions. Drunvalo and [others] talk about it in more depth.

To my mind, the way of Sahaj Marg is creating a sense of one family amongst us and bringing unification. We have to transcend our differences of race, religion, culture, judgment… things which so often separate us. It offers us the means to find our true identity so that we can know love, thereby creating harmony and respect for one another (which are so badly needed).

Kim: We just had the end of 2012 and everyone was all excited about the number 12-12-12 and seeing all the different predictions of cataclysm, etc. I think, some people, when nothing happened, kind of went "boink, now what"?

THE JOURNEY WITHIN

It wasn't supposed to just happen overnight, but the idea is that we are gradually moving into the next transition or "phase" of life. An acceleration of changes will start to happen in the coming years; some (e.g. natural disasters) are already happening. Other changes may also affect life as we know it. For instance there are intense storms on the sun at present, and this activity is causing solar flares which are powerful bursts of radiation. This radiation can disturb the atmosphere in the layer where GPS and communication signals travel. This would seriously affect communication technology, so we may have to learn a new form of communication. The Hopi and Kogi Indian elders and other visionaries are advanced souls all saying the same thing about what lies ahead.

Kim: And what are you doing about that?

I figure it's necessary to live more sustainably and to set up places for people to live in the future that are independent from the current system. Babuji has said that we need to create spiritual refuges; and people will come and raise these places. He also said that we need to start living in communities because it will help to protect us in the future.

All my life (even when I was young), I've been craving to be part of a community. We're fortunate that, in Sahaj Marg, we have that common goal or connection; it's very special. It is like a big extended family somehow, isn't it? That sense of brotherhood and sisterhood.

Sometimes I find it difficult to live in the current system of living as it seems to be going against nature-- and it's hard sometimes to relate or fit in. There is disturbance from different forms of pollution; electrical, radiation, chemical, noise, contamination, etc. Many people are sensitive to these disturbances, creating a lot of imbalance and illness.

THE JOURNEY WITHIN

I do think the day will come and all will change due to the big wake-up call from nature. People will have to re-evaluate and re-think our values and the way we live. Babuji keeps referring to it; that things have to change, it can't go on the way it's going, you know? The scales are tipping and the balance of the world and the ecosystem are being seriously affected. So, we'll just have to look at taking another road soon enough.

Kim: Do you have any advice for someone who is trying to lead a new lifestyle, to stop drinking alcohol, for example, or stop eating meat...or do you find those habits drop off without you having to make a conscious effort as you try to lead a more pure lifestyle? What do you have to do in your personal lifestyle to feel that you're taking full advantage of the practice?

I know myself, when I started this practice, when somebody told me meat wasn't a great idea, I thought, "No way can I give up meat!" but over the years, my taste started to change, and I couldn't eat it anymore. It gave *me* up; I didn't try to give *it* up. As Master says, sometimes if you try too hard or feel forced to give these things up, you're giving them more power. Some things just fall away naturally on this journey. Things fall away by degrees if they're not meant to be there, if they're obstructing our path.

Kim: Can you talk more about vibrations and the idea of resonance?

Quantum physicists are discovering more of this complex system of life, what everything is made of, and that we humans are made up of molecules, particles and vibrational energy. We exist and are connected in a quantum unified vibrational field. The true reality is probably beyond the current knowledge of scientists.

THE JOURNEY WITHIN

The higher our vibration, the lighter we feel internally and so I try to avoid things that are more base in nature – as they lower our vibration. An idea in spirituality is that we're trying to rise up and connect with the higher aspect or the higher self. So these things like negativity, addictions, anger, being hurtful to others and other lower tendencies of us humans; all can lower our vibration. I have heard that eating meat can lower our vibration and create more denseness or heaviness in us. Especially these days with the way meat is produced, for instance, many animals are raised in huge pens at an industrial level to cater for mass human consumption. These poor animals never get to live a natural life, eat the grass or roam the land, so imagine the pain they're in, you know?

Kim: Coming from a Catholic upbringing, how do you reconcile Jesus Christ on Earth and Master? Are there any parallels, or have they had the same role?

I think that Jesus and all the Masters who graced this planet were, and are still, working for the Creator, the Source. They came at different periods in history when Nature needed and all were teaching more or less the same message. Who can say which of them is greater or what their role is? There are other very high souls at present on the planet who are helping nature and humanity.

Kim: Can you tell me more about constant remembrance and how that works for you?

I suppose, for me, I can only be in remembrance when I tune in and become present in my heart where I feel love and connected to the Source. After years of struggling, and being through many lessons and tests, I know the difference between being up in the head and being in the heart. Life is certainly easier living from the heart space and I can operate from a better place. Drunvalo describes exercises in his <u>Living</u>

THE JOURNEY WITHIN

in the Heart book of how to bring the focus down from the head to the heart. He says that being in the head is male (male energy) and being in the heart is female. The Mayans and the Kogi's have said that we've moved back into the divine feminine energy after being 30,000 years in the male energy. I suppose that's why we go back more into the heart now; feminine energy. So perhaps men may become more in touch with their feminine side as well. [We're] shifting into a new paradigm, the next stage of evolution, to bring us to a higher state.

Babuji has said that Sahaj Marg will change in its teachings and practice when humans are ready for it. At the moment, it's quite simple because it is what people can understand. It's a process of evolution. As we become more awake and aware, we will become more open and able to use the information given. It doesn't mean that Sahaj Marg is for everybody but it is said it will become a huge movement in the future. It's unprecedented that these messages come directly from the Brighter World. I feel so blessed to be exposed to all these wonderful messages and information from the higher realms.

There are many portals or sacred high points of vibrational energy on this planet, or places with zero point gravity, like Sedona in Arizona, Stonehenge, The Uluru mountain in Australia, the various Pyramids throughout the planet -- the ancients such as the Druids and monks, for example, were more aware of the energy grid of the planet and the dimensional doorways to the higher worlds and seemed to be more in tune with the spiritual energies. They were aware of the higher dimensions and so they constructed pyramids, temples, standing stones or stone circles at these sites. And now we also have these ashrams all over the planet that are great points of light, built to help humanity rise.

Kim: What is your vision? What do you personally plan to do in this new age that is coming?

THE JOURNEY WITHIN

I suppose [my vision] is to be in a community with like-minded souls, all living together in a more harmonious setting and in direct connection with the land, in tune with nature. I happened to be with Master in India when the news broke of the tsunami in Japan and the damage to the nuclear plant back in 2011 and he said that we have now passed the point of human solution and we have to go back to nature, to a more simple way of living.

So, what I would love is for a group of abhyasis to have a place somewhere in Europe with land. We could build eco-houses, communal spaces and become self-sustainable. There are all sorts of amazing energy efficient houses being built now, even ones that can actually create their own energy source. It would be lovely to have a communal space for meditation, as well. I know someday it will happen. We just have to start the ball rolling and get together with other abhyasis who have the same vision. Master said recently, on hearing of this plan, that he is all for these kinds of projects and that we have to act fast. A friend and her husband are living 'off the grid' and have been homesteading for the last 20 years, but they are realizing the need for community support. So, there are lots of people who are being brave in this way of living and people like that have the knowledge to teach the rest of us.

Kim: A wonderful dream. Let's make it happen. Thank you.

Chapter 15   **A Grain of Sand**

Thomas (Tom)

U.S.A. American, male, late 60's, retired mortgage banker

Preface: Thomas and I met at the ashram canteen when mutual friends introduced us after meditation one morning. I immediately liked him and wanted to spend time in his company. He felt like a fun-loving older uncle to me, full of jokes and insights. He twinkles. We agreed to meet at the canteen and walk nearby to a quieter place for the interview but it was difficult to tear Thomas away from all his friends at the canteen. He was instantly "nabbed" again when we got back. He clearly is much-loved and appreciated. Laughter seems to follow him everywhere, yet he has experienced a great deal of personal tragedy.

In this chapter, Thomas talks about early experiences with spirituality that are unique and quite personal -- starting when he was only nine years old, later as a young man in the military, and now during his golden years as he seeks to bring others to an awareness of the importance of "in-volution." He also discusses the difference between religion and spirituality, race in America and the importance of being our brother's keepers. Pithy, irreverent, kind and loving, Thomas described his "journey on the train" and his awareness of being just "a grain of sand on a 7-mile beach." Enjoy!

I'm a mixture of Hopi Indian and Irish and I just recently turned 69 years of age. I retired after 40 years in the mortgage banking business, including owning my own company of 56 employees. I've had two experiences with cancer. I had the right upper lobe of my lung removed and they gave me six months to live in 2008: I told them they didn't have a Master like my spiritual master and I lived through that. Then I had ablation surgery approximately six months ago and I came through that -- now my oncologist and my radiologist have both joined Sahaj Marg.

My first experience with spirituality was when I was around nine years old. My brother and I were walking down the railroad tracks and, at the railroad station, I saw who I later came to know as Paramhansa Yogananda [the first yoga master of India to permanently live and teach in the West, arriving in America in 1920]. As I crossed over the train trestle and came upon him, he and I began to talk. I felt very comfortable talking to him because he looked like my Aun Tiny; he had long black hair and he was about 5 feet 2 [inches tall]. I had no idea that he was the spiritual master of his own organization. I remember that my brother coaxed me on, "C'mon because we have to go to church!" and I remember Paramhansa Yogananda saying to me "I will see you later in life. We will meet again." and that was my first introduction to spirituality. As I became an adult I saw his book, Autobiography of a Yogi, and I remembered it was him. The warmth that I felt when I was a little boy came over me again. I read his book several times.

I had another experience with a spiritual master when I was stationed in Turkey. I had an experience that brought me to Sahaj Marg but 25 years later. I had gone to sleep and, while I was asleep, a little Indian man came to me and he took me up and showed me how to fly, effortlessly. I remember that very vividly. That was in 1964. We flew over the trees, we flew over the telephone wires, and I remember saying to my roommate the next day, "I learned how to fly last night." He says, "Well, I don't think you should eat or drink what you had last night!" But the very next night, this little Indian man came to me again. This time he takes me over the ashram in Molina, Georgia, which was not built yet. Then he took me on a trip of infinity. I was high up enough that the planet looked flat; it didn't look round. I remember saying to him, "this is too far up!" (I was afraid that I might fall) and he says, "Do not worry because you are attached to me with a string."

THE JOURNEY WITHIN

Going back after that point I went in a bookstore called "Manifestations" in Cleveland, Ohio and Bob, who owns the store, says, "Hey, I have a book for you. It's called <u>The Complete Works of Ram Chandra</u> (Chandra, 2009). When I opened the book and saw the very first picture it was of Babuji Maharajah [who had taken me flying] and I immediately knew at that point that I was home. I called the contact number on the back of the book and asked how I could get started and was told I would have to have three sittings. I asked if I could start but, "Was I ok to start?" because I didn't think I was clean enough to come into a spiritual organization. She said, "Whatever you have, everyone has." That was 26 years ago and I've been here (in Sahaj Marg) ever since.

Kim: Did you have a history or background of spiritual messages, or family orientation toward spirits?

Our family are Hopi Indian and I always felt that we were intuitive about certain things but I had no idea that this man who I met [was a spiritual leader]; and I doubt I would have stopped if he didn't look like my Aun Tiny. As I said, his hair was about 4 feet long. Frankly, I never did research to find out why he was at that train trestle unless he was just there for me.

Kim: Did your brother see him too?

Yes, but he told me, "come along, come along, come along." I felt such warmth, such <u>love</u> from this man that I wanted to go with him; I didn't want to go with my brother. So that was the beginning of what I call "The Trip on the Train."

THE JOURNEY WITHIN

Kim: I'm going to ask you this because you brought up the illness: Are you afraid of death?

Not now. Not at all, not now. I think I came to the conclusion in meditation that everything is by choice and, if in fact you choose to die, then you will die -- but if you choose to live after this life then you will live. It's all a matter of choice. This is a good question because we hear many times people write books and say that after this life there is no more life -- and if that is your choice that's absolutely correct -- but if you do believe that there is life after this life then this body will drop off like a coat that is too heavy and you will go to the next level, if you are prepared.

Kim: And what are your personal goals as a practitioner of Sahaj Marg?

My goal is basically the will of the Master. I can't say what's in store -- I just want to reach the next level; but I do have enough common sense to know that light attracts light and we know that God is light. We know that Jesus had reached a pinnacle of light that became the "sun" of God (not the S-O-N of God but the S-U-N of God) and merged with the infinite. I imagine that I would like to achieve the same goal and give God as many souls as I possibly can for his pocket.

Kim: How have you changed since you started the meditation practice?

I think that I've become more aware of feelings within myself, attitudes with other people, the craving of other people and the need for a spiritual, simple way to the goal for all mankind. So I think it's given me the intuitiveness to believe that I'm one of the recruiters of Sahaj Marg because, if I see that you have the desire, then I will try to help you come this way.

THE JOURNEY WITHIN

Kim: Do you have any comments on being a person with black color skin living in America?

I think that America has created its own albatross in not identifying with human actions, human reactions rather than colors, ridiculous colors, of people's skin. I think that's the most offensive thing that America could ever do to human beings and, consequently, we will either move along as a root race or we will be stopped in our tracks.

R-o-o-t, just like as in a garden where all the flowers are being watered and all the flowers will shine. If you only water a certain segment of flowers then the others will become weeds. So I think that America has to stop the <u>fear</u> of color and move into the next level.

Kim: Do you feel that Sahaj Marg is a social movement, that it can provide help for a world that's gone wrong?

My answer to that question, as best I can give, is that I believe that Sahaj Marg is the speech that Dr. Martin Luther King gave, "I Have a Dream," and this is the reality of the dream.

Kim: Would you have any advice for someone who has never really considered spirituality as an important part of his or her life?

Try spirituality -- because the car becomes old, the clothes become old, the house becomes old. You can only use one bed, one toilet and you can't take the money and put it in the casket. My spiritual master has said repeatedly that books are for the brain, food is for the body, spirituality is for the soul. In order for the soul to expand and grow to

THE JOURNEY WITHIN

a level of peace and calmness, one <u>must</u> and has no choice but to come to spirituality.

Kim: I want to go back to your comment about not being pure. Do you feel that leading a pure lifestyle is something that's important for spirituality?

I think, in spirituality (especially in Sahaj Marg), what happens is that those things that are not important will fall off the tree. So it's not so much what you have to do; if you do the practice, if you're disciplined in the practice, the unnecessary things will fall off. An example is [the person] who was my spiritual Master's preceptor: He had somebody who had stopped coming to meditation and he said, "Why is it that you haven't been coming to meditation?" and he [was told], "I've done so many bad things since I've been here." And the response was, "What could you have done as a human being? Anything and everything that you have done is not new. Please come back to meditation."

Kim: Could you explain the concept of "Master"?

I think the problem, especially with Americans, is the interpretation of the word "master." There are two negative connotations of master, one being a "massah" to slaves [and] the other one representing 'master' [as authority]. However, looking at the English version of master, master means "teacher." When I asked Master Chariji this question he explained to me that he is just a spiritual teacher and that his spiritual teacher was a teacher to take you from here to the goal of human life. We have reached the highest evolutionary state in the human body. The state that we reach is that we will get no more arms, no more legs and no more body on the planet. The actual goal of human life is: we go from a state in a physical body through an *in*volutionary journey of this body. We travel through the *chakras* (see glossary) to reach the highest chakra to merge with the ultimate. Like the salmon does; when it reaches its goal it has its babies.

THE JOURNEY WITHIN

I came to Sahaj Marg like a moth does to the flame; I've never been without the warmth. The tragedies of life were just life's experiences. I remember an incident that happened when I first came into Sahaj Marg and I was in Molina, Georgia. I had an experience where Babuji came to me and he said to me, "The soul takes on the body to experience experiences." So tragedies, even though they happened to me, I understood they were experiences. I lost my mother, I lost my wife three months later, I lost an old girlfriend (all during that period of time), but I was able to keep myself submerged in Sahaj Marg and I was able to move on to the best of my ability as a human being. The fact that there is humor in me still, means I'm still on key.

I remember Master saying that it's important to do the practice. It's about the morning meditation, the evening cleaning and the prayer before going to bed. He also gave an example of why some people don't feel the vibration and it's mainly because they're not doing the practice; it's like having wet wood versus dry wood to burn. So if they are not feeling it in their hearts, are they really doing the practice? It's a question that everyone should ask himself or herself. We in America have a wrong concept about becoming and, in Sahaj Marg, it's about *un*becoming. We're goal-orientated in America -- that we are going to become a preceptor or we are going to be a master -- and all this accumulation is merely accumulation and the whole purpose of Sahaj Marg and living in Sahaj Marg is to become *un*accumulated. So the good and the bad have to drop off and we become what it is that God wants us to be.

Kim: Do you think all those masters are up there working together (Krishna, Mohammed, Jesus…)? What's your take on that?

Yes, I believe, if they are all within God, then they are all one -- and if there's a separateness then it's not God. The difference between religion and spirituality is that religion separates; spirituality unites.

THE JOURNEY WITHIN

That's why you have a million trillion religions but there's only one spirituality. When we look at the Billy Grahams and all the television ministries, we see the exploitation of people who are only trying to reach the garment of Lord Jesus. We keep hearing, over and over and over again, how Jesus is the Way. But he has a flaw -- and that flaw is, he's always broke. He always needs money [laughter]. In Sahaj Marg, we don't ask for money. God does not ask for money. He only wants to take the soul to the next level in the boat so we can all move (like the Mayan people who all take another along).

We are our brother's keeper. We are responsible for one another and we have to take that attitude on a day-to-day basis. We are responsible: We are the mother, we are the father, we are the son. We have to start taking responsibility.

Kim: What are the hardest aspects of growing into an evolved person? What have been the biggest challenges?

Being an American, probably being goal oriented, wondering if I've made progress or not made progress. The progress in Sahaj Marg is by other people seeing the radiated light in you, not in yourself. I'm just a grain of sand on a seven-mile beach. An Indian brother recently asked me at the swimming pool of my complex why I was going to India, and I said I was going to my ashram and he says, "Are you a teacher?" I say, "No, I'm just a student." He says, "How long have you been a student?" and I said, "26 years." I started laughing and he said, "Well that's long enough to be a teacher." and I said, "Well, maybe so, but I'm still learning."

Kim: Could you comment on the idea of the human family and spirituality? Or some people would use the word "brotherhood" and spirituality?

THE JOURNEY WITHIN

I think in Sahaj Marg or not in Sahaj Marg, we are all brothers and sisters, as I was saying before about the root race; we're in the boat together. If you read the history in Hindu books you will find that we go into a 25,000-year cycle -- and we're in the boat so it is <u>all</u> of our responsibility that <u>everybody</u> in the boat moves along.

Do you have anything else you'd like to add?

Wake up, wake, up, wake up. Wake up, brothers. Wake up, sisters. If what you're doing is not bringing you to the point of peace, give this a try. Give it six months. If it doesn't work, don't do it anymore. But I, Thomas, believe for 26 years this is the most wonderful ride that I've been on, at 186,000 miles per second. I'm just a grain of sand on a seven-mile beach.

THE JOURNEY WITHIN

Chapter 16 **Don't Waste Time**

Kali

North American, female, 60's, therapeutic bodyworker & preceptor

Preface: Kali introduced herself to me after meditation and offered to give an interview for the book. I foolishly almost said "no," as I already had twice as many interviews as I was anticipating. Luckily, Kali forgave my initial lack of enthusiasm and gave one of the most fascinating interviews of the entire collection. I was later to learn that she is quite a well-known abhyasi "from Babuji's times," as people like to say. She was among the first Westerners to travel to India, doing it as a young adult traveling overland from Europe. She has been visiting ever since, typically staying the entire three months of her visa.

We meet near the lotus pond near the back gate of the ashram and Kali is a good sport about invading ants and mosquitoes. We busily wave our fans in a vain attempt to stay cool as we talk. I quickly become mesmerized as Kali explains how, as a young adult, Sahaj Marg meditation 'found' her. Over forty years later, she is now a retired therapeutic body worker and an active meditation guide (preceptor). Kali encourages those new to the concept of spirituality to have an open mind and to recognize that mind, body and spirit need to be in balance. She asks that we avoid dogmatism. When the heart changes, everything changes. As she explains, the biggest revolution is to change yourself.

Kim: Could you tell us a little about your background and how you got involved in spirituality?

I grew up in the United States of America, in a Catholic background with a patriotic father who was in the U.S. navy. At age 12, my mother and I moved to California. I had grown up in the Catholic religion but, when I turned 16, I knew something was not quite right: so I informed my mother that I was leaving the Catholic religion - much to her sadness - but I knew something was "off." I never tried anything further until I just happened to be taken to Sahaj Marg, literally, when Babuji and Parthasarathi (Chariji) came to Denmark in 1972.

There really wasn't too much happening back then about spirituality or meditation: it was just beginning. There were very few preceptors in all of Europe at that time. A friend of mine who had somehow come across Sahaj Marg meditation when he was in Germany told me that Babuji was coming to Copenhagen [to the home of a preceptor] for three or four days. We were maybe, at the very most 20 people, maybe only 15. I went to get my second sitting and Babuji gave a group sitting; so before I got my third sitting I got a group sitting with Babuji. I went, I got three sittings, I met Babuji; but I was a blank slate because I hadn't read or [learned] anything about meditation ever. I was really a blank slate [and] I'm glad because I had nothing that was coloring my experience. I had just been three days with Babuji and Chariji and afterwards I didn't really do the practice that much. There was no written material back then; you were just told how to meditate. I'm glad I started that way because I had no expectations, no pre-conceived ideas.

My first sittings were by a preceptor from India who was temporarily living in Copenhagen. I just found the sittings out of this world, literally; I was gone. I was in my young 20's, a very mixed-up 20-year-old that had moved from California to Denmark. That was in June of 1972 in Copenhagen and the following March there were a few of us who thought, "Well, let's go to India and see who this Babuji is and what all this was about." March the following year (6 months after the Copenhagen gathering), I traveled overland from Denmark to Greece, Greece to Turkey and onward to India. It took 30 days by train, by rickshaw, by everything, and we finally got to Babuji's house. We

THE JOURNEY WITHIN

arrived (but) we had no address; we only knew Shahjahanpur (the city). We were some of the first Westerners.

The bicycle rickshaws were there (at the train station) and we just said, "Do you know, Ram Chandra mission?" but there was another Rama Chandra mission! So we really didn't know where we were going. We were so naïve and stupid. We got into the rickshaw. We were extremely tired and we just thought, "Okay, we'll just go wherever he's taking us and then maybe we'll find out where we <u>really</u> should go."

When we arrived there, I asked the person in the rickshaw to get out and go see (I was a little unsure). We had travelled down an alley that had big pigs in it and it was really strange. We came to a gate and walls in front of the house before you walked into the compound. There was no name on the gate so we thought this probably was not the correct place. The abhyasi that went [to see] came back out and said, "Oh yeah, he's in there," we got out of the rickshaw and went in. We were rather tired after 30 days and we both had been very, very ill so we were not really with it. When we entered, Babuji greeted us, and then he sent us to different rooms and said, "You take a shower and please sleep." That was the beginning. I was there for a month; that was my first trip overland to Babuji and we were there a month. I think two other Westerners, or maybe three, may have come at that time. That was my beginning with Sahaj Marg.

I had been brought up, like I said, in the Catholic religion, which I felt did teach me about God and faith. My mother was a very devout Catholic and I was grateful. I was grateful that I had learnt about prayer and God and faith. These were good elements and that was (from my birth) my religious beginnings -- then Sahaj Marg for 41 years now. I was made a preceptor by Babuji in 1975, when I was in Shahahanapur at that time. I had just gotten married so I knew I was going to be leaving Denmark and returning to North America.

THE JOURNEY WITHIN

Kim: So would you have any advice to somebody who's new to the idea of spirituality, who hasn't really thought about it very much?

Well, I'm sort of torn because I don't think it's really great to give advice. One of the things my master/teacher has taught me over the years is that you can't force anybody; there's no idea of force. Normally, if there's interest, you can talk with somebody. I work with people all the time and we end up having conversations (me and my clients) about God and spirituality and things in general. We'll talk from wherever it is they're coming from. I usually end up speaking with them about Sahaj Marg if it comes up naturally. They all know I meditate because I work out of my home and there's Master's picture hanging up -- so, they may have questions about the meditation I do.

For a young person, I think it just depends on the conversation and where they're at and where they're leading you. I would hope, in general, that younger people are looking for something beyond this world. They are realizing that the world is offering money, position. But nowadays, you can't even get a college education and get a job. All these challenges are there. So if they're looking beyond that, knowing that this isn't really satisfying everything, then they might feel that there is something more. Something more is that divinity or spark or consciousness inside of us. It's just like when we pursue anything (whether it is a job or anything we're interested in), that side [spirituality] also has to be researched and pursued, however they want to go about it.

We are mental, physical, emotional and spiritual beings. So we're body, mind and spirit. Usually, people in general, in the world, know very much about the body. We're very much involved with our bodies in various ways, our health and how people look and things like that – same with our mind, the intellectual, the schooling and all. But then we have the spirit; we have all three. So we have to pay attention to the spirit because if we don't, that's what makes us out of balance. I think even health-wise more persons are becoming aware of the body-mind-

THE JOURNEY WITHIN

spirit aspect. The spirit, I call it, is that light, that divinity, inside yourself. You can look into that in whatever way possible but it's important to look inside, otherwise you'll be out of balance.

Kim: How important is it to have a master? I know some people take issue with that term...

I frequently hold introductory talks about Sahaj Marg. We have pamphlets and announcements in the local paper and people call to inquire about meditation. They come, have a cup of tea; I talk with them, show them a little video, and then answer any questions. I always use the term 'teacher' because I think that's easier for people. I say spiritual teacher, a spiritual guide because that's what he is. I share with people that, like with anything, when we want to get help with our health or need our car fixed – anything -- if we want to learn a new language we go to a teacher; we go to a person who already has experience and they help us. I work in the health field so people come to me when they're looking for help with their health. If you're looking for help with spirituality, why not have a guide or a teacher? I think that's important because otherwise it's like trying to teach ourselves Russian when we don't know Russian. The North American idea, that we can do everything ourselves, well we can see how far that gets us, you know. Normally we end up realizing, "Well, maybe I could use a little help." It's not a master-slave thing. A master is a teacher. Master just means guru and Master is a teacher who is helping us, that's all.

Kim: How would you say that you personally have changed since your time in Sahaj Marg?

Well, that's a tricky one to answer. I definitely feel I have changed; I know I've changed. I came in as a young 20-year-old. I'm now 66 this year. That's a lot of years. At first, I just found it gave me so much peace. Back in the '70s, I was just a screwed up 20-year-old like so many of us; I didn't even know I was looking for spirituality. Thank

God, Master found me because I wasn't even smart enough to know I should go look for it! So it was handed to me. I found it gave me some peace. I mean, I didn't change overnight or anything. I still had a lot of things to work out over time, but I just kept doing the meditation, I kept doing it. No matter what else I was doing in my life, I just kept doing the meditation – because somehow it made me feel good. With time, slowly you start changing and you begin to realize some things, you begin to grow.

I always compare it to, if you're a mother or a father: you know about having a child because you've had parents, you see parents all around you -- but until you have a baby yourself you don't know really what it is about. You *become* a parent. Just like when you get married – you *become* a husband, you *become* a wife -- because you're learning as you go. To me, in any spiritual practice, I don't care which one it is, Sahaj Marg or anything, you are learning as you go. So it's a process. Many years later, I'm <u>still</u> in this process.

When I started in Denmark I said, "Okay, why not? It sounds good, and I'll do it for as far as it can take me." I didn't know what it was. Well see, all this time later, I'm still doing it because it keeps continuing to broaden and broaden the vision and the horizon. So change is a process, you know? Now it is the priority in my life; I can't imagine life without it -- not because my mind can't or that I've been indoctrinated or anything -- it's because it gives you everything in your life that you need. You start feeling you can handle situations better. You get rid of all the attachments that might not be very healthy for you, all the patterns that we learned from our culture, our religion, our parents, everything – the world -- you begin to see a different view.

In general, I see people becoming more compassionate. You can dislike a person's behavior, but you still feel love towards them. So what is meditation? What is this Divinity? It's just really, really pure love. I guess, in a simple way, you just keep learning how to love and that keeps expanding.

THE JOURNEY WITHIN

Kim: How important is <u>purity</u> in terms of being able to progress spiritually?

First of all, there are no "Do's" and "Don'ts" in Sahaj Marg. The second thing is, Babuji used to say, any bad habits (and he never would say what a bad habit is) will leave you; they'll drop off. I find that, with this particular practice of meditation, that's true. A bad habit can be something really pleasurable and nice, but you're still attached to it (doesn't have to be something that's terrible or wrong). When I started as a young girl in Denmark, are you kidding? I mean, I didn't even <u>know</u> we were not supposed to have a drink. I didn't know that; nobody told me. I never did drugs nor did I really drink very much.

Basically, what I see happening with this practice is that naturally, as you do the practice, you get disinterested in these things and they sort of leave <u>you</u>. It just falls away. Sahaj Marg means "the natural path" – there are no commandments, as in "Thou shalt not…" I think if you give anybody a list of 'do's and don'ts' they will rebel, depending on culture. I feel you grow <u>into</u> a purer lifestyle.

As a preceptor, when someone comes to me to start the practice, I have to check use of medications and anti-depressants because it's like mixing oil and water, they don't mix well <u>together</u>. But I simply explain the practice, make sure they understand, and then we just start. Everything falls off naturally. Everything fell off for me, not that I was a wild person or anything but, all just falls away because you no longer find it interesting. In fact, worldly habits get sort of boring, you know?

There's a whole world inside your heart -- and most people don't know it. When they start the meditation, this world starts revealing itself and that becomes so much more interesting than the worldly world outside, it starts pulling your attention. It really is a whole universe inside and because of the way our meditation works, you get to access that

THE JOURNEY WITHIN

universe and to explore it and discover it on a regular basis. So those experiences are much higher than anything you can do with a drug. I don't think you can tell people 'don't do this, don't do that'. There are suggestions we can give; or as they read the books or things come up in conversation, we can then talk about whatever comes up for them.

Babuji has said meat-eating is not conducive to spirituality. He never would say, "Do this, do that." He'd never say that. He would give you hints: "Well this doesn't really help your progress very much." So then it's up to you to sort it out. Drinking or doing pot (or whatever people do nowadays; I'm out of date, so I don't know), it gives you a sensation -- it gives you a different type of experience in how your brain is working. But that is not the same as a meditative spiritual experience. If you're having drugs or pot – it's not saying that that's wrong or impure or you're bad, definitely not. But it doesn't allow you to have the full spiritual "high" and spiritual experience that you can have; it sort of blurs it.

Kim: Could you speak to the idea of vibrations and the "inner universe"? Have you yourself had any experiences out of the ordinary realm that may be tied to spiritualism or this concept of other worlds that we may have access to if we could use the full capacity of what we've been given by the Divine?

That's really a good question. There are different vibrations, I think, that are going on all the time. So what I find, with doing the meditation, as you grow and change, you become more in tune with a lot of those vibrations and you become aware of them, number one. There are so many books and theories out there. Of course there are vibrations in the earth, the plane, everything. Life is a vibration. There's life in everything. I lived in Arizona, about an hour from Sedona, and (other than being with Master) Arizona is my favorite place on earth because, to me, it's just a spiritual state (chuckles). You can feel something going on in the atmosphere. Sedona itself, you know, has these vortexes.

THE JOURNEY WITHIN

It's a tricky one for me to answer because, first of all, yes of course, I think all this is real. "Do I care much about it?" No. Because I think the inner divinity and where that's coming from, that type of work is actually much higher than any other vibration. I mean, everything is a vibration, yes, but it's of a different category, or state. So for me, yes, you can be very sensitive. When I go to Sedona, in the red rocks and walking, I love all those places. I feel very close to Master there, in a different way (because I always feel close to Master).

Someone just sent me a YouTube video, a documentary made in Canada. It was very encouraging, a documentary about cultural evolution. Nothing really big deal but they actually believe we create the whole world and universe, everything, from our thought, what we think. Babuji and our teachers, they always say, our meditation is just about thought. We can't meditate if we don't have a mind, and so the mind plays very much a part in our heart-centered meditation. Our thoughts create everything, everything. So, if you have the Divine will behind your thoughts that could be amazing. If you have negative thinking, if we think we're having a bad day or whatever, it's our thought. The whole world (war, religions, the money system, whatever), it's all been created by our thoughts -- and our samskaras, our impressions. Our thoughts leave impressions. If you really want to get into the 'woo-woo' details about it, our thought has a lot to do with it and that creates vibration. But I do think there are other worlds, if you want to say that -- inner worlds and worlds that are much higher evolved --and that's what we're going towards in this particular practice of meditation, is evolving to that and being within that.

Babuji used to say, all the books he's written, and everything he speaks about Sahaj Marg, they're actually for the <u>future</u> future. People will understand this <u>in the future</u> because we have to <u>grow up</u>. The societies, the culture, we're growing. If you look back in the '60s and hippies and all that, they had a great idea about peace and love. Did they know how to go about doing it? I don't think so. But as we

THE JOURNEY WITHIN

evolved, then more spirituality came, then more meditations came and we evolved. This practice helps us evolve <u>much</u> more quickly.

Kim: Do you have any comments on the idea of liberation or any experiences of past lives?

First of all, liberation, by many teachers, including our own, is always considered the first rung of the ladder. To be liberated, not to come back into this life – there's nothing wrong with that – but it's not a higher goal. There's much, much more <u>past</u> (beyond) liberation. So, as you do meditation and grow, you find out that, even if you started with that idea (Oh, let's get the hell out of this world, right?), you begin to realize that, well, that is possible with Sahaj Marg (to be liberated), but it's not a really high goal to aspire for. Then you find out that, as you grow and change, you can more easily live in this world, even with everything going on. You don't feel like, "I just want to get out of here," because you change. You can live in this world and not be a part of this world also. Each person, they find out for themselves, how that changes. [There's] nothing wrong with being liberated but it's not the top goal. There's so much more than that. There's so much more depth than liberation. So that's one thing.

As far as past lives: Well, I had an experience when I was in California in 1977, at a school to learn about polarity therapy, a type of body work (a recognized practitioner's course). I stayed and lived at the school for six weeks. It was a very intense program. While I was there, going through all this learning, cleansing and things like that, I ended up getting blood poisoning or septicemia and had a near death experience. They had doctors at the school and my roommate was actually a nurse. I had a high, high fever, and I knew that they were wrapping me in cold sheets (a natural means of bringing down fever). My experience was that I had left my body and I saw myself in my bed. First, I experienced my own birth of my present life with my mother. What was interesting was that it was what you hear about collective consciousness. I was in the birthing room in the hospital because it

THE JOURNEY WITHIN

was 1947. I knew – it wasn't just knowing – I <u>was</u> really my mother's consciousness. I was also the nurse and the doctor's and my father and my brother (my one sibling who is older than me), their consciousness. My father and brother weren't even at the hospital (my father was someplace else with my brother), but I knew and felt everything they were feeling and thinking -- and it wasn't thinking with the mind. It was being really part of them, so in a way I guess you could call it the collective mind. I'd never had that experience. I was just this soul or energy.

My mother had a difficult birth – I mean she was birthing me, so my birth was difficult for her. The doctors, back in those days (out of ignorance, probably) at the end of the birth used forceps -- but I knew what they were feeling and thinking. I also knew what my mother was feeling and thinking as this soul came into this world. That was the beginning of my near-death experience, my own birth. That actually released me (I'm skipping forward now), that actually helped me a lot in understanding certain things about the medical profession that they only do what they feel they must. I didn't have a bad feeling towards them as they were doing their best.

So it was interesting. From that, I went into another phase where it was almost like being on a train. You look out the window and see scenes going by. That was the feeling I had, but I saw this scene (I'm assuming it was India). I saw my mother from that life rocking me in a large shawl or swing that was tied to a tree. I saw her swinging me and I knew that was my mother from my last life and I knew that was me as a baby. It was just a passing scene.

The next thing that occurred was what you always hear about near-death experiences. I felt like I was going upward and there was this kind of special light and then Babuji was there. (Now at this point Babuji was still alive.) So Babuji was there and it was such a wonderful experience and I was so happy -- this energy, this soul -- I was going and going upward. And then he spoke to me and said, "You have to

THE JOURNEY WITHIN

go back because you have more work to do." I didn't know what he meant by that, but when he said that I had to go back, I felt like I was tumbling backward through space and then eventually I was jerked back into my body.

I didn't want to come back. Now, when I came back I knew everything that had happened. I knew I knew it but my mind couldn't think about it until the next day. My body was like this gigantic 10-ton weight; it was so heavy compared to where I had just been. And so I came back -- to me. I had died and was leaving but then I was supposed to come back. [So] I was thrust back into my body.

Now, the interesting thing about this was, in a couple of days, when as I was more back into my body, I sat up and I wrote down this whole experience - everything. I wrote every single thing. The nurse lady who was in the room, my roommate, said, "Well, I wrote down everything we had observed." While they were doing whatever they were doing on me, she had written down everything I was saying, my body language (I have no idea why she decided to do that – maybe legally for a report or something). She had written everything down that they were observing and doing in real life time.

We traded our writings of the experience. The funny thing is, everything matched up. It was a confirmation. She said that, when I was reliving my own birth of this life, my body was of a baby birthing. I was in the fetal position, I was kicking out [and] she said it looked just like a birth. Luckily, she had written this. I had written my account and they matched up. Very different experiences but they matched up. And that was a confirmation. That was my near death experience. I don't really talk about it much. I know sometimes scientists and doctors say there's something else that happens but it doesn't really matter; I know what happened and that's all that counts. I think I did write Babuji about it as well.

THE JOURNEY WITHIN

There's a book by Anita Moorjani, she's of Indian descent, and it's called Dying to Be Me. I would recommend reading that book. It's about her near-death experience. Some of the things [in her book] I really related to and then, of course, she had her own experience. Her story in general is interesting because of her parentage and all. She had cancer and was dying, and should have been dead. It's a very interesting book that will tell you about spirituality. I like the way she describes things, and that we cannot get dogmatic. We cannot get dogmatic, whether it's Sahaj Marg or anything. Do not get dogmatic. Do not get into rules and regulations. Yes, we have guidelines. Yes, there are certain things that need to be done so that we can progress, but dogma isn't helpful.

Kim: Do you have any other memories to share?

That was the second or maybe the third time I almost died. When I was 5 years old, I broke my neck and the doctors thought I was going to die. My first (or maybe my second) visit to Shahjahanpur, to meet Babuji, I got deathly ill with sunstroke as well as heatstroke. I remember, after about the fourth day, I was really out of it with an extreme pounding headache. You can't see and you're really ill when you have sunstroke and heat stroke. You don't ever want it. I went crawling downstairs into Babuji's room from where I was staying up in the guest rooms; literally, I crawled in there. I said, "Babuji, I think I'm really sick." I hadn't wanted to bother him but finally I decided I'd better bother him because this might be it. He came over and was so sweet, this sweet little man. He touched my forehead and [said], "Oh." He called his doctor from the village who, I think, was a homeopathic doctor.

There are cots made out of rope called charpoys, so all that evening I was outside Babuji's little room, out in the courtyard, lying on this charpoy cot. There were a few others around. Every two or three hours, I had to take doses of medicine. As it became cooler, more people would come out there. Babuji used to laugh, get lively at night and tell stories. I remember this going on (in my dazed condition) and I remember saying something about, "Please, if I die, don't forget my mother."

The night before I got ill, he had been talking about souls that had passed on and things like that and my mother had just died about a year before, at age 48. When he was talking, it caught my ear when he was talking about souls that had passed on so I asked him, "Is there anything that I can do for my mother?" He said, "When did she die?" I said, "About a year and a half ago." He laughed (he had a sweet little laugh) and he said, "Well, there's nothing you can do but I can do something." I told him the date and he sat there and he was looking up, his head tilted up. I almost had this image he was looking through an old rolodex looking for her name. Basically, the gist of it was, he told me she hadn't been reborn yet and so, therefore, he could do something for her. The next life could be her last life, so she could be liberated. It brought tears to my eyes because she was a very good mother and I felt like, finally, I could do something for her through Babuji doing something for her.

When I became ill and felt I wasn't going to be around much longer, I remember saying to him in my dazed state, "Just remember my mother" and he patted me on the shoulder and sort of chuckled. So I took the homeopathic medicine doses and I was better the next day, very weak but back to normal. Babuji came out in the morning and said, "How do you feel?" I said, "I think I'm ok, better now." I said, "That doctor sure had some good medicine. I didn't think I was going to make it." Babuji laughed and said, "Well, I think I was a little bit of your doctor too."

To me, he saved my life. Actually, he was the one who was doing the work. The medicine may have helped my physical body but I knew -- even in my young, stupid, naïve way -- I knew that he was the one who did it all and saved me. That was one of my very sweet experiences with Babuji. When I returned to my room later that day, Babuji

THE JOURNEY WITHIN

climbed the steps all the way up – this little old man – and brought me tea and toast. That was Babuji. That was humility. That was real, pure, universal love. Our present teacher, Parthasarathi, is the same way. The teachers, the guides -- you see that they really are universal, pure love. They are just here to raise humanity to that state. And they give and they give and they give.

Kim: Do you think they're working with similar souls? Do you think Krishna and Jesus and all of them are there working together?

Babuji's always had communication. Back then, he'd talk about Jesus and various things. To my understanding, there have been different teachers and they know each other in this other realm, the spiritual hierarchy. Of course, there are a lot of different souls working for humanity and this particular world -- maybe for other worlds too. Normally, there can be one Master or teacher at a time but that does not negate that they work with others. Jesus was the living Master of his time, Buddha maybe the living teacher of his time, whoever else. I think they [each] have different work they do.

Kim: Some people think there is possible catastrophic change coming, that we may have to learn to live life in a different way, even communicate in a different way. Some people see Sahaj Marg as important to help us evolve. Do you have comments on Sahaj Marg as a social movement, as hope for the future?

Well, I wouldn't still be in Sahaj Marg if I didn't think it was working. I've lived all over the world, in Europe, in India three or four months out of the year, in Canada, in the U.S.A. I've traveled. And I have this one big, gigantic family of Sahaj Marg family that is worldwide. I think that, for me, I find (I can only speak of my own experience) that this is all part of that change that is happening, that is taking place. You have from the past Nostradamus, the Hopi Indian writings – and the Hopi's actually are quite connected to Sahaj Marg in a funny way. If you read the Hopi's, some of the messages the elders give will actually mention

THE JOURNEY WITHIN

"Our brothers in the East." My first spiritual book ever, when I was young and before I knew anything about spirituality, was <u>Book of the Hopi</u> by Frank Waters. The Hopi live in Arizona. They have a very peaceful lifestyle and a lot of their visions and prophecies are quite in synch with Sahaj Marg.

I think there are many cultures that are working together in different ways. Yes, there is change; we already see that. We see a lot of the negative things happening and that probably will continue to happen until people realize that we have to change our hearts, our lifestyles, our thinking, and come to spirituality. There will probably be a lot of cleaning out, like when you're ill and you're cleaning out toxins. Our world, our humanity, is sort of ill. [We're] going to go through a lot of purging, which we already see -- all the disasters, nature being crazy, the wars, all of that, it's a type of purging – until we get so desperate that we <u>have</u> to come to spirituality. It would be nice if it changed before then. I feel there are other people and practices, besides Sahaj Marg, that realize this. Yes, we are all part of that change, of changing the world.

Even back in the 60's, I always liked that slogan, back in the hippie days: "The Biggest Revolution is Changing Yourself." You have to change yourself and then the world changes with you. When each heart changes, you look at life differently. You can't kill animals and eat them; they're your brother and your sister. You can't kill a human being (if you can't kill an animal, you can't kill a human being). So the change begins with you. And how do you change? You have to do something dynamic. You have to do something <u>spiritual</u>. You have to change your heart -- not just nice thinking, and workshops that last a day or a week. It's work. It's progressive work that keeps going on. I think there are a lot of things happening.

Me personally, I find this path of Sahaj Marg to be the quickest and the most efficient tool of change. I've stuck with it. I've done other workshops and seminars. They're good but they're just steps to take you to something that works even deeper and that brings permanent change.

Kim: Anything more to add?

Don't waste time. Don't waste time, don't waste time. Whatever you want to do -- if you want to start Sahaj Marg, start Sahaj Marg. Whatever you want to do. Just <u>do</u> something and start changing yourself. Even me, even with Sahaj Marg, I feel I've <u>wasted</u> so much time -- even in this wonderful system that was given to me, just given to me! The more the years go by, the more I appreciate it and see, really, even more change, but I also know I've wasted a lot of time. We can only do what we can do — what we're aware of -- but just start something to work on yourself spiritually. I found (for myself) Sahaj Marg the most effective system that keeps going on and on -- into infinity it seems.

THE JOURNEY WITHIN

Conclusion

I hope you have enjoyed these stories, presented as "journeys" to a more evolved Self. I would like to take this moment to thank the interviewees. They gave freely not only of their time but, more importantly, their deepest thoughts and feelings. They taught me, as a newcomer to spirituality, the importance of placing my spiritual life at the forefront and center of all I do. They also helped to better understand the self-fulfillment that could be ours as followers and members of a global spiritual community.

A number of interesting concepts are worth further reflection. Bani's chapter on the method itself, as well as her humorous and honest portrayal of early experiences at the ashram, are fun and enlightening. We hear from people quite new to the practice, as they discuss fundamentals such as being able to sit still and "rest" the brain. We hear from some who have tried a number of meditation or other spiritual practices. Meant to be simply a sharing of experiences, there is no attempt to compare practices. Instead, many advise to just try anything as a movement away from materiality and toward both a simpler lifestyle and one which is more spiritually-oriented.

A practical reason to focus on Sahaj Marg is that it is the only method with which I personally have experience. I have found it to be amazingly effective, but one must have the willpower and discipline to do all aspects of the practice and to be really working on character development. Beyond that, faith and love move mountains. Another reason to focus on Sahaj Marg is because little has been publicly or readily available until now about this method. The most important reason, however, is that it really works. No longer is rapid progress available only to those who lead a hermetic or monastic lifestyle.

THE JOURNEY WITHIN

Michelle put it well: "In my opinion, Sahaj Marg is the simplest and most efficient system to spiritual progress. My experience has proven it to me. Now, my heartfelt desire is to spread this well-kept secret of Sahaj Marg among as many heart-sensitive humans as possible."

Sharing by people with months versus decades in the Sahaj Marg practice shows common trends of change: change in lifestyle, increased feelings of balance, reduced reactions to stress, and an improved ability to simply manage life from a more self-filled perspective. A number of the interviewees are "ashram kids," remarking on what it's like to attend meditation gatherings from an early age and later starting their own relationship with a spiritual master (teacher). Some difficult concepts have been explained to us, as well, including: past lives, samskaras, evolving as a human (self to Self), the role of past and present Masters, connections with worlds or dimensions beyond this Earth, surrender and constant remembrance. The most important themes throughout have been the role of transmission and the need to cleanse (and avoid creating) samskaras. Overarching all we hear anecdotes and lessons from or about Babuji Maharaj and the living Master, Chariji, our loving Tender. May we ever be thankful for their guidance, as well as that from other loving souls and Greats. Imagine us all, dear sisters and brothers, growing together and individually in faith and love.

Resources Referenced and Recommended

Babuji Maharaj (1899 -1983), also known as Ram Chandra of Shahajahanpur, founder president of Shri Ram Chandra Mission (SRCM). http://www.sahajmarg.org/babuji-maharaj

Bhavnagari, Khorshed (2009). Laws of the Spirit World. Mumbai: Jaico Publishing House.

Braden, Gregg (2007). The Divine Matrix: Bridging time, space, miracles and belief. Hay House. Also see www.greggbraden.com/videos

Chandra, Ram (quote): http://www.sahajmarg.org/babuji-maharaj

Chandra, Ram (2010 reprint; first published 1954). Reality at Dawn. Kolkata: Spiritual Hierarchy Publications Trust. See http://www.sahajmarg.org/publications/ebook/reality-at-dawn

Chandra, Ram (2012 reprint; first published 1959). Commentary on Ten Maxims of Sahaj Marg. Shri Ram Chandra Mission, Manapakkam, Chennai.

Chandra, Shri Ram (2010). Whispers from The Brighter World - A Third Revelation. Rajagopalachari, P. (Ed). Spiritual Hierarchy Publication Trust for Sahaj Marg Spirituality Foundation, Kolkata, India.

Chandra, Shri Ram (2012). Whispers from The Brighter World - A Fourth Revelation. Rajagopalachari, P. (Ed). Spiritual Hierarchy Publication Trust for Sahaj Marg Spirituality Foundation, Kolkata, India.

Chandra, Shri Ram (2013). Whispers from The Brighter World - A Fifth Revelation. Rajagopalachari, P. (Ed). Spiritual Hierarchy

Publication Trust for Sahaj Marg Spirituality Foundation, Chennai, India.

Constant Remembrance, the global spiritual quarterly magazine of the Shri Ram Chandra Mission: https://www.sahajmarg.org/publications/bookstore/constant-remembrance

Gormley, Claire (2012). The Divine Spark: A Miracle of Human Transformation. Galway, Ireland: The Divine Spark Project. www.thedivinesparkproject.com

Hesse, Herman (1922). Siddhartha. Can be found at: http://www.gutenberg.org/ebooks/2500?msg=welcome_stranger

Hodges, Benjamin (1982). The Tao of Pooh. New York: Penguin Books.

King, Martin Luther Jr. (1963). I Have a Dream. See http://www.youtube.com/watch?v=smEqnnklfYs

Lalaji, Maharaj (1873-1931). Also know as Shri Ram Chandra of Fatchgarb, is adi-guru (first spiritual master) of Shri Ram Chandra Mission.

Lewis, C. S. Perhaps best known for The Chronicles of Narnia series. See https://www.cslewis.com/us

Melchizedek, Drunvalo (2003). Living in the Heart: How to enter the sacred space within the heart. Flagstaff, AZ: Light Technology Publishing.

Moorjani, Anita (2012). Dying to be Me. Hong Kong: Hay House, Inc.

Nostradamus, Michel de (1555). The Prophecies. See http://www.freeinfosociety.com/media/pdf/2426.pdf

Pearsall, Paul (1998). The Heart's Code: Tapping the wisdom and power of our heart energy. NY: Broadway Books.

THE JOURNEY WITHIN

Pockets of the Future video blog:
https://www.youtube.com/watch?v=tLwdXpuWJww

Rajagopalachari, Shri Parthasarathi (1989) My Master. Kolkata: Spiritual Hierarchy Publication Trust.

Rajagopalachari, Parthasarathi (2011). Heartspeak 2011. Kolkata: Spiritual Hierarchy Publication Trust.

Rajagopalachari, Parthasarathi (2013). Wisdom to Wonder: Talks and informal conversations with abhyasis and prefects in Malaysia, Europe and the United States, 1994 to 1996. Kolkata: Spiritual Hierarchy Publication Trust.

Rinpoche, Patrul (2003). Words of a Perfect Teacher: A complete translation of a classic introduction to Tibetan Buddhism. Published by Motilal Banarsidass, India

Romano, Paul (2013). The Choice. Bamboo Grove Press.
http://www.amazon.com/The-Choice-Art-Remembrance-ebook/dp/B00EBC8P4G/ref=sr_1_1?s=digital-text&ie=UTF8&qid=1375741309&sr=1-1&keywords=the+choice

Sahaj Marg (The Natural Path) Learn to Meditate:
http://www.sahajmarg.org/seeker/home

Sai Baba: More information can be found at
http://en.wikipedia.org/wiki/Sai_Baba_of_Shirdi

Shri Ram Chandra Mission. See www.sahajmarg.org for more information.

Shri Ram Chandra Mission: www.sahajmarg.org

SRCM Bookstores online: http: www.srcm.com/bookstore/index.jsp

The Ten Maxims: http://www.sahajmarg.org/sm/practice/ten-maxims

Tolkien, J. R. R. (1954). Also adapted into a film. See
http://en.wikipedia.org/wiki/J._R._R._Tolkien

Tolle, Eckhart (2004). The Power of Now. See sample quotes at http://www.goodreads.com/work/quotes/840520-the-power-of-now-a-guide-to-spiritual-enlightenment

Waters, Frank (1963). Book of the Hopi. Viking Press.

Weiss, Brian L. (1988). Many Lives, Many Masters. NY: Touchstone, Simon & Schuster.

Weiss, Brian L. (2004). Same Soul, Many Bodies. NY: Free Press, Simon & Schuster.

Yogananda, Paramhansa. More information can be found at http://www.crystalclarity.com/authors.php?author=Paramhansa%20Yogananda